Knowledge for the People:

The Struggle for Adult Learning
in English-Speaking Canada,
1828-1973

Michael R. Welton, editor

Symposium Series / 18

OISE Press

The Ontario Institute for Studies in Education

The Ontario Institute for Studies in Education has three prime functions: to conduct programs of graduate study in education, to undertake research in education, and to assist in the implementation of the findings of educational studies. The Institute is a college chartered by an Act of the Ontario Legislature in 1965. It is affiliated with the University of Toronto for graduate studies purposes.

The publications program of the Institute has been established to make available information and materials arising from studies in education, to foster the spirit of critical inquiry, and to provide a forum for the exchange of ideas about education. The opinions expressed should be viewed as those of the contributors.

© The Ontario Institute for Studies in Education 1987
252 Bloor Street West
Toronto, Ontario
M5S 1V6

Canadian Cataloguing in Publication Data

Main entry under title:
Knowledge for the people

(Symposium series ; 18)
ISBN 0-7744-0303-9

1. Adult education — Canada — History. I. Welton, Michael Robert, 1942-   II. Ontario Institute for Studies in Education.   III. Series: Symposium series (Ontario Institute for Studies in Education) ; 18.

LC5254.K56   1987   374'.971   C87-095191-2

Cover: *A WEA float at the annual Labor Day Parade in Toronto, date unknown. (Ontario Archives, Toronto.) Printed by permission of the Workers' Educational Association, Toronto Branch.*

CMID #116376

Printed on
Recycled Paper

ISBN 0-7744-0303-9   Printed in Canada

1   2   3   4   5   AP   19   09   98   88   78

In Memory

Of My Father

R. C. Welton

Contents

Contributors

Nora Robins is Head of the Humanities Division of the University of Calgary Library System, Calgary, Alberta.

Carol J. Dennison completed her M.A. in History at the University of Victoria, Victoria, British Columbia.

George L. Cook is Head of the Department of Arts and Science at Bermuda College, Bermuda.

Juliet Pollard is an Assistant Professor in the Department of History of the University of Saskatchewan, Saskatoon.

Michael R. Welton is an Assistant Professor in the Department of Education of Dalhousie University, Halifax, Nova Scotia.

Sandra Souchotte is a freelance journalist.

Ian MacPherson is a Professor in the Department of History of the University of Victoria, Victoria, British Columbia.

Jim Lotz is a freelance journalist.

Ian Radforth is an Assistant Professor in the Department of History of the University of Toronto, Toronto, Ontario.

Joan Sangster is an Assistant Professor in the Department of History of Trent University, Peterborough, Ontario.

Preface

This collection of essays takes its title from that of a famous pamphlet, *Knowledge for the People: A Call to St. Francis Xavier College*, written by Father Jimmy Tompkins, one of the peskiest of Canada's pioneer adult educators, in 1921. Though dated and scribbled on the run, this pamphlet was fired by a vision of the power of adult education to transform lives and society. Our pioneers, gifted amateurs out to change the world, had little time to reflect and perhaps not much inclination. Getting on with mobilizing the "common people" to become masters of their own destiny took precedence over patient theoretical work.

In the last two decades, however, as adult education has attempted to establish itself in the Academy, it has become evident that the world has not been moving in an emancipatory direction. Our theoretical resources have not been adequate to the task of comprehending the complexities of adult learning or of knowing how to change the world. Our neglect of theory has contributed to the neglect of the adult learner. Our intellectual garb is tattered, shabby, flimsy.

Knowledge for the People has been constructed to add to our conceptual arsenal. Among our necessary theoretical resources is historical understanding. This collection of essays explores the struggle between the common people in community, on farm, and in factory who want a life and problem-centred pedagogy and élites who want to provide for and determine the direction of their subordinate's learning. It is hoped that *Knowledge for the People* will contribute to the debate about the meanings of our past and the renewal of our liberatory traditions in the present.

Michael R. Welton
Dalhousie University
Halifax, Nova Scotia

Introduction: Reclaiming Our Past: Memory, Traditions, Kindling Hope

Michael R. Welton

This introduction tries to accomplish several things. In the first part, I grapple with the problem of the invisibility of adult educational thought and practice within mainstream Canadian historical writing and the historical amnesia of the Canadian adult education community. Can history provide a vantage point to understand present trends and practices? Does the past speak to the present? Does historical consciousness provide us with essential insight and understanding? Is history, as Nietzsche suggested, really a "costly and superfluous luxury of the understanding" in a world that seems accommodated to an "eternal present"?[1]

These questions press upon us with some urgency. The twentieth century has not been particularly hospitable to the historical consciousness.[2] Social science has dislodged history from its pre-eminent role as purveyor of humanist values. Psychology has been the discipline of great promise for many adult educators. In this milieu it is difficult for adult educators and researchers to understand how a "vision of the past" might turn them "toward the future."[3] This task is made doubly difficult because the dominant Canadian historical consciousness has paid little attention to adult learning. Our traditions are largely ignored in Hurtig's pathbreaking *Canadian Encyclopedia*, a work supposedly acutely sensitive to the new social history. There are no entries under Frontier College, Mechanics' Institutes, or the Canadian Association for Adult Education (CAAE), and no biographical sketches of E. A. Corbett, Alfred Fitzpatrick, and Edmund Bradwin (where's Ned, Ed, and Alfred?), to cite three of hundreds who should be included. A recent volume in the Canadian centenary series, *Canada 1922-1939: Decades of Discord,* does not even mention the Antigonish movement or the CAAE. Nonetheless, in spite of the fact that the history and historiography of Canadian adult education is underdeveloped and undertheorized, there is renewed interest within the Canadian adult education community in opening up a dialogue with the past. This interest was registered in the 1985 regional meetings celebrating the CAAE's fiftieth anniversary and the June 1986 meeting in Montreal, "Building the Social Movement." We appear to be seizing hold of forgotten memories as they flash up in a moment of global danger. By fanning sparks of hope in the past, we are kindling the vision that "justice will yet come . . .''[4]

In the second part of this introductory essay, I shall provide critical commentary on the selected essays. We must recognize at the outset that we are in the midst of constructing our past — of marking it out, defining its contours, identifying the elements in its field, of discerning the kinds of relationships that obtain among them.[5] We do not yet know with certainty how we should constitute the past. Nevertheless, we do know that we must locate learning forms, sites, and processes within multiple contexts and that we must conceptualize learning in terms of the social-historical construction of knowledge within societies that are riven by class, gender, ethnic, and bureaucratic divisions. To paraphrase Marx's famous aphorism in *The Eighteenth Brumaire of Louis Bonaparte*, people learn, but they do not learn just as they please; they do so under circumstances not chosen by themselves, but under circumstances directly encountered, given and transmitted from the past. The unfulfilled learning capacity of all dead generations weighs like a nightmare on the brains of the living.[6]

My general purpose has been to select essays written by those sensitive to the need to contextualize educational history and to break from our romantic historiography.[7] These essays inescapably implicate adult education in the economic, political, and ideological tensions of the day and illustrate the importance of considering the relationship of adult education to political organization, official educational institutions (especially universities), influential religions, and other groups. More specifically, I have selected case studies from English-speaking Canada that examine, implicitly or explicitly, the complex question of how adults in a range of learning sites develop their own understandings and skills to control their life situation within a particular set of constraints (ideological, cultural, social, political, and economic).

The choice of subtitle — The Struggle for Adult Learning in English-speaking Canada — captures the tension, continuing into the present, between a constrained and managed adult educational process and a learner-centred, legitimated, and emancipatory learning process. Learning, then, seen as autonomous, has four moments: it must be centred in the life situation and needs of the learner; it must be legitimated by the learners themselves; it must be critical of the status quo; and it must articulate an emancipatory project. Autonomous learning is not found in pure form in history; indeed, the historical record ought to dampen any easy optimism about human capacity to learn to act autonomously. But this concept, as roughly hewn as it is, can provide us with a reference point to scrutinize adult learning processes and forms across time and in multiple contexts. Within this fundamental problematic, two central themes, and several sub-thematics, are selected for commentary: (1) Modes of Adult Educational Discourse: From Paternalism to Transformation; and (2) The Role of the State as Knowledge Legitimator.

I: Rendering the Invisible Visible

Adult educational thought and practice has been largely invisible to the Canadian historian. But we know that what we see often reflects the questions we are asking and not the inadequacy of the data or the insignificance of the human activity. "Historians looking at the past," Anne Firor Scott has observed, "do not see all that is there."[8] Even when they do see, they do not necessarily think about what they have seen.

It is no secret among Canadian adult educators that we find ourselves confronting a paradoxical and confusing situation. Despite the fact that Canadians have been innovative creators of adult educational forms and movements and imaginative adaptors of received ones, the field of Canadian adult educational history is seriously underdeveloped. One will search in vain for a systematic history (or histories), a rich body of scholarly literature and serious debates about the meaning of our past. There are too many silences in our history. Movement activists like J. Roby Kidd have, to be sure, served as docu-mentors to the adult education community. The importance of our popular inspirational tradition ought not be be underestimated.[9] But history written by insiders or movement activists suffers from a number of flaws: it is insufficiently critical, seldom self-consciously interpretative and overly focussed on the achievements of individual men and women. Our history has been viewed largely as romance: a "drama of the triumph of good over evil, of virtue over vice, of light over darkness, . . ."[10] The situation is lamentable, the costs to current practice severe. How can we account for the invisibility of adult educational thought and practice in Canadian historical writing?

Let us begin by noting that the dominant Canadian historiographic tradition has cast great shadows over other important areas of human thought and practice. Until quite recently Canadian history has been overwhelmingly biased towards political history: the evolution of the nation-state and the axial role of heroic individuals in this process.[11] Social, cultural, and intellectual history are relatively late arrivals on the scene. The new social history of the 1970s did succeed to some extent in making children visible in school and out. We began to see the world from their knee-high perspective. But Canadian social historians have not been very interested in either the education of adults (the educative dimensions of economic, political, social, and cultural life) or adult education (intentional educational forms transmitting knowledge, skills, attitudes in a variety of sites).[12] A brief examination of the work of several labor historians illustrates this latter observation.

In spite of ringing declarations about the need to reconceptualize their field as cultural and social history, labor historians have not strayed far from the workplace or factory gates to embrace familial and associational life.[13] Desmond Morton, a reputable scholar, can still write a book entitled *Working People* in 1980 without including one reference to educational forms or processes. This would be utterly inconceivable in the British context. Bryan Palmer's work is the exception to the Canadian rule. In *A Culture in Conflict* (1979) he actually sees Mechanics' Institutes and challenges the conventional wisdom that they did not serve working-class needs. His recent synthetic work, *Working-Class Experience* (1983), incorporates data on cultural life in the process of postulating the emergence of an autonomous working-class oppositional culture. This Gramscian-style reading has great potential for adult education historians.[14] But not unexpectedly, Palmer does not ask educational questions of working-class cultural experience, that is, the learning process whereby working-class individuals acquire a set of competencies and understandings that differ from yet interweave with dominant modes of understanding and acting.

Nor is the industrialization process itself conceptualized as educative: requiring profound new modes of self and world understanding and the acquisition of new skills, attitudes, and sensibilities, differentially experienced by class and gender at particular historical moments. Only one work, the late H. Clare Pentland's long neglected *Labour and Capital in Canada, 1650-1850,* places knowledge creation at the heart of the movement from pre-industrial to early industrial society. The fundamental educative process at work in mid-nineteenth-century Canada was the "transformation of Canadians" — remaking of the labor force — into industrialized minds and bodies. This process, Pentland observed, was conducted "largely in the school of experience with the goad of harsh impersonal penalties for failure."[15] Through the "harsh but hardening school of labor," the primary pedagogue according to Marx, workers were learning really useful knowledge about the nature of work, wages, contractors, where their security and power lay, the rules of the game in a capitalist market. In their families, churches, clubs, unions, and libraries, working-class people received their secondary education, reflecting on the meaning of the formative deep structural process at work reshaping the configuration of societal life.

Perhaps it is understandable in our age of specialization that social history would consist of partial and selective visions of the past. However, one might assume that historians of education would see what their colleagues have chosen not, or been unable, to see. The publication of *Canadian Education: A History* in 1970 marked something of a turning point in Canadian educational historiography. The editors sought to reconstitute the field of educational history as social history. Rejecting the filio-pietism and institutional romances of writers like Charles Philips, they declared:

> We maintain that educational history should be regarded as social history in the belief that education is at all times and everywhere a reflection of the social order. As corollary, we maintain that the political, economic, social, cultural and intellectual aspects of Canadian history are vital to an understanding of Canadian educational development.[16]

Profoundly influenced by Bernard Bailyn's seminal *Education in the Forming of American Society* (1960), the editors wanted to contextualize[17] the analysis of educational forms. They also wanted to follow Bailyn in broadening the definition of education to embrace processes and activities operative outside formal schooling. Bailyn had demonstrated convincingly that if one analysed education in colonial society there would be little to see if one were looking only for formal schooling. Further, it was "bad history" to find only the seeds of the present in the gardens of the past. *Canadian Education: A History* did not succeed, however, in redefining the boundaries of education. As John Calam pointed out, the work suffered a "prefatory disharmony with its own major themes."[18] The book turned out to be mainly about schools, all kinds, with little attention to "uncommon schools" for adults. If they had wanted models for the latter task, they had J. F. C. Harrison's *Learning and Living, 1790-1960* (1961) and Brian Simon's *Education and the Labour Movement, 1870-1918* (1965). But this criticism is unfair: English working-class educational traditions were much more visible, the historiography more developed, monographs extant. Synthetic works build on the monographic labors of others. Even if Canadian educational historians had wanted to write about the labor movement as a learning site they would have found few scholarly works to draw upon.

Nor is it at all clear that the Canadian working class, unlike its British counterpart, has a vital tradition of adult education. The fragmentary evidence we do have does seem to suggest, though, that Canada has a weak university-based liberal adult education tradition, and that voluntary associations providing knowledge for the working people have met with resistance or indifference.[19] However, if educational historians had looked at agrarian and co-operative movements, and known how to think about the role of learning in social movements, they would have begun the process of recovering a vital and dynamic popular adult education tradition. But they have not.[20]

Bernard Bailyn's work — in a paradigmatic sense — was especially significant for historians of adult education. The way was now open to see those educational processes operating outside the formal school system. Although most Canadian educational historians in the decades following the publication of *Education in the Forming of American Society* would choose to write about the life experience of children and adolescents inside and outside formal public schools, there was nothing stopping them from analysing the workplace as a learning site (mine, mill, factory, shop, office), or specific educational forms for the diffusion of special kinds of knowledge (libraries, lyceums, fairs, museums).

Indeed, the American educational historian Lawrence Cremin would demonstrate in *American Education: The National Experience, 1783-1876* (1980) an unusual sensitivity and interest in comprehending the way knowledge, values, attitudes, and sensibilities rooted in an agrarian society were transformed as men and women and children adapted to the new world of the factory. Cremin shows how the educative influence of the workplace increasingly mediated the influence of all other education during the years of adult employment. With the development of the factory system in mid-nineteenth-century New England, the values and attitudes traditionally associated with Poor Richard (discipline, hard work, punctuality, frugality, sobriety, orderliness, prudence) were taught with renewed vigor and growing intensity by churches, schools, and voluntary associations. Cremin's genius, like de Tocqueville's, lies in his ability to see unity in the breathtaking multiplicity of cultural, political, and religious institutions and in his intellectual agility which enables him to see the significance of the evangelical voluntary associations' contribution to the forming of the "popular paideia." Cremin also recognizes that alternative and, at times, oppositional values and practices exist within the framework of the established but never totally incorporative hegemony. In a chapter simply titled "Outcasts," he introduces the notion of a "discordant education": through family and clandestine religious assembly, black slaves survived as a people and maintained a sense of identity as black human beings. Canadian educational historians have not yet followed Cremin's pathbreaking and subtle work.

Canadian Education: A History had set an exemplary model of carefully crafted writing, but it had not achieved any interpretative breakthroughs. How, precisely and analytically, did education reflect the social order? The appearance of Michael Katz's *The Irony of Early School Reform* in the late 1960s signalled the emergence of a new paradigm for educational history — the revisionist social control model. Focussing on the intentions of élites, Katz argued that early school reform was imposed from above against the wishes of those below. No longer the engine of democracy, schools were now perceived as central institutions for the reproduction of a classist, racist, sexist, and hierarchical society. The social control paradigm fit the mood of graduate students and professors who were doing history in a period of economic recession and quiescent politics. Works written in the 1970s reflected this pessimistic ethos, this loss of faith in the progressive role of formal schooling. Historiographic style shifted from romantic to ironic, mechanistic argumentative modes gained the day, and radical ideological stances confronted the conservatism of the old histories.

But even this skepticism about the reform potential of formal schooling did not drive revisionists outside formal schooling to search for critical traditions. Although often conceptually crude,[21] revisionist works played an effective demythologizing role. Rather than simply documenting, narrating, or celebrating the work of school promoters, analysts implicated schools in the maintenance of structures of domination. Everyone was forced to sharpen up analytically. However, if we were becoming more critical of schooling, we were also less certain about what role the teaching of educational history should be playing in the training of teachers.

Revisionism was a mixed blessing for those interested in the history of adult education. The good news was that the stormy historiographic debates of the 1970s revealed rather pointedly to adult educationalists that their own historiographic house was not in order, that their work had to be informed by conceptual and methodological developments in social history, social sciences, and literary criticism. They had to stop celebrating and start analysing! Ron Faris's *The Passionate Educators,* written in the early 1970s, reflected these new developments. But this was not an easy lesson for adult educators to learn. Hived off intellectually, at times spatially, from current modes of intellectual discourse, adult education's theoretical practice has been consumed by the practical, captive to a professional ideology of ''needs, access and provision'' and prone to psychologizing.[22] The professionalization and psychologizing of the field has prevented adult educationalists from seeing the importance of socio-historical modes of thought and the necessity of analysing adult learning forms and processes in terms of the social construction of knowledge. When we do write history, it is all too easy for us to write pietistic chronicle. Nonetheless, historians of adult education can learn from the errors and successes of their revisionist school-oriented colleagues. The essayists in *Knowledge for the People* have learned from the social control paradigm without becoming its captive.

The bad news in revisionism from an adult educator's perspective was that Katz and his followers forgot Bailyn's challenge to broaden the boundaries of the field. In this sense revisionism was reactionary: the school was still on centre stage, only the moral of the play had changed. My argument is this: adult learning is more central to societal reproduction, resistance, and transformation than that of the children. Resistance to and transformation of societal structures emerges from the adult population, and is premised upon men and women's ability to learn new ways of seeing the world and acting within it. In our restriction of educational discourse to inter-generational transmission we have failed to understand the most powerful ''educational'' mechanisms operating within the social order. We ought to think of all of society as a vast school and begin to understand how autonomous learning emerges or is blocked and distorted within our political economy. ''The subject of adult education,'' the editorialist of the *Saskatoon Star-Phoenix* observed in 1946, "contains more political dynamite than most Governments can safely play with." This observation is more than amply exemplified in the essays collected in *Knowledge for the People*.

In 1970 J. D. Wilson wrote that Bailyn's reconceptualization of education "spelled doom to the 'history of schools and schooling'."[23] This doomsaying was premature. Few Canadian historians have strayed very far beyond the realm of formal, public schooling. When they have, they have focussed on the life experience of children and adolescents and have not extended their notions of the human life cycle. Writing about organized, institutional schooling remains at the heart of the historian of education's enterprise. A new way of seeing the boundaries and content of the field has not taken hold of the educational historian's mindset.[24] The title of a recent collection of essays, *An Imperfect Past: Education and Society in Canadian History* (1984), captures ironically the state of the art. The book is still about schools and children. The subdiscipline of the history of education is at an impasse and in desperate need of new historiographic styles and a reconceptualization of the nature of human learning across the life cycle.

II: Critical Dialogue with Tradition: Silences and Significances

All of the writers in *Knowledge for the People* recognize with varying degrees of self-consciousness that the historian must emplot (emplotment refers to the *kind* of story narrated) his or her narrative sensitive to the contextual surround, make arguments in theoretically reflexive ways, and be conscious of the ideological implications of one's narrative and argumentative choices. Indeed, following Hayden White's characterization of historiographic styles, we note that the essays in *Knowledge for the People* are *emplotted* as comedy (they take seriously the "forces which oppose the effort at human redemption naively held up as a possibility for Mankind in Romance"[25]), that the *argumentative* form is largely contextualist ("In this operation the aim of explanation is to identify the 'threads' that link the individual or institution under study to its specious sociocultural 'present' "[26]), and the *ideological* stances a mix of liberal and radical positions ("Just as every ideology is attended by a specific idea of history and its processes, so too, I maintain, is every idea of history attended by specifically determinable ideological implications"[27]).

All of the authors empathize with the struggles of the "common people," who want a life and problem-centred pedagogy, against the dominant interests, who want to determine the content and process of their subordinate's learning. The danger in this ideological populism is that identification with the protagonist (person, association, movement) may prevent the historian from a rigorous analysis of the forces opposing human redemption through educational practice. One moves inside the protagonist's world view and takes over the blindnesses! As noted, the authors do not share a common position on the adequacy of the fundamental structures of society or the nature of the transformation needed to usher in an equitable and fully co-operative society. Their visions of emancipation tend to be restricted to those of their protagonists. In this commentary, then, I question my co-authors about the silences and significances in their texts through scrutinizing two central themes.

Theme 1: Modes of Adult Education Discourse: From Paternalism to Transformation

The presence of the preposition "for" in the title of this book signals the existence of a deep-rooted tension in the discourse of Canadian adult education: between a patronizing rhetoric of provided for learning and a transformative rhetoric that is learner-centred, learner-legitimated, and critical. In the Mechanics' Institutes, an increasingly self-conscious middle class, undergoing its own cultural revolution as it learned to be a hegemonic class, reached out to the subaltern artisans and proletariat. This curriculum for the (male) artisans and proletariat is framed by the knowledge code (self-improvement and paternal humanitarianism) articulated by the emergent professional strata. It is they who are defining what "useful knowledge" is for the workingman.

The discourse of the professional classes censored and constrained the learning of the workers, skewing it in a particular ideological direction through particular pedagogical forms (lectures, classes, and library). Yet, in this conscientious seeking to educate workers and apprentices, the Montreal city élite admitted that the new scientific knowledge and technical skills were not the possession of one class alone. Here, then, one detects a glimmer of an egalitarian impulse. Knowledge for more people, albeit framed by a class which believes that its world view and values are universalistic. But before one too easily adopts a blunt social control analysis of Mechanics' Institutes, I would insist, as Bryan Palmer has in *A Culture in Conflict*, that we need to know how and to what ends working people appropriated the knowledge and skills provided. The Mechanics' Institutes failed to reach the workingman. But in this failure — noted by many writers — we also see the need to understand the kind of adult learning occurring within the workplace and cultural life of workers of various sort and type. And what were the women learning? The silence of mid-nineteenth-century male middle-class discourse on women's learning capacity begs for decoding. Does the absence of educational provision for women in early nineteenth-century Canada mean that women were not learning?[28]

In the educational vision of Alfred Fitzpatrick we see very vividly the tension between patronizing and transformative discourses. With Fitzpatrick we enter a different world — a turbulent period of class, ethnic, and gender conflict as Canada underwent her "great transformation." Rooted in the social regenerative assumptions of the reformers of late Victorian society,[29] Fitzpatrick argued that education was for all men, and not for a privileged class alone. Appropriating Marx's notion of humanization through labor but not his radical politics, Fitzpatrick criticized the universities for their ivory-tower separation from the real world and the state for its laissez-faire posture. Fitzpatrick — the early twentieth-century social gospeller — thought the solution to structurally rooted problems lay with the redemption of the individual through empathetic provision of basic adult education by laborer-teachers. There are still traces of paternalism and mid-nineteenth-century moralism present in his vision. Yet Fitzpatrick stands outside the establishment, unlike the patrons of the Montreal Mechanics' Institute, and with the voiceless and mute. His discourse is still patronizing but speaks with a deeply humanistic accent. His social gospel ideological frame moves him towards the neglected while simultaneously constraining his educational practice, repressing more overtly political education for social transformation and alternative conceptions of citizenship.

Originating in a time of labor militancy and radicalism on an unprecedented scale, the Workers' Educational Association's (WEA) university-based tutors saw the WEA as a "propaganda vehicle for imperialist doctrines." Like Fitzpatrick, the University of Toronto dons saw the purpose of the WEA as curbing radicalism — adult education to guard the status quo. A liberal education, they believed, could improve society by contributing to a new concordat between Capital, Labor, and the State. They were educating men for citizenship. But this discourse — "educating for citizenship" — masked some very significant differences within the association from the start. Some workers were suspicious of education and social mores being imposed from above and did not ascribe to the view that the interests of Capital and Labor could be reconciled. University professors were perceived as ideological gatekeepers. By the early 1930s the discourse shifted from patronizing to transformative. Wren believed that teaching the workers "how to think, not what to think" was "revolutionary" because the "application of critical judgment to existing social and economic wrongs would eventually eliminate . . . all injustices."[30] Workers' education was now fought for as a right of the oppressed classes and as a stimulant to working-class radicalization. Knowledge for the empowerment of working people (males?) and not their containment. But this rationalistic emancipatory vision, resonate with awakening elements in the working class, confronted bureaucratic and ideological resistance from both the university extension department and trade union leadership. The union leadership, particularly in the war years and edging into the late 1940s, opted for an authoritarian pedagogy, repressing and silencing the WEA as a critically reflective associative space. The union leadership, I surmise, was just as fearful of a critically educated membership as were the professors at the end of the First World War. The undermining of autonomous workers' education points to the need to analyse the structural preconditions for learner-centred and legitimated transformative education.[31]

The struggle for autonomous learning, manifest in the conflicts of the WEA with universities and union leadership, is also aptly illustrated in the Women's Institutes of B.C. Learning, to be sure, in an environment of constrained possibility, and sharing prevalent beliefs in the regenerative power of education, rural B.C. women grasped at club membership and participation in order to exercise some control over their lives. Excluded from the public realm by definition, women creatively manipulated the "ideology of domesticity" to insert themselves into the realm of the forbidden as a moral influence. "We start out to reform the world," one member lamented, "and very often cannot conduct a meeting." Through the Women's Institutes away from male scrutiny and fear of intimidation, women acquired important knowledge and skills pertaining to the law, politics, household management, and community building. The Women's Institutes can be profitably viewed as an early form of community education and development — educational action oriented towards concrete problem-solving. And this invisible action needs to be understood in relationship to larger social change processes. Yet, we need to ask to what extent the "ideology of domesticity" prevented women from developing an analysis that would have helped them undermine the patriarchal naming of their world. The Women's Institutes must be seen as constrained associative spaces. That they succeeded, to some extent, in enabling women to cope with their lives certainly challenges easy assumptions about women's victimization.

Canadians, Toronto professor Peter Sandiford observed in 1935, appeared to be on the eve of a great mass movement. Though exaggerated, Sandiford's observation captures the utopian spirit of Canadian adult education in the depression and war years. Seeing themselves as "amateurs out to change the world,"[32] adult educators in a range of settings thought that adult education could be a "vitalizing force in any movement toward the realization of social justice . . ."[33] To argue that the Canadian adult education movement was animated by a vision of participatory and economic democracy based on the principle of self-education in groups and direct action in local communities would not be inaccurate. This impulse fired the co-operative movement in its pre-Second World War phase, the early CAAE experiments, the WEA under Wren's leadership, the CAAE's great national mobilizing projects, the National Film Board's (NFB) film circuits, and Thomson's provocative initiatives in Saskatchewan. But we must recognize different accents and emphases in the discourse of Canadian adult education in the depression and war years. Knowledge for people to change the world. What kind of world? Under what conditions? Utilizing what pedagogical modes? While the Antigonish Movement embodied system-transcending elements in its vision, the deeply conservative political culture of Nova Scotia and a mildly liberal Roman Catholic Church pressed the movement in a liberal reformist direction and away from socialist solutions. To what extent did Coady and other leaders demand a "radical restructuring of the social order"? How conscious were they of the limitations of co-operative solutions in a capitalist political economy and culture? To what extent did the Antigonish Movement challenge patriarchal domination — in local congregation, in family, community, and emergent co-operative institutions?[34]

Watson Thomson's linking of personal development and social action, his commitment to community-based, participatory forms of social organization placed him in critical tension with the communists, social democrats, and the liberal democratic co-operative movement. Thomson's vision and practice, while obviously sharing much with that of Antigonish, is more explicitly socialist and aware of the problem of "false consciousness" in liberal democratic capitalist societies. Thomson recognized the depth of the cultural hegemony of capitalism, and that the acquisition of emancipatory subjectivity was an intentional educational practice.[35] The Antigonish leadership assumed that the transformation of the capitalist into a co-operative character structure was a by-product of participation in co-operative enterprises. Some individuals were shaken out of passivity and catalyzed into action through study and collective work. But, to what extent were the "relations of production" in society really transformed and, even if they were, did this new spirit spill over into other spheres of society (for example, creating the egalitarian family)? Though his emancipatory project ran aground, Thomson understood in a way his Antigonish colleagues did not that cultural/attitudinal revolution was central to any deep material transformation of society.

By the end of the Second World War with Canada on the eve of a great mass consumer society, adult education discourse would lose its "biting edge." The idiot winds of the Cold War blew numerous adult educators out of the action. The transformation of the Canadian economy, rapid urbanization, and the seduction of consumer ideology pressed the adult education movement into "narrowing limits." A new professional discourse began to replace the old. The struggle to maintain the old transformative vision in culturally unreceptive times is captured in the struggle to build a co-operative college in Saskatchewan. Contrasting with the original approach, which envisioned expanding the consciousness of ordinary Canadians so they could reform the nation if not the world, Canadian co-operators in the 1950s and 1960s became increasingly preoccupied with their own internal needs. The pedagogy of the College organizers underwent a "subtle but vital" shift from education for mobilization to education for human relations. By the end of the 1960s, the co-operative movement had capitulated to bigness, centralized control, and bureaucratic procedure. Is the failure of the co-operative movement to transform society (or fulfil its own norms) fundamentally an educational problem, or are there inherent limitations in the co-operative vision and social change program?

Theme 2: The Role of the State as Knowledge Legitimator

We have scrutinized the role of the state in the rise of the common school. We seldom reflect critically on the role of the state in the management of adult learning. To focus this theme, we note that the capitalist state plays three fundamental roles in societal and cultural reproduction: it aids in the capital accumulation process (the accumulative function); it maintains law and order (the coercive function); and it assists in legitimating the rule of the dominant class, or class fractions, through managing societal learning processes (the knowledge legitimating function). While the third function, that of legitimation, is central to our discussion of adult learning, the other two forms obviously interweave with that of the legitimation function, and impinge in their own way on the practical learning of adults. Here we enter the under-theorized realm of adult education and public policy. Before providing some general provisional formulations regarding the role of the state in adult education, we will offer commentary and observations.

For Fitzpatrick, the laissez-faire state of the late nineteenth and early twentieth century neglected the campmen. Through silence and lack of intervention, the Canadian state legitimated the exploitation of the campmen's labor and their maintenance as uneducated wage-slaves. Their fate was left to the logic of the market place, and the state was essentially instrumentalized by the railway companies. Continually calling on the state to intervene by deploying resources for neglected adult learners, Fitzpatrick would be repeatedly rebuffed, despite his powerful moral argument that the state derived its funds from frontier industries. The state was not going to interfere with the capital accumulation process in the frontier industries, and did not see that it had any responsibility for the men's lives and learning. Yet the state's laissez-faire stance was only maintained as long as the accumulation process was grinding along unimpeded. When labor tensions threatened social stability and the accumulation process, the state used its coercive apparatus to quell rebellion. It is also suggestive to see the university as part of the state apparatus and to note the way the university will legitimize certain knowledge forms and delegitimize others. However, Fitzpatrick's move to ensure that the campmen did not turn into Lenins suggests something of the complexity of the legitimation process. Should voluntary associations like Frontier College play a legitimating role for the dominant interests?

If Fitzpatrick cried out like John the Baptist for the state to intervene on behalf of the destitute, the Women's Institutes of B.C. were constituted, at least in part, by the state. The B.C. government clearly intended to contain women's learning, in response to problems of capital accumulation, rural depopulation, and an emergent suffragette movement. What the women did, however, was to collaborate with the government where they agreed with their policies and, at the local level away from state scrutiny, to resist state and patriarchal definitions of what they should learn and do. The extent to which their collaboration with the state undermined their collective empowerment begs further analysis and research. We need to think creatively about the tension between centralized state control of learning and development and local control of learning and development.

The essays on Grierson and Thomson focus on another fascinating dimension of the relationship between the state and adult education, namely, the attempts on the part of educators to use the state apparatus to mobilize the people for social change. In the fall of 1944 Watson Thomson actually believed that he had state support for his vision of creating a communitarian socialist society. For Thomson, the Saskatchewan experiment was a grand opportunity to mobilize the people towards laying the foundation for a "really new people's society"; for M. J. Coldwell, CCF national leader, a grand opportunity to show the Canadian electorate that the Saskatchewan CCF was a moderate reform party, ruled by humanistic bureaucrats. It is difficult to escape the conclusion that Saskatchewan parliamentary democracy, like other parties capitalist or communist, wanted to marginalize any movement at the base, however innocuous. In the exuberant first few months of the regime, Douglas thought he wanted to "launch the biggest adult education program in the country." There is no evidence, however, that he or Woodrow Lloyd shared Thomson's commitment to a socialist learning society. Under pressure from an increasingly conservative and Russophobic national leadership, the Saskatchewan government lost whatever imagination it had, discouraged creative and innovative experiments in self-management and community-based development, and opted instead to be a party of order and respectability. Any mobilization of the people in liberal or social democracies is potentially threatening to the élite managers of the system.

Motivated by the conviction that "only if the state is fighting for democracy" does it have a "dog's chance of coming through," Grierson grasped a truth understood by both Lenin and Thomson. Yet, it is not clear how Grierson really understood the relationship between the social movements of his time and the achievement of state power, whether he had even a faint glimmer of Gramsci's understanding of counter-hegemonic educational struggle.[36] The depression had weakened faith in free enterprise; war and collectivist controls had restored a prosperity of sorts and a sense of common purpose. To many the importance of the rough equality of wartime seemed to demonstrate the real possibility of social justice in the postwar world. Canadians were increasingly confident that "collective action could and should create a far more stable and equitable society."[37] At this historical juncture the liberal democratic state faced a legitimation crisis. The ruling Liberal party, facing its own internal crisis, needed someone like Grierson to win the people for its policies, and Grierson thought he could use film to motivate Canadians "towards a more egalitarian and co-operative society." The state, in

Grierson's view, was to be the people's tutor. To what extent did Grierson's bargain with the liberal democratic state constrain his emancipatory project, and even channel social protest away from radical restructuring?

Grierson believed that art was a hammer and not a mirror with which to forge a new "socialist" sensibility. This view of art — as an "instrument of artistically viable political instruction" — was shared by the workers' theatre advocates. Sacrificing aesthetic form to didactic content, workers' theatre and Grierson's documentary were inserted into the social struggle as weapons for justice. Workers' Theatre wanted to "expose and ridicule" bourgeois values and corruption; Grierson framed reality for the masses he believed were incapable of "making sense" of modernity. Here we need to disentangle the complex relationship of adult education to propaganda and art. The danger in documentary (film or theatre) is in the way reality is framed for the recipient: truth is not arrived at through dialogical process. Documentary does not enable the non-expert "reader" to go to the same sources. Dialogical process, says Dominick La Capra, must "stimulate the reader to respond critically to the interpretation it offers through his or her own reading or re-reading of the primary texts."[38] We note, however, that grassroots adult educators, sensitive to this problem, created innovations like the film forum in order to create dialogical contexts for learning, and the Theatre of Action tried to overcome the distinction between propaganda and art.

These provisional formulations suggest themselves. First, the case of Frontier College highlights the low-profile status of adult education within educational policy formation. This should be attributed to two basic reasons: the "structural location of its potential clientele, and its clientele's lack of power."[39] It does appear that the capitalist state assesses the strength of particular sectors in its resource allocation decisions. The weaker the clientele, the fewer the resources. Here the state can move in two directions: it can neglect the less powerful's needs and demands (often voiced through an advocate) or, as the women's institutes illustrate, utilize the voluntary sector to provide services it cannot or will not provide, services minimally necessary to ensure either the capital accumulation process or political legitimation.

Second, we suggest as a general rule of the capitalist state (in liberal, social democratic, and democratic socialist variants) that "adult education policies and programs should never promote the political participation of its clientele in the civic culture and government affairs."[40] Of course, democratic socialist parties tend to be more open to participative adult education. But even here, they are leery of increasing citizen participation because of the difficulty and problems of control and co-optation. Participative research or participative planning will seldom be advanced as a policy of the capitalist state. That both the Saskatchewan CCF and, to a lesser extent, the federal Liberals, were open to participative planning from below indicates that at certain turning points the state can be reformed. More insight is needed into which forms of state and what kind of political regime support what kind of adult education and for what state purposes? And, under what specific conditions is the capitalist state vulnerable to popular initiatives?

Third, our historical case studies reveal that popular social movements can embody in their internal practice participative adult learning and win some gains and support within the state. To understand more fully how this occurs, we need a theory of social movements which accounts for the "ongoing creativity of social actors in developing a plurality of new forms of democracy such as councils, local assemblies . . ." and the potentiality of "reform of the political/economic steering mechanisms." As Jean Cohen observes, "Social movements are not political movements, but without reform of political/economic steering mechanisms the very social space in which they operate and which they seek to expand is endangered."[41]

*   *   *

I shall conclude by reiterating the commitment of Canadian adult educators to open up dialogue with the past in order to illuminate present predicaments and possibilities. Historical consciousness can provide depth and context for current discourse about the possibilities of autonomous learning in our world. *Knowledge for the People*, it is hoped, will contribute to the retrieval of our history and the fanning of sparks of hope in the present.

Footnotes

1. Nietzsche is quoted in Alfred Schmidt, *History and Structure: An Essay on Hegelian-Marxist and Structuralist Theories of History* (Cambridge, Mass.: The MIT Press, 1981), p. 3. The citation, the "eternal present," is from Theodor Adorno, cited by Schmidt, p. 2.

2. See Hayden White, "The Burden of History," in *Tropics of Discourse: Essays in Cultural Criticism,* edited by Hayden White (Baltimore: Johns Hopkins University Press, 1978) for a brilliant discussion of this issue.

3. Nietzsche, cited in Schmidt, p. 3.

4. The quotation is from Nietzsche, cited in Schmidt, p. 3, and the fanning metaphor is drawn from Walter Benjamin, *Illuminations* (Fontana Books, 1973): "Only that historian will have the gift of fanning the spark of hope in the past who is firmly convinced that *even the dead* will not be safe from the enemy if he wins." (p. 257, italics W.B.)

5. Hayden White suggested some of the dimensions of this constructivist process.

6. The actual quotation is as follows: "Men make their own history, but they do not make it just as they please; they do not make it under circumstances chosen by themselves, but under circumstances directly encountered, given and transmitted from the past. The tradition of all the dead generations weighs like a nightmare on the brain of the living."

7. For a discussion of romantic emploment, see Hayden White, *MetaHistory: The Historical Imagination in Nineteenth-Century Europe* (Baltimore: The Johns Hopkins Press, 1973), pp. 8-11.

8. Anne Firor Scott, "On Seeing and Not Seeing: A Case of Historical Invisibility," *The Journal of American History*, vol. 71 (1), June 1984, p. 8.

9. Adult education activists like Moses Coady, E. A. Corbett, and J. Roby Kidd, and journalist fellow-travellers like George Boyle, Bertram Fowler, and Leo Ward, have kept the memory of Canadian popular education alive through bleak times. Rather than denouncing this unscholarly, popular, enthusiastic tradition from the unsullied groves of the Academy, we ought to affirm their belief that history has exhortatory value.

10. Hayden White, *MetaHistory*, p. 9.

11. Carl Berger, *The Writing of Canadian History: Aspects of English-Canadian History Writing: 1900-1970* (Toronto: Oxford University Press, 1976), provides a useful guide to the dominant historiographic tradition. For a rather acerbic critique of Berger from a Maritime perspective, see E. G. Forbes, "In Search of a Post-Confederation Maritime Historiography, 1900-1967," in *Eastern and Western Perspectives*, edited by David J. Bercuson and Phillip Buckner (Toronto: University of Toronto Press, 1981). Viv Nelles, "Rewriting History," *Saturday Night*, February 1981, is a valuable popular explication of the emergence of the new social history.

12. Here the reader will recognize the influence of Lawrence Cremin who defined education as the "deliberate, systematic, and sustained effort to transmit, evoke, or acquire knowledge, attitudes, values, skills, or sensibilities, as well as any outcomes of that effort." See *Public Education* (New York: Basic Books, 1976), p. 27.

13. See, for example, Gregory Kealey and Peter Warrian, eds., "Introduction," *Essays in Canadian Working Class History* (Toronto: McClelland and Stewart, 1976), and Bryan Palmer's bibliographic observations in *Working Class Experience* (Toronto: Butterworth, 1983).

14. The works of Antonio Gramsci and, more recently, Raymond Williams (*Marxism and Literature*, 1977) have great potential for historians of adult education. Until we have a comprehensive, dynamic theory of culture along Williams's lines (dominant, oppositional, alternative, residual), we will not be able to conceptualize adequately the multiplicity of adult education forms and processes.

15. H. Clare Pentland, *Labour and Capital in Canada, 1650-1850* (Toronto: James Lorimer, 1981), p. 176.

16. J. D. Wilson et al., *Canadian Education: A History* (Scarborough: Prentice-Hall, 1970), p. viii.

17. In a recent book, *Education and the Social Condition* (London: Methuen, 1980), Harold Silver rejects the concept of "social context" because "it is too inert, as if education is surrounded by, framed by, perhaps even affected by the big out-there, but is not in any serious kind of relationship with it, in but not *of* it" (p. 3).

18. John Calam, review of Wilson et al. in *The Journal of Educational Thought,* vol. 5(1), 1971.

19. See, for a comparative perspective, Richard Taylor, Kathleen Rockhill, and Roger Fieldhouse, *University Adult Education in England and the USA* (London: Croom Helm, 1985).

20. See Ian MacPherson, *Each for All: A History of the Co-operative Movement in English Canada, 1900-1945* (Toronto: The Macmillan Co., 1979) for a history sensitive to the role of education in social movements.

21. Harold Silver, "View from Afar: An Afterword," *History of Education,* vol. 7(3), 1978, provides a useful critique of the conceptual crudities of the revisionists.

22. Kjell Rubenson, "Adult Education Research: In Quest of a Map of the Territory," *Adult Education,* vol. 32(2), Winter 1982, is the best critique of the psychologizing of the field, and Colin Griffin, *Curriculum Theory in Adult and Lifelong Education* (London: Croom Helm, 1983), ch. 3, "An Ideology of Needs, Access and Provision," provides one of the most devastating critiques of the ideology currently dominating adult educational thought and practice.

23. J. D. Wilson et al., *Canadian Education: A History,* p. vii.

24. This may be changing a little. *Canadian Woman Studies,* vol. 7(3), Fall 1986, actually includes several essays on women's learning in voluntary associations!

25. White, *MetaHistory,* p. 10.

26. Ibid., p. 18.

27. Ibid., p. 24.

28. Barbara Taylor's *Eve and the New Jerusalem* (New York: Pantheon Books, 1983) is a pathbreaking text in that she does not merely discover the absence of adult education provision for women in early nineteenth-century England, but painstakingly reconstructs women's learning in the context of the Owenite movement.

29. See Ramsey Cook, *The Regenerators: Social Criticism in Late Victorian English Canada* (Toronto: University of Toronto Press, 1985).

30. Cited in Michael R. Welton, " 'The Depths of Despondency': The Struggle for Autonomous Workers' Education in the Vancouver WEA, 1942-1948," *CASAE History Bulletin,* May 1986.

31. In "The 'New Social Movements': Moral Crusades, Political Pressure Groups, or Social Movements," *Social Research,* vol. 52(4), Winter 1985, pp. 886ff, Klaus Eder says that it is useful to examine the form of sociality that permits the construction of a social world by "means of communicative conflict resolution." This type of sociality "leads to rational social movements; social conditions are established which force those involved into learning. Its rationality consists in being a form of associative practice which is based upon communicative social relations."

32. Alexander Laidlaw, " 'Return of a Native' — Lecture Notes on Adult Education" (1970), in Laidlaw Papers, Public Archives of Canada, vol. 10, file 62.

33. E. A. Corbett, "The Canadians March," *Adult Learning,* September–October, 1939, p. 12.

34. The evidence suggests that men continued to dominate in the co-operative movement. See, for instance, Ida Delaney, *By Their Own Hands: A Fieldworker's Account of the Antigonish Movement* (Hantsport: Lancelot Press: 1985).

35. This theme — the acquisition of emancipatory subjectivity as intentional educational practice — is pursued in Erica Sherover-Marcuse, *Emancipation and Consciousness: Dogmatic and Dialectical Perspectives in the Early Marx* (Oxford: Basil Blackwell, 1986).

36. See, on Gramsci's counter-hegemonic project, Walter L. Adamson, *Hegemony and Revolution: A Study of Antonio Gramsci's Political and Cultural Theory* (Berkeley: University of California Press, 1980).

37. Cited in Michael R. Welton, " 'An Authentic Instrument of the Democratic Process': The Intellectual Origins of the Canadian Citizens' Forum," *Studies in the Education of Adults,* vol. 18(1), April 1986.

38. Dominick La Capra, "Rethinking Intellectual History and Reading Texts," in *Modern European Intellectual History: Reappraisals and New Perspectives,* edited by Dominick La Capra and Stephen Kaplan (Ithaca: Cornell University Press, 1982), pp. 67-68.

39. Carlos Torres, "The Political Economy of Adult Education in Latin America," *Canadian and International Education,* vol. 13(2), 1984, p. 31.

40. Torres, p. 32.

41. Jean Cohen, *Class and Civil Society: The Limits of Marxian Critical Theory* (Oxford: Martin Robertson, 1982), pp. 226-27.

"Useful Education for the Workingman": The Montreal Mechanics' Institute, 1828-70

Nora Robins

The story of the Montreal Mechanics' Institute, the first institution of its kind in British North America, covers 159 years and falls into two distinct periods. The Montreal Mechanics' Institution operated from 1828 until 1835 when it lapsed due to social and political pressures. Revived in 1840 as the Montreal Mechanics' Institute, it continues to this day as the Atwater Library of Montreal.

A mechanics' institute, simply defined, was meant to be a voluntary association of mechanics who gathered together for instruction in the elementary and scientific principles underlying their work. As the movement gained in popularity, membership was expanded to include "every man who earned his living by the work of his hands."[1]

The origins of the movement have been the subject of continued and often contradictory debate. While the work of George Birkbeck in early nineteenth-century Glasgow laid the foundations of the movement in its recognizable form, the truth is that the movement was not the work of one man but, like most large undertakings, was the result of a number of events which worked to produce similar results in a variety of places. By 1823 the London Mechanics' Institute had been founded in England. The publicity inevitably resulting from any large London venture gave initial impetus and later cohesion to the movement as a whole. By the 1850s there were almost 700 Institutes with a membership of more than 120 000 in Great Britain.[2]

Even before the movement was fully established in Great Britain it reached out to influence adult education all over the world. France, Germany, and the United States had such movements prior to 1823, but all adapted some of the ideas of the British Institutes. Mechanics' Institutes were opened in Boston and Philadelphia (1820), St Petersburg (1831), Sydney (1833),

Canton (1837), Calcutta (1839), and in British North North America.

That the worthy citizens of Montreal should consider establishing a society of this nature in 1828 is not surprising. With a population between 22 357 and 27 297, the city was outgrowing its origins as the centre of the fur trade and developing into "the metropolis of a commercial state."[3] The city possessed a wealthy and influential group of merchants, a growing professional class, numerous craftsmen and laborers. Many workers, both skilled and unskilled, were employed on the construction of the Lachine Canal, on the railway, in factories and in shops. By 1831, some 675 families were considered to be engaged in commerce and trade.

For the common man the hours of labor were long and hard. In 1833 a journeyman carpenter remarked, "I don't know what a Master carpenter would call a fair and honest work day, but this I know, after working 12 hours a day, sleeping 7 hours a night, I cannot do as much work the next day than if I had worked 10 hours."[4] That same year the Montreal Mechanics' Mutual Protective Society for Carpenters decided to organize for the purpose of discovering "the most efficient (means) for accomplishing a diminution of the hours of labor."[5] The unanimous decision was that ten hours a day was as much as any man could be expected to work.

Many of the factors that contributed to the development of the movement in Great Britain were present to some degree in Montreal: increasing need for skilled workers who possessed at least an elementary understanding of mathematics and science to help them grapple with the growing technology of machines; popular interest in science and the formation of societies to meet this interest; a general move towards the provision of popular education for all regardless of class; and the fight for democratic government with its need for a literate .electorate.

The need for an organization that could supply practical knowledge of the three "R's" and of the sciences was evident when one examined the limited educational facilities available to the English-speaking population. There were a number of schools and small private establishments for the children of Montreal's affluent citizens but nothing for the working class. While the British and Canadian Schools had been founded in 1822 for the purpose of promoting the education of working-class children, there was no institution capable of providing for the education of adults. McGill College, although granted its charter in 1824, did not begin teaching until 1828, due to protracted litigation, and it was not viewed as a place for the workingman.

The level of literacy of Montreal's population had some bearing on events. The majority of the non-francophone population were from the British Isles where, in 1839, illiteracy was rated at 33.7 percent for men and 49.5 percent for women.[6] Immigrants from Scotland, of which there were many in the city, were probably better educated since compulsory schooling had existed there prior to 1800. Lord Durham, in his famous *Report*, was of the opinion that adults from the "old country" were more or less educated. This has been borne out by recent studies which show that the level of literacy among the English-speaking population of Lower Canada was higher than among the French Canadians.[7] All of which would seem to indicate the need to provide the means of encouraging and sustaining literacy.

On the evening of 21 November 1828, a group of influential citizens gathered at the home of the Reverend Henry Esson, minister of St Gabriel's Presbyterian Church, to discuss the formation of a society called the Montreal Mechanics' Institution whose object would be "to instruct the members in the principles of the arts and in the various branches of science and useful knowledge."[8] This would be accomplished in seven ways: formation of a voluntary association of mechanics and others, with payment of a small fee; donations of money, books, and apparatus; a library of reference and a reading room; a museum of machines and natural history; a school; lectures, experimental workshop, and laboratory. The aims of the society and the means of achieving them were expressed in terms identical to those used by the London Mechanics' Institute in 1823.

Esson was clearly the guiding light and, as a Scot who had arrived in Montreal in 1817, had probably been exposed to the idea of education for mechanics while at home. Other concerned individuals would doubtless have read or heard about the movement in the United States or Britain. Bosworth, writing about Montreal in 1829, stated that the Institution was formed "after the model of those at home."[9] Certainly the motivation would appear to be similar: the desirability of useful education for the workingman, thereby making him a better worker and a better Christian. English Montrealers believed, as did their British counterparts, that

> by inducing those who would otherwise spend their earnings at the tavern, to pay some attention to the improvements of their minds, and by placing within their reach the means of becoming acquainted with the principles of their art, and of gaining otherwise useful knowledge, a great advantage is conferred upon them.[10]

The founding of such an institute can also be seen as part of the broad social service and philanthropic endeavors which were characteristic of the reforming attitudes of the period. The Ladies Benevolent Society, Protestant Orphans' Home, Public Dispensary, and Montreal General Hospital were all founded in the first quarter of the nineteenth century.

Within a month, notices of meeting had been printed in newspapers, rooms rented, a constitution drawn up, and a committee of management elected. The importance attached to the enterprise may be gauged by noting the calibre of the men elected to the first executive on 9 December 1828. The president was Louis Gugy, sheriff of Montreal, while the vice-presidents were John Molson, banker and merchant, Horatio Gates, merchant, Esson, minister, and Louis-Joseph Papineau, politician. Sir James Kempt, governor of Lower

Canada, agreed to serve as patron. Thus from its inception the institution had the support of Montreal's foremost citizens.

The Montreal Mechanics' Institution lost no time in putting into practice the three most popular means of "diffusing knowledge": lecture, class, and library. At the inaugural meeting, it was decided to offer half-hour lectures on a wide variety of subjects: natural and experimental philosophy, practical mechanics, astronomy, elementary civil history, political economy, philosophy of the mind, literature, and the arts. The first lecture was delivered by Esson, appropriately enough, on the advantages of mechanics' institutes. Over the next seven years lectures were given in such widely diverse subjects as the "Causes and Cure of Cahots," "The Boiling of Grain for Feeding Cattle," "The Principles of Architecture," "Prison Disciplines," and "Lime Stones." They were delivered by members, free of charge.

The lecture program was subject to criticism. The frustration incurred by occasional lectures with no follow-up finally found expression in Professor J. Clark's proposal that since

> such information cannot be duly appreciated or received with that general benefit as it would if received in a regular way and a proper salary paid to the lecturers . . . in order to have a regular course of information during the subsequent Winter Sessions, I beg to recommend that the committee of Management come up with a plan.[11]

The institution never did get around to setting up regular lectures. However, members were invited to attend those given at the Natural History Society, an organization to which many of the executive, at least, belonged.

There is ample evidence that the weekly meetings were used as information sessions at which questions were posed to members who were then expected to provide answers at succeeding meetings. Suggestions were also made on ways to improve business and factory techniques. For example, on 2 December 1828, Mr Shand spoke of the importance of introducing into "the Parent-Country the Canadian Gin for raising large logs of timber as being a savings of labor and expense." At subsequent meetings, Clark demonstrated his improved scuttle pipe while Mr Ayres reported that he had tried a "bathing machine to obviate the unseemly practice of immersing hands and arms in the material in the preparation of breads,"[12] and requested the formation of a committee to examine it. The topic proposed for 5 May 1829 was "What is the reason . . . rivers running southward have not the abrupt rapids that exist in those that run in a northerly direction?" And so much interest was aroused by Mr Cooper's geometrical staircase that he was obliged to invite member to his home to view it!

Classes were not formed as speedily as some members would have liked. A school for the sons and apprentices of members opened in December 1833 and ceased in April 1834, due evidently to a lack of students and inadequate quarters. The library was, from the outset, dependent upon donations. It seems to have done quite well, for by 1835 it contained five hundred volumes. The reading room was stocked with Canadian, British, and American newspapers and journals and was reported to be well attended. There is no evidence that there were any strictures against religious discussion, as was the case in other institutes, for subscriptions were held to the *Religious Observer* and to Paley's *Natural Theology*. The museum got off to a rather dubious start with donations of a petrified snail, stuffed hummingbird, the tail, hind, and fore-foot of a beaver, and an ancient Roman coil — all kept in a glass-fronted cabinet!

The incompleteness of the early records makes it extremely difficult to form an accurate picture of the composition of the membership of the Institution in its first phase. We cannot even be certain of the size of the membership nor do we know how many people attended the weekly meetings. In 1828 the secretary estimated the membership at two hundred, predominantly English and all male. Socially they ranged from officers of the garrison to grocers. The founders and directors were clearly affluent business and professional men. In this the movement was no different from that in Great Britain and certainly no different from what is know of the individuals whose names were associated with the institutes in Upper Canada.[13] There were a wide variety of occupations recorded against the names of members: distiller, attorney, joiner, teacher, miller, hatter, and minister. The term "mechanic" or "craftsman" did not occur. However, it is reasonable to believe that the institution accepted as members those who, because of their work, were most likely to benefit from the instruction offered. This was after all the course of action taken by the London Mechanics' Institute and, as has been shown, the Montreal Mechanics' Institution did not hesitate to follow that Institute's example.

The ethnic composition of the institution was overwhelmingly Anglo-Saxon. There were only two local French-speaking members, albeit distinguished ones, on the executive: Louis-Joseph Papineau and F. A. Laroque (Gugy was Swiss). The membership lists record only four French names, although that is no guarantee that there were not more. One can only surmise that the founders, themselves anglophone, felt that their first responsibility was to their employees and apprentices. French members were welcome provided they spoke English.

Lack of money clearly plagued the Institution and severely affected the quality of much of what the organization planned. Heavy reliance was placed on the annual grant of £25 from the provincial legislature, on membership dues of 20s. 7d per annum, and on donations.

By 1832, the *Minutes*, or rather lack of them, indicated that something was happening that was severely limiting the effectiveness of the Institution. Between 1832 and 1835, only sixteen meetings were held, the last on 24 March 1835. Since Montreal suffered cholera and typhoid epidemics as well as political unrest during this period, it is not unreasonable to assume that members were too ill, too busy, or too fearful to attend meetings, lectures, or classes.

Records for these early years are scarce but they do provide a picture of a group of earnest gentlemen, members of the city's élite, who conscientiously sought to educate workers and apprentices. The degree to which the Institution was able to attract mechanics or artisans is unclear; they certainly were not part of the executive. It did, on the other hand, attract the small businessman, the clerk, and the skilled worker. That the Institute was reinstituted in 1840 indicates that its usefulness was recognized and that its founders had laid the foundation from which was to develop a healthy institution.

The 1840s were important ones in Montreal's growth and economic development. Recovery from the economic distress and political troubles of the previous decade was rapid and a flood of immigrants helped swell the population to more than 44 000 by 1844 and to 57 715 by 1852. The *Census of 1851-52* did not list mechanics but it did record 2458 workers in the commercial class, 4659 industrial, 451 professional, and 1622 domestics. The first mention of "mechanics" occurred in the *Census of 1860-61* when thirty-seven were listed as working in Montreal. One wonders just how the term "mechanic" was used by the government for in 1871 there were four hundred in the city.

This was a period of "great improvements in transportation and the dramatic expansion of the industrial activity of the city." It saw the establishment of new banking, insurance, and telegraph companies, as well as significant expansion in older companies. Work resumed on the Montreal docks and on the Lachine Canal. The water power of the enlarged canal was such that "several established Montreal industrialists and many new men were induced to erect large factories employing some two thousand workers."[14] The 1850s witnessed the construction of the Victoria Bridge, the Grand Trunk Railway, and the Montreal Waterworks. These were substantial undertakings, creating employment and maintaining payrolls quite without parallel in the city's history. This was also the period that saw the founding of at least three fortunes: John Redpath turned from contracting and real-estate to sugar refining; A. W. Ogilvie established his flour mills; and Hugh Allan formed the Montreal Ocean Steamship Company.[15] All three gentlemen were to be involved with the Montreal Mechanics' Institute. Such activity would seemingly reinforce the need for adequate training in the practical sciences, training that it was felt a mechanics' institute could provide.

On 8 February 1840, there appeared in the *Montreal Transcript* the following notice addressed to:

> the public generally, but more particularly to the Master and Journeymen Mechanics of this city, and requests them to meet at the School Room of Mr. Bruce . . . to take into consideration the best means of reorganiz-

ing and re-establishing the Mechanics' Institute (formerly existing here) with a view to benefitting the Mechanics, whether Masters, Journeymen or Apprentices by establishing an institution that will improve their conditions, socially and morally.[16]

The first meeting was held on 11 February 1840 with John Redpath in the chair, and, as the *Minutes* succinctly report, "after lively discussion, the Institute was forthwith formed." Subsequent meetings witnessed the approval of a constitution and by-laws (the contents of which were, to all intents and purposes, those of the 1828 institution), setting of subscription fees, and election of Redpath as president.

The aims of the Montreal Mechanics' Institute were in accord with those of their British counterparts: "to unite in the diffusion of knowledge and intelligence, to aim by such means at what is called a sound and healthy public opinion."[17] The founders believed that less fortunate nations than Canada would look to her as a country whose middle class, the best and greatest portion of whom had recently been recruited from the ranks of mechanics and citizens, possessed a sound moral public opinion broadly based on education and knowledge. In days of rapid and startling improvements in all commercial, mechanical, and scientific matters ". . . the humblest trade will yet require for its successful conduct a much wider intellectual range than was ever imagined — mental cultivation in itself, and for its own sake, is our highest, our ultimate aim."[18] The founders believed that the education of the working class would promote peace and prosperity and would make a man a better mechanic (and possibly a mechanic a better man). However, increasingly avowels of the purpose of the Institute were preceded by plaintive laments over the inadequate number of mechanics who cared to join.[19]

The first task facing the officers was to meet with those in charge of the previous organization's effects with a view to amalgamation. Arbitrators set the value of the property at £20.10s.6d. Amalgamation took place on 1 June 1840, and the Montreal Mechanics' Institute was free to begin its work.

The government of the Institute was in the hands of a general committee composed of president, four vice-presidents, one corresponding and one recording secretary, treasurer, librarian, cabinet keeper, and twelve members. All were elected by majority votes. The Institute was incorporated on 29 March 1845 as the Mechanics' Institute of Montreal. The act of incorporation was amended several times, notably in1860, when the governing body, by then deemed unwieldy, was decreased to thirteen members by the elimination of three vice-presidents and seven members.

The Institute lost no time in recruiting members. Information regarding weekly meetings was placed in newspapers and in shops. Membership was open to all men, regardless of party, position, or creed, upon payment of a subscription fee. By August 1840 there were 223 members, of whom six were listed as apprentices and twenty-four as members of the previous institute. The size of membership fluctuated, the high point occurring in 1856 with 1245 members. Unfortunately, only 924 of these had paid up subscriptions. Non-payment of dues was evidently a perennial problem. An 1859 report found the average duration of membership or time members paid fees was 2½ years. After 1848, the *Minutes* also recorded the number of members who left. Reference was made to their loss because they moved, were expelled for "improper conduct," or failed to pay dues. It is also possible that people left because they lost interest, or found the lectures and classes not to their taste, or were unable to obtain books of their choice, a frequent complaint throughout the 1850s.

The occupation of individuals was seldom mentioned before the 1860s at which time we find clerks, carpenters, and butchers rubbing shoulders with engineers, politicians, and men of the cloth. Members were noticeably anglophone as was the case with the previous institutions. The explanation may be found in the lack of advertising in French-language newspapers, lack of ability and money to provide lectures and books in French, and the predominance of English in business and factories. Reicher feels that "the French Canadians tried to prevent linguistic assimilation by creating the Institut Canadien which, though eventually defeated by the Church, brought modern ideas into Quebec."[20]

It is evident from all available information that the Institute was never able to attract what the executive felt was a sufficient number of mechanics and apprentices. There are frequent comments strewn throughout the *Minutes* complaining of apathy and lack of interest on the part of mechanics. This was particularly aggravating because they were the ones for whose particular benefit the organization had been founded.

The move in 1843 to amend the constitution to permit the admission of ladies "to all the privileges" could be interpreted as a response to the drop in membership the previous year. The immediate result was the admission of twenty ladies. The ladies paid the same fee per annum as apprentices while journeymen mechanics paid 10s and ordinary members paid 15s.

The Institute was continually on the move from one set of rented rooms to another in its search for a suitable location. After seven moves in eleven years, a lot, situated on the east side of St James Street, was finally purchased for £2521. Work began on the building in the fall of 1853 and the cornerstone was laid with imposing Masonic ceremony the following spring. The Mechanics Hall was completed in 1855. Built at a cost of £5236, it was designed "in the Italian style" and comprised three floors, the top floor housing a lecture hall capable of seating eight hundred people. The opening was attended by more than five hundred ladies and gentlemen, many of them "of the first standing in the city: we should however, have preferred to see more mechanics present."[21]

The Montreal Mechanics' Institute endorsed the idea that lectures were the best means of awakening a desire for knowledge. Free lectures on a wide

MECHANICS INSTITUTE, MONTREAL. 1854.

variety of topics were to be delivered by respected professional men on a regular basis. They were to be one-half hour long, delivered in a clear, distinct, agreeable style, and technical terms were to be, if possible, avoided when addressing a mixed audience. Lecture topics were approved by the executive who did not hesitate to reject those they deemed inappropriate. The first one was given by attorney Christopher Dunkin who spoke on the subject of "Self Improvement and the Education of the working Class." It was attended by two hundred and fifty ladies and gentlemen who unanimously agreed that the topic was most appropriate for "it was calculated to remove anything like a sense of inferiority excepting only in external circumstances."[22] One wonders how the working-class attendees, if any, felt! By 1844, the Institute was offering lectures on such diverse subjects as natural philosophy, philosophy of education, chemical science, vegetable poisons, Greek history, savings banks, and the ventilation of buildings.

Attendance must have been a matter of concern for there were frequent references to the lack of it. While it is clear that members of the middle class attended the lectures, the lack of working-class members among those who set policy and the numerous comments upon the apathy of the working class leads to the conclusion that they were not present in any significant numbers. For the middle-class members, however, the lecture proved useful, educational, and a means of social intercourse. However, by 1851, the number of lectures had declined to three or four a year, owing in part to a lack of suitable speakers. In 1857, the Institute finally relinquished its lectures to the Board of Arts and Manufactures which had been formed by the government "to promote the development of mechanical talent among the prople . . . by disseminating instruction in mechanics and kindred sciences."[23] The Board continued to give lectures with varying degrees of success until 1868 when it was disbanded because of inadequate funding.

Classes proved even less successful than lectures. Evening classes began in 1841 but were evidently not as well attended as had been expected. One reason given for poor attendance was the unwillingness of employers to grant time off to their apprentices. The Committee of Education could hardly believe that the employers (many of whom were members of the Institute) would be so blind to their own interests as to act so inconsiderately. In 1854, the Institute observed that "during former years the classes were attended by but a very small number of members, perhaps not averaging more than twelve to eighteen"[24] and resolved to abolish the admission fee in the hope of attracting the working-class youth. Classes were offered in French, architectural and mechanical drawing, writing, bookkeeping, and arithmetic to about one hundred students. Attendance fell drastically in 1856 when the Institute reintroduced a nominal fee of £1. In 1858 free classes were again offered in French, drawing, writing, bookkeeping, arithmetic, and mathematics. They lasted four months. Classes limped along until 1870 when they were taken over by the School of Arts and Design which had been formed upon the demise of the Board of Arts and Manufacturers.

When the executive presented its first *Annual Report* it showed a modest start at the task of assembling a library — "the sheet anchor" of the Institute. They reported a library of four hundred volumes, thirty of which were termed "reference" books, all in good order, "the whole representing a repository of literary and scientific knowledge of which amassed as it has been during a short period, the Institution may well be proud."[25] A committee to purchase books had been formed in March 1840, and by June they reported that they "had procured as many of them as can be had in town" to the tune of £7.11s.8d. An additional £50 was spent on books, a commendable effort considering that the total income for the year was only £91.3s.5d. Unfortunately, despite declarations to the contrary, the library clearly ranked third to lectures and classes and frequently bore the brunt of the Institute's indebtedness. Between 1841 and 1850 only thirty-five books were purchased. During the same period, however, the library grew to over 1200 volumes, thanks to donations which proved to be the lifeblood of the collection. The *Minutes* are sprinkled with requests to members "to intensify vigilence in procuring dontations . . . the library would be a fine one if each member were to donate one book a year."[26]

By 1855, the library had become a popular feature of the Institute and in recognition of this, 189 titles were purchased in an effort to fill the shelves with the newest publications as they arrived. Such a course of action would, the executive felt, increase at once the value and attractiveness of the library. The results of a members' survey taken in 1859 reported that the library and reading room were the most popular as far as the members were concerned and they felt that the manner in which these departments were run would always have a great influence upon the membership. The popularity of the library can be appreciated when one realizes that, unlike the situation in Ontario, there were few libraries to meet the needs of the English community (or French, for that matter). The library of the Montreal Mechanics' Institute was, together with the Montreal Library and the Mercantile Institution, providing a service unavailable elsewhere.

A glance at the sixty-six page *Catalogue* of 1859 shows a varied collection of more than three thousand volumes covering history, religion, travel, biography, and science, as well as the works of such "popular" novelists as Jane Austen, Charles Dickens, Alexandre Dumas, and Sir Walter Scott. There were also works of interest to young people, fairy tales, and books by Marryat and Ballantyne. Attempts in the 1850s to purchase popular fiction, while in keeping with the trend in other institutes, did not meet with the approval of the executive of the Montreal Institute. They were quite upset over the fact that "novels and fiction received more perusal than all the other branches of the library combined" and declared that they would prevent as far as possible the introduction of such works. They would rather purchase "those which are more healthful and beneficial to the rising generation."[27] In the end they were obliged to bow to members' demands and to acquire more fiction.

In 1869, the library underwent a major renovation in an 'effort to halt the exodus of members. The room was cleaned, painted, papered, shelves added, books weeded, and many "useful and valuable books" added, including a large number of "standard historical and modern novels." In 1870, of 9368 volumes in circulation, 6314 were novels.[28] It would appear that the library was destined to receive considerable attention from the executive whenever membership declined. Membership declined in 1854, 1858, and 1868, and the library expanded in 1855, 1859, and 1869.

The Library Committee had overall charge of the library and reading room while the day-to-day work was done by the librarian. The duties proved too much for Mr Maxwell who, when hired in 1843 as schoolmaster and librarian, found that his library duties included full responsibility for the library, collection of all monies, delivery of all notices, and attendances in the library from 7:00 a.m. to 8:00 a.m. and 4:00 p.m. to 10:00 p.m. He resigned in 1844. Succeeding librarians were also responsible for organizing the collection, preparing the printed catalogue, repairing damaged items, and checking out books. The loan period was quite unusual: an octavo or smaller volume was allowed out for two weeks, a quarto for three weeks, and a folio for four weeks.[29]

In addition to the library there was a reading room which housed a representative collection of Canadian, British, and American newspapers and periodicals. Susanna Moodie's remark that "a Canadian cannot get along without his newspaper any more than an American could without his tobacco"[30] was borne out by frequent statements in the *Minutes* that the reading room was very heavily used and "much frequented by Gentlemen of Education and Science." By 1870, the initial twenty newspapers and journals had increased to more than seventy.

There are occasional references to a museum of minerals but it never really made an impact. This is not surprising when one considers the chronic shortage of money and the nature of the donations: a map of Quebec on rollers, a phrenological chart, seven specimens of conchology, and a stuffed crocodile. There is no mention of a workshop or laboratory.

It is evident that from the beginning the directors of the Montreal Mechanics' Institute took themselves and their work quite seriously. The provision of library facilities and the impressive list of lectures on a wide variety of subjects, delivered by respected professional men, left little room for anything bordering on the light and frivolous. The occasional soirée, social reunions, and the annual Mechanics Exhibition were the only social activities. Mechanics' Institutes in Upper Canada, on the other hand, participated in numerous social activities in their efforts to attract and keep members. The Toronto Mechanics' Institute had inaugurated a series of summer excursions on Lake Ontario, while the Hamilton Mechanics' Institute had established an annual music festival.[31] The Montrealers appear to have been models of Victorian respectability imbued with the Protestant work ethic. Many of them were on the boards of such charitable organizations as the Irish Protestant Benevolent Society and the Workingman's Widows and Orphans Benefit Society as well as being members of the Temperance Society, the Sunday School and Bible Societies, and, of course, the Masons.

Fortunately the Mechanics' Hall, completed in 1855, became one of the principal cultural centres of the city thanks to its large lecture hall and central location. The list of distinguished scientists, politicians, and men of letters who spoke there included Charles Kingsley, Henry Beecher, Goldwin Smith, Sir John A. MacDonald, Thomas D'Arcy McGee, and P. T. Barnum.

It was quite clear that the ambitions of the founders were severely curtailed by lack of funds. Dependent upon government grants, local fund raising, and monies from the rent of the lecture hall, existence was frequently precarious. In 1855, it was reported that the amount of indebtedness was large enough "to supply a powerful stimulation to its members for further exertions, but not so large as to render its security doubtful to its creditors."[32] By 1870, the point at which we leave the Institute, it was in much better shape with assets of $53 030 and liabilities of $26 117.

A product of educational borrowing, the Mechanics' Institutes of British North America consciously adopted the aims and methods of the British Institutes. The motives that inspired their middle-class founders were as varied as the ways in which the Institutes originated. Employers sought better education and more industrious workers; politicians sought an educated electorate; ministers sought better Christians; philanthropists hoped for the alleviation of poverty and misery. The Institutes would provide a place where "the leisure of the mechanic, which would probably be whiled listlessly away or squandered in a manner destructive of both mind and body, may be spent with profit and advantage."[33] Control of the Montreal Mechanics' Institute was always in the hands of its upper- and middle-class members. Its principal object of offering practical instruction by means of lectures and classes in technical subjects of value to workers was only partially successful. It was never able to attract or hold workers in any great numbers. Explanations for this failure are many and varied: unsuitable lecture topics, lack of teachers who understood the needs of adults, irregular and long hours of work, fees, shortage of money with which to carry out programs, and perhaps most important of all, a lack of identification with the Institute on the part of the very people for whom it had been created. There was not the same spirit or sense of fellowship that could be found in unions or workingmen's societies. The fundamentally middle-class policies of the Institute never really came to grips with the needs or interests of the Montreal workingman.[34]

The Institute did attract and keep skilled workers and members of the middle class. The programs met their cultural aspirations and so received their support. In the 1870s lectures and classes faced stiff competition from outside agencies, and the Institute was forced to make changes and modifications in its programs in an attempt to adapt to changing times. It was the Institute's library, so long a stepsister to the other offerings, which remained and assumed paramount importance. It did so because of the dearth of library facilities available to Montrealers.

The situation with respect to public libraries was quite different from that in Ontario. That province had been the fortunate recipient of library legislation since 1882 whereas Quebec had to wait until 1959 for its Public Library Act. In the meantime, the reading public had to be content with small parish libraries and municipal libraries (of which there were only eleven by 1930). Consequently, the library of the Montreal Mechanics' Institute, while a subscription rather than a public library, met a serious need.

In its modern guise as the Atwater Library of Montreal, the Montreal Mechanics' Institute is still guided by the words of Frances Bacon which so greatly inspired its founders — "Knowledge is Power."

Footnotes

1. Thomas Kelly, *George Birkbeck* (Liverpool: University Press, 1957), p. 86.

2. J. W. Hudson, *The History of Adult Education* (London: Longmans, 1851), p. 55; Kelly, *George Birkbeck*, p. 259.

3. D. S. Creighton, *The Empire of the St. Lawrence* (Toronto: Macmillan, 1956), p. 211.

4. *The Vindicator,* 29 January 1983.

5. Ibid., 1 February 1833.

6. *Encyclopedia of the Social Sciences,* volume 9 (New York: Macmillan, 1937), p. 519.

7. Alan Greer, "The Pattern of Literacy in Quebec, 1745-1899," *Histoire Sociale/Social History,* November 1978, p. 331.

8. Montreal Mechanics'Institution (M.M.I.), *Minutes,* 21 November 1828.

9. N. Bosworth, *Hochelaga Depicta* (Montreal: Craig, 1839), p. 93.

10. Ibid., pp. 192-93.

11. M.M.I. *Minutes,* 15 December 1829.

12. Ibid., 31 March 1829.

13. Foster Vernon, "The Development of Adult Education in Ontario, 1790-1900," unpublished Ph.D. thesis, University of Toronto, 1960, p. 268.

14. J. Tulchinsky, "The Montreal Business Community, 1837-1853," *Canadian Business* (Toronto: McClelland and Stewart, 1972), p. 126.

15. J. I. Cooper, "The Social Structure of Montreal in the 1850's," *Canadian Historical Association Report* (1955-56), p. 63.

16. *Montreal Transcript*, 8 February 1840.

17. M.M.I. *Minutes*, 3 November 1840.

18. Ibid., 1 February 1842.

19. Ibid., 2 November 1841; 3 May 1842; 1 August 1843; 3 November 1846; *Annual Report* 1853; 16 September 1867.

20. D. Reicher, "Les bibliothèques québécoises d'avant 1970," *Canadian Libraries in Their Changing Environment* (Toronto: York University Press, 1977), p. 141.

21. *Canadian Mail*, 23 May 1855.

22. *Montreal Transcript*, 12 May 1840.

23. Province of Canada, *Statistics*, 20 Vic, Cap. 32, 1857.

24. M.M.I. *Minutes*, 6 November 1854.

25. M.M.I. *Annual Report*, 2 February 1841.

26. M.M.I. *Minutes*, 1 November 1945.

27. Ibid., 2 September 1864.

28. Ibid., 5 September 1870. That year six volumes were lost and seven members of the Montreal police force joined the Institute. The two events were not, one hopes, connected!

29. Ibid., 20 December 1847.

30. Susanna Moodie, *Mark Hurdlestone* (London: Bentley, 1853), vol. 1, p. 20.

31. Vernon, "Development of Adult Education," p. 304; see also Bryan D. Palmer, *A Culture in Conflict* (Montreal: McGill-Queen's University Press, 1979).

32. M.M.I. *Annual Report*, 5 November 1855.

33. J. M. Kerr, *Essay on the Nature and Objects of Mechanics' Institutes* (Montreal, 1855), p. 2.

34. For a discussion of working-class associational life between 1800 and 1880, see Bryan D. Palmer, *Working-class Experience: The Rise and Reconstitution of Canadian Labour, 1800-1980* (Toronto: Butterworth and Co., 1983).

Educational Justice for the Campmen: Alfred Fitzpatrick and the Foundation of Frontier College, 1899-1922

George L. Cook

"The Frontier College instructors go a step further than Froebel, who said: 'Come, let us live with our students'. Its instructors say: 'Come, let us work with our students'."[1]

Canadian society at the turn of the last century was guilty of "the crime of the desertion and demoralization of the frontiersman, the crime not only of robbing him of . . . the right of an education, but the equally damnable crime of licensing men and institutions to degrade him."[2] That was the opinion of Alfred Fitzpatrick, the founder of Frontier College. His charge was based upon years of personal experience in the mining, lumber, and railway camps of the Canadian frontier. In undertaking the amassing and presentation of the evidence of society's neglect, Fitzpatrick acted as a trailblazer; to reform the "criminal" elements was an impossible undertaking, for Canadian society would never plead guilty to his charge. Almost alone, Fitzpatrick waged his personal crusade to secure justice for the campmen. He had the passionate idealism of the reformer and the crusading zeal of the missionary, but his foundation of the Reading Camp Association in 1901, and its evolution into Frontier College, represented eminently pragmatic responses to the human needs of the frontier.

Fitzpatrick's innovation of the "laborer-teacher," who not only lives with, but works with, his students, is a teaching method which has seen broad acceptance in recent years. Few realize that this method is a Canadian creation, whose origins lie in Alfred Fitzpatrick's efforts to alleviate the conditions facing the campmen of Canada's frontier industries at the beginning of the century. The legacy of Fitzpatrick's work is Frontier College, an educational institution which to this day maintains the principles initiated by him and evolved and tested by his associate and successor, Edmund Bradwin.

Canada has been peculiarly dependent upon frontier development. More than any other country, she has had to contend with the human problems of frontier existence arising from huge projects undertaken in isolated surroundings with a nomadic labor force. In Fitzpatrick's day the frontier condition was most clearly exemplified by Canada's third great wave of railway building which saw the country's railway lines increase from fifteen thousand to forty thousand miles between 1891 and 1921, an immense undertaking for a few million people.

But the human cost of these spectacular feats has to be calculated, among other things, in the price paid by thousands of unskilled and uneducated laborers working in virtual isolation and cut off from even the most rudimentary social and educational services that were beginning to be offered in cities and towns. Most Canadians remained oblivious, however, of the living conditions of the thousands of railway laborers, large gangs of "navvies" laying track or constructing bridges, and "stationmen" in their twos and threes building up the grade in "stations" of one hundred yards. Because the churches, the labor unions, and the universities could not, and the state would not, act on their behalf, Fitzpatrick did. He became, in the words of Stephen Leacock, "a pioneer of social justice" in Canada.[3]

Ostensibly, Canada was a religious or at least a church-going society, but in an age of unrelieved materialism Christians with a social conscience were not common. Fitzpatrick was one of the few who would not condone Canadian society as it existed at the turn of the century. Like most social reformers of the day, his background lay in the Protestant churches which had become imbued with the spirit of the "social gospel." Social gospellers like Fitzpatrick aspired to realize the Kingdom of God in the very fabric of society. A Presbyterian who remained faithful to the principle that all social and economic relationships were subject to divine direction, Fitzpatrick insisted that, while his ideas were not ecclesiastical, they were not any less religious. The point was that "the mere oracular expression of God's love is not the whole Gospel."[4] To teach men the dangers of filth and the causes of disease was equally to preach the gospel. This religious sentiment was at the heart of Fitzpatrick's every act.

Born in 1862, Alfred Fitzpatrick was the product of a modest Presbyterian and United Empire Loyalist household from Pictou County in Nova Scotia. In this Anglo-Saxon, Protestant, and patriotic environment, he also learned to appreciate the value of hard work and individual initiative and the regenerative effects of education. Intending to become a missionary, he went off to the seat of Canadian Presbyterianism, Queen's University, where another son of Pictou County, Principal George Munro Grant, became his mentor. Between 1892 and 1899, he carried on his mission amongst the loggers in the California Redwoods and in the Algoma district of northern Ontario. But he soon saw the futility of attempting to minister to men's spirits without first attending to their social needs, and he left the church to devote his whole life to the men in the camps. Other more famous social gospellers, like J. S. Woodsworth, were to leave the church to pursue the political road to social reform, but Fitzpatrick chose the moderate and decidedly more limited objective of persuading society to change life in the frontier camps.

Large frontier undertakings required large numbers of workers. In 1918 more than 3700 camps existed in Canada, 1500 in northern Ontario alone. Their inhabitants, between 200 000 and 250 000 strong, constituted 5 percent of the total labor force. Here was a significant, if ignored, quarter of a million unskilled men. They had largely been imported from overseas by employers with the assistance of an obliging immigration policy. Over the period from 1906-1907, when the railway building began in earnest, to 1913-1914, immigration was at its peak. Unskilled laborers increased from 31 percent to 43 percent (an average of 34.1 percent) of the total male immigration over the period. During those same years, immigration from Central and Southern Europe increased from 29 percent to 48 percent of total male immigration and more than half of these immigrants were unskilled. While most swelled the ranks of an emerging industrial proletariat in the cities, many went straight to the frontier, where they stamped an indelible imprint on the camps.

Fitzpatrick's surveys of the camps reflected in miniature the ethnic and vertical mosaic of Canadian society. The racial composition of the camp varied with the degree of skill required in the work: in the winter lumber camps the foreign-born comprised 25 percent of the work force (15 percent were French Canadian, the remaining 60 percent being the so-called "English-speaking" group); on the summer railway gangs, aside from the "big six" (foreman, clerk, straw boss, cook, cookee, and choreboy, who were usually Canadians), the navvies made up 80 percent of the 90 percent foreign-born. Typically, a distinction in function was drawn between the "whitemen" — all Canadians, all the English-speaking, the Scandinavians, and anyone who had procured sufficient education, skill, and responsibility to be accepted in "white" company — and the "foreigners" who did all the heavy, dirty, and menial work. Because the Slavs so predominated in the railway work (over three-quarters of the labor force on the National Transcontinental), all "frontiers" were casually referred to as "Russians," "Bohunks," or "Galicians," and occasionally as "Douks" or "Hunkies." Italians were "Dagoes." Each language group, even within the same bunkhouse, tended to segregate itself for mutual support and protection and sustained the ethnic hierarchy. None would work with the "Japs," "Chinamen," and "Hindus."

Campmen were treated as "mere hewers of wood and drawers of water," whose labor was so degraded that "whitemen fearing loss of self-respect cannot be induced to perform it. What a fearful travesty on human life . . ."[5] Canada was in danger of creating a foreign-born frontier labor force who were condemned to live permanently under "a species of sweating system." Canadian society, because of the free hand permitted to employers in determining conditions of frontier employment, "curse[d] our fellow men by selling them into slavery." That state of affairs was "nothing short of criminal."[6]

Whatever the stridency of his moral indignation, Fitzpatrick could always sustain his position by an unmatched and commanding knowledge of the facts of camp life and work. Here was one long catalogue of depravity and deprivation. Transiency marked its every aspect. The work was seasonal. Ten hours was a normal working day on the frontier; twelve to fifteen were common in the railway camps. It was always at the mercy of the vagaries of the weather. The men were nomadic, gravitating easily from rail gang to bush camp, to mine, perhaps toting supplies, "skinning" (driving) mules, track laying, mucking on the grade, or "bucking" (sawing) timber, "chickadeeing" and "beavering" (clearing and cutting trails), or wheeling dirt or gravel. Housing was temporary.

The average bunkhouse in a winter bush camp lasted two and a half years, while the railway gangs were communities on wheels, moving from one isolated siding to the next as the work progressed, and the stationmen's shacks lasted only the season from April until freeze-up. The work itself was regarded simply as a chance to build up a "stake" before moving on to bigger and better things. However, a life in constant flux and devoid of any permanent attachments to a family, a home, or a piece of land, engendered an attitude which led the men to squander their stakes and doom themselves to a continuing camp existence. "The trouble is," explained Fitzpatrick, "that when men occupy the slave's position, the slave's spirit naturally develops."[7]

To the "slave's spirit" was added the thraldom of lack of education and a form of wage slavery. In the prime of life and physical condition, the campmen's only asset was their bodily strength. The prospects of ignorant and unschooled men acquiring skills were slim. Their vocabulary seldom exceeded four hundred words. In Fitzpatrick's experience, 30 percent were entirely illiterate, 50 percent did not know the multiplication tables, and 75 percent could not calculate their time or whether they had been fairly paid by their employers. Command of English was certainly not a prerequisite for the job, but the "foreigners" were imprisoned by their ignorance. On the railways, the system of pay was "tantamount to lesser forms of serfdom," wrote Fitzpatrick's associate, Edmund Bradwin. Here, the system of subletting was turned into a veritable art, with the navvies and stationmen at the bottom of the ladder. Pay rates promised good stakes, barring loss of time because of wet weather or sickness, but the rub came at the "measuring up," when the common experience was excessive charges for advances on tools and supplies, transportation, clothing and board, or misrepresentations in the employment agreement and in the classification of the material moved on the grade. The senior contractor had the unquestioned power of a satrap.

It was not unknown for Slavs to be paid by contractors whose loaded revolver lay conspicuously on the table. This was the "relation of boss and hireling."[8]

The seemingly unending routine of working, eating, and sleeping made for a solitary and spiritually deadening life. Of necessity, the day ran with military regularity to the tune of the cook's gong. Social contacts were restricted entirely to the campmen themselves. Recreational and cultural facilities did not exist. Gambling, drinking, and disease might relieve the humdrum existence, but these carried their own rewards. The desire for riches and freedom from the camp could lead to the gambling away of a month's pay in a single night of poker. Weeks of disciplined asceticism would be relieved by a riotous spate of revelry in the nearest frontier community. It was the absence of women, however, which cut most deeply into men's souls. That "certain indescribable vacuum" drove men to seek female companionship, if not of "a healthy kind," to use Fitzpatrick's phase, "then of any kind."[9] The incidence of tuberculosis and other respiratory diseases, all the manifest result of filth and lack of sanitation, was "appalling," thought Fitzpatrick, who knew that medical attention was generally unavailable, despite monthly pay deductions for a camp doctor. The whole environment induced a pervasive and sullen resentment.

Resentful though they were, the debilitating ennui and the mental sluggishness created by the camp atmosphere made of campmen a very passive group. Transiency, illiteracy, and ignorance of language and rights aborted any attempt for change within the camps. The seasonal work regime was an added obstacle to any effective labor organization. That there was no pressure for change from outside was Fitzpatrick's concern. Less was thought about the campmen, he complained, than about any other group of people, although many of the state funds supporting education and culture in the cities were derived from frontier industries. Fitzpatrick's accusation that "by a life of filth and disease, of physical and mental and spiritual bondage, as also by his untimely death, the frontiersman helped to pay for your education and mine"[10] was ignored by all the important social institutions.

Organized labor appeared to speak "very audibly for the workers in the cities where more permanent conditions are found," protested Bradwin,[11] but it took no interest in the immigration policies which supplied a steady flow of foreign labor for the camps (other than in restrictions against skilled British workers and Orientals who threatened Canadian jobs). It paid attention to camp working and living conditions only when radical political movements became active. The churches, who devoted their efforts to the cities and the western homesteaders, had no remedies for frontier conditions. They were badly divided along denominational lines and lacked the resources to do much. Fitzpatrick, the erstwhile Presbyterian missionary, knew from his own experience that the spasmodic efforts of the occasional Protestant itinerant missionary were "love's labour's lost." There was simply no point sermonizing to men who were largely Catholic or Orthodox and who were unable to understand either the language or the message. Even the most eloquent sermon could change nothing of the campman's living conditions. More importantly, to proselytize was to take a fundamentally wrong approach, warned Fitzpatrick. "Vital religion is impossible on a foundation of ignorance and barbarism."[12] On the other hand, it was not legitimate, he felt, to delegate to the churches what was the duty of the state.

Dominion and provincial governments recognized no such duty. Pressure from the railway companies assured a compliant immigration policy. By their acts of omission, governments appeared to condone the camp conditions. After the occasional investigation, the contractors were invariably exonerated. As Bradwin knew from his own experience, Ottawa was not "overzealous" in protecting the campmen, even with the limited legislation that did exist. During all his years in the camps, Bradwin never saw a Department of Labour representative in a bunkhouse. "I did hear once of one having been at the office."[13] Even when Fitzpatrick began to focus on the political responses which ultimately emerged from camp conditions, governments remained unmoved. To Fitzpatrick, the state which neglected the campmen "as if they were horses and cattle" did so at its own peril. The camps, "idle intellectually and degenerating morally," would breed enormous social ills which were "a menace to any state."[14] By 1910, the warnings were going out that "the seeds of revolutionary socialism" were being sown, flourishing best in the foreign-born seedbed.[15] By 1919, as Fitzpatrick had warned, the camp soil proved ripe for the blossoming of the anathema called "Bolshevism."

To Fitzpatrick it was axiomatic that there could be no life without labor: the true object of life was to "make men, not money"; the true object of labor was the development of "the whole man — body, mind and soul."[16] Labor directed in such a spirit was an extension of God's work, for men grew towards perfection only as they cultivated their physical as well as their intellectual and spiritual faculties to the fullness of their "God-given potentialities." No labor, therefore, should be demeaned by venal conditions. Rather labor, which was dignified by humane conditions and which was in the mutual interests of worker, employer, and society at large, Fitzpatrick believed, could be the salvation of mankind and "the key to the industrial, educational, social and religious problems of our time."[17]

In his view of education, Fitzpatrick reflected the current and "almost universal principle that education is for all men, not for a privileged class alone, that it means development of the whole man . . . and that it is primarily the duty of the state to educate."[18] There was nothing extraordinary in the view that it was the state's duty to provide education for all people. Surely, Fitzpatrick and others argued, no one could quarrel with the view that the right to an education must become a reality for all citizens, since "an enlightened and healthy citizenship is a better asset than ignorant and filthy slaves."[19] The enormity of the problems facing the campmen — the working and living conditions which prohibited individual improvement for those desiring it, and the effective restriction of educational opportunity to the organized regions of the country — could be dealt with only by the power of the state. The task, Fitzpatrick knew, was "Herculean." Yet he remained convinced that it was essential to "bring education to the man, not man to education." If education left its cloisters and went to the workers in the frontier camps and on the remote homesteads as well as in the city factories, the vision could become a reality. Practically speaking, education would dissolve that "greatest menace to civilization," the hours of idleness spent by campmen in drinking, gambling, and "worse evils."[20]

Unemployment would be tackled and city slums combatted by enabling men to take their families with them to a decent livelihood in the frontier camps and homesteads, but only if frontier conditions so improved as to make them habitable by women and children. Only if practical efforts were made to reach out to foreign workers, to welcome them into Canadian society as functioning citizens, would their contribution to that society be recognized and would Canada's well-being be advanced. Either "foreigners" would receive education in the English language and in the ideas and ideals of the Canadian nation or, bitterly, they would return home, their place being taken by unassimilable Oriental workers, a thought which, like most Canadians, Fitzpatrick abhorred; or, what was worse, they would drift into the saloons, shacks, and hovels of the frontier or the slums of the city, there to compound existing social ailments. The lack of education for all men, therefore, carried with it social consequences from which no one could escape.

At the core of Fitzpatrick's response was his sense of Christian service. Although only the power of the state could possibly bear the enormous burden of educational and social reform, the vitality of society could be rejuvenated solely by the individual's spirit of service. Individuals grew only as they were prepared to give of themselves in service to their fellow beings. The Presbyterian in Fitzpatrick told him that each man was called upon to work for "something outside himself, for the sake of society at large in order to purify it of its evils and its sins, and advance it on its path of future progress,"[21] and that the struggles of man to accomplish good through service was but God working through human agencies to accomplish the salvation of man. Consequently, Fitzpatrick, who had himself of course answered the call, appealed to others, and especially to young university men, to take up the challenge of service to one's fellow man, even if he be the foreign campman, who was generally despised by most middle-class Canadians. Indeed, no greater service could be rendered by Canada's university men than that "of working in our frontier camps and factories, side by side with the native and foreign workingmen, for the purpose of convincing them that we are deeply interested in them, teaching them our ideas of citizenship and our ideals of life."[22] Here, in a nutshell, was the ideal and the driving force behind the Reading Camp Association and its laborer-teachers: each laborer-teacher answered the call of service to his fellow workers in the camp, setting a personal example for his students and growing in character as he learned from those around him. In this way the Association answered the call of service to society, and set an example for the state and for society to follow.

What form service to campmen should take was a continuing concern of Fitzpatrick, for he always regarded the means that he pursued to effect a system of frontier education as an experiment subject to constant refinement. Thus, what began as one man's service on the frontier grew into a national organization by natural stages. Its genesis lay in Fitzpatrick's own search in the Californian Redwood camps for his lost brother, Tom, and his subsequent mission to the bushmen in the Algoma district of northern Ontario. Having decided that proselytizing was futile, he began in 1899 to carry in his back pack reading material for the men of the bush camps who would "treasure the wrappings from a patent medicine bottle because it gave them something to read."[23] Because of the impossibility of reading in the bunkhouse, Fitzpatrick persuaded James Playfair, a prominent lumberman near Nairn Centre, to raise in early 1900 a log building entirely separate from the "eat camp" and the "sleep camp" and devoted solely to reading, writing, and other leisure-time pursuits. This was the first "reading camp" in Canada. From this modest beginning, forty-two such unsupervised reading camps were raised before the practice was discontinued in 1904. In the summer railway camps, reading tents were in use as late as 1924.

To supply the reading camps, Fitzpatrick secured changes in the Ontario Public Libraries Act which enabled municipalities to establish branch libraries in neighboring unincorporated areas where camps were to be found. Concurrently, he organized lumbermen to support the construction of reading camps and to press the government of Ontario to establish a library commission, which in 1901 inaugurated a proper scheme of travelling libraries for the camps. From many lumbermen, like John Charlton, MP, he received support for his "important and philanthropic work," based upon the improved morale created amongst the men in their camps. The railways provided Fitzpatrick with travel passes and donated camp equipment, books, and magazines. However, in a day when the concept of adult education was not widely accepted, some library boards objected that uneducated men would only destroy the books and that the illiteracy and the long hours of work would doom the scheme to failure. Moreoever, an outbreak of smallpox obliged the Board of Health in 1902 to prohibit the circulation of books whose binding paste could carry the disease.

Having demonstrated the feasibility of reading camps, Fitzpatrick hoped that the government would then establish proper, supervised branch libraries in the camps. He had intended only to expose camp living and working conditions in order to enlist the support of social and welfare agencies who were better equipped to tackle such problems. He received no encouragement whatever from the government. The only solution, advised the keenly interested Principal Grant of Queen's, was to "trust to the Christian Public" for support. A public association was the only alternative to doing nothing.

National Archives Canada/NA-C 54480

Class of Miners in Frontier College Reading Room,
Mond Nickel Co., Levack, Ontario, c. 1917.

The decision in July of 1901 to form the "Canadian Reading Camp Movement" was rationalized by Fitzpatrick on the grounds that "at least partial organization" was necessary to mobilize public support, but with no other object, he insisted, than to interest the government. Prominent lumbermen like the Charltons and J. R. Booth, railwaymen like Thomas Shaughnessy of the Canadian Pacific, Charles M. Hayes of the Grand Trunk Pacific, and D. B. Hanna of the Canadian Northern lent weight to his appeals and drives by serving in honorary roles of Officers and Councillors, while Sir Sandford Fleming and later the Governors-General served as patrons. Fitzpatrick's response to the wave of railway construction getting under way was to make the "Reading Camp Association" a legal entity in 1906. A lumberman, H. L. Lovering, became the first Chairman of its Board of Governors, which began to take on a national character with the addition of eastern and western members a year later. Fitzpatrick felt that his duty had been done simply by demonstrating, with the co-operation of enlightened employers, how the task on the frontier could be confronted. Since it was as unrealistic to expect frontier employers, as it was city manufacturers, to educate their workers, the Association "simply asks the state to perform its duty,"[24] whereupon the Association would be perfectly "glad to get out of the business."[25] This, of course, was not to be.

The illiteracy, disease, and apathy in the camps impelled Fitzpatrick to bring greater sophistication to the service he had accepted. The "indispensable thing," Principal Grant had advised, was the "right man" to supervise each reading camp, some of which had, of course, failed for want to supervision. Because of the severe problem of disease, Fitzpatrick first looked to fifth-year medical students, who could concurrently offer basic medical care and act as reading camp instructors. Believing that "wonders could be accomplished, by young men of culture and good common sense, conducting evening classes in every camp," he successively recruited qualified clerks and laborers already in the camps and then professional teachers — including women — to conduct camp schools for the men and their families.[26]

None of these early forays proved particularly effective in terms of reaching the campmen themselves; Fitzpatrick's problem was to find some way to establish good relations between laborers and teachers. The teacher who also worked with his students was the simple but radical solution. It was also cheap. The germ of the laborer-teacher idea is supposed to have been planted when Angus Gray, unable to bear the daytime idleness in the camp, decided one day in the summer of 1902 to pick up tools and work alongside the men. Whatever the foundation for this event, the laborer-teacher approach was Fitzpatrick's creation. It remained for Edmund Bradwin, who would "rather teach than eat," to test and refine the idea in the field over the next twenty years. As early as 1906, he concluded that Fitzpatrick had the "best solution, not preaching but contact by men who can influence. . . ."[27]

Contact rather than indoctrination was the vital principle in the laborer-teacher's relationship with his fellow workers. An exchange of experience was the mutual reward. The workers, of course, could not be obliged to have any contact with the laborer-teacher. Fundamental to any success in teaching, therefore, was the establishment of mutual respect and rapport. Laborer-teachers worked and lived on exactly the same level as the workers: they received no special favors from the employers; they held the only jobs they could, the lowest paying, unskilled jobs, in which they survived only by learning how to work from the other workers; they received the same pay, plus expenses, and from ten to twenty dollars a month for teaching. Only when he was accepted as a fellow-worker would the men begin to acquire from the instructor the learning they wanted, whether it was English, fractions, or something about Canada. The experience was mixed. On the one hand, letters from the instructors referred like a refrain to the isolation, the toil, the monotony, the hours and other camp conditions, the jumping, and the consequent problems of initiating and sustaining classes or other cultural or recreational activities. On the other hand, the letters also contained full acknowledgement of the enormity of the problems, of the sense of challenge, of self-discovery, of the dignity of labor and the laboring man, and of the sheer pleasure in learning from others while helping others to learn. For the typical laborer-teachers, middle class, usually English-speaking and Protestant (although there were French-speaking and Catholic laborer-teachers from the earliest days), the experience itself was a real education. As one instructor wrote: "The instructor's work cannot be reported. It is limitless."[28]

One such instructor was the young medical student, Norman Bethune, who worked in a bush camp near Whitefish, Ontario, in the winter of 1911-12. Another was the theology student, James Ralph Mutchmore, later Moderator of the United Church of Canada, who from 1911 worked on the railways in northern Ontario for five consecutive summers. Bethune, reporting on a restraining combination of "work, lack of time, and sore hands — the latter possibly being the greatest," worked on a bush road with the inevitable results: "blisters and fully developed symptoms of a kink in my vertebral column. However I enjoy it, and am sure I shall like it immensely later on." He opened his reading room, but to begin his teaching he needed books, magazines, posters, song books, records, and story books in simple English for Germans, French, "Pollacks," and Hungarians. Later, he reported on the success of the reading room, but at Christmas "the usual jumping took place reducing to a great extent the classes." He requested some materials in Polish and French for a dozen men who could not speak English. "It is extremely desirable that they know something at least about the language when they leave in the spring."[29] Well could Fitzpatrick appreciate the strength of such words and the effects of the experience on the instructor. Mutchmor placed his years on the railway gangs on a par with his experiences overseas in the war. "They helped me to know and love my fellow man. They provided for involvement and identification." Indeed, the insights gained, he felt, were in some ways akin to those of Bonhoeffer and Niemöller in prison. "Upon a foundation of good pioneer work has been erected the superstructure of wise counsel, practical training and education and Christian service."[30] Fitzpatrick would have revelled in such an assessment of his works, but his major concern remained always with what actually happened in the classes in the camps.

Since men could not be made to attend classes, or made to learn, the laborer-teacher had to offer what the men themselves recognized as a need. He therefore attempted to teach anything practical which men could immediately put to use themselves, like basic English or French and arithmetic, most often in a very informal manner by exploiting such tools and items of clothing as happened to be at hand. Illiteracy, being such a profound camp problem, received special attention. Frequently, an instructor would employ Professor S. W. Dyde's (of Queen's University) method of structuring classes around group readings of poetry and prose from the classics. What benefits the laborer-teacher provided could not, of course, be measured. The only testimony to practical success was the use made by the men of the reading camps and of their attendance at classes, while the occasional laboriously written letter from a campman would encourage Fitzpatrick and confirm the value of the laborer-teacher approach. In the more stable lumber camps, 50 percent of the men would attend classes more or less frequently, but on the volatile railway gangs, attendance of from 2 percent to 10 percent was far more common. Almost invariably, the reading rooms would be used by 90 percent of the literate men (about 50 percent of the camp). Likewise, "healthy" recreation, counselling, friendship, and sheer human kindness were important elements of the laborer-teacher's role in camp.

"No hyphenated Canadians"[31] was another of Fitzpatrick's refrains, but he cried in vain. Frontier College was the only Canadian organization which made any attempts to provide a program of "Canadianization" for the high proportion of foreign-born campmen. Since existing materials were entirely unsuited to adults, Fitzpatrick produced in 1919 his own *Handbook for New Canadians*. Very largely based on techniques evolved by experience in the camps by Bradwin, here was one of the earliest Canadian attempts to teach adults everyday English by illustrations and actions. Simultaneously, it attempted to provide the immigrant worker with "an intelligent conception of Canadian citizenship,"[32] by informing the learner in simple English of Canada's geography, history, and government, and by attempting to impart commonly accepted, English-Canadian notions of patriotism, democracy, morality, and personal cleanliness, as well as providing detailed advice on naturalization. The realities of the camps demanded toleration of different religions and cultures. A Catholic "Galician" or an Orthodox "Russian" could no more be made to accept a particular view of life or of Canada than he could be made to learn English or fractions. A doctrinaire approach would no more do for the laborer-teacher than preaching had for the Presbyterian missionary.

Laborer-teachers were already working outside Ontario by 1904. Fitzpatrick believed that he was performing a nationalizing exercise, and this required a national organization. By 1919 over 40 percent of the work was in the remainder of the country. French-speaking laborer-teachers were working in Quebec and northern Ontario by 1904. The peak of operations was reached in 1913, when seventy-one laborer-teachers were placed in camps, and by 1919 over six hundred instructors, including a small number of women, had served in every province and territory except Prince Edward Island. In that year, there was also a brief international excursion when a few instructors served in Washington and Michigan states. Always experimenting, Fitzpatrick sought to demonstrate how improved living conditions could be brought to frontier homesteads, thereby making them more habitable for women and children. The project, delayed by the First World War, was inaugurated in 1922 with women field workers. During the war, instructors went overseas with the Forestry Battalions, but were withdrawn when Canadian universities organized a university extension program for servicemen.

As the work extended in scope, so did Fitzpatrick's claims on behalf of his laborer-teachers. They represented a bridge between urban centre and rural settlement, rich and poor, educated and ignorant, Canadian and immigrant, in short, between civilization and the frontier. When strikes swept the camps in 1919, Fitzpatrick contended that the laborer-teachers' activities would determine whether the camps would produce "Lenins or Lincolns." Because of their initiative, example, sensitivity, and absence of doctrine, laborer-teachers demonstrated "what it really means to be a Canadian."[33] Working under the banner, "Welfare — Instruction — Canadianization — Leadership," their objects were: "(1) to educate the worker and give him a fighting chance; (2) to educate and citizenize (*sic*) the immigrant; (3) to meet the 'Red' agitator on his own ground."[34] Fitzpatrick emerged from the war, with all its social dislocation and political ferment, more convinced than ever that "the personality of a strong-minded, well-trained teacher . . . is the most effective means of meeting the educational and social needs of the men . . . [Instructors] do a national work, not only in Canadianizing foreigners, but also in diffusing education generally."[35]

National though the scope of the task and the effort was, Fitzpatrick failed to evoke a national response to his crusade. He had been successful, as Principal Grant had advised back in 1902, in "going to the people." Frontier College, which was now well established in the public mind, was financially supported by all three transcontinental railroads and by large lumbering enterprises, by the leaders of the Montreal and Toronto business establishment, by the churches (particularly by the Methodists and the Presbyterians), by eight of the provinces, and by hundreds of small donors in large and small communities all across the country. The result was donations, which rose from $49.50 in 1900 to $22 000 in 1914. However, Fitzpatrick could not, as Grant had also admonished, stay within his means. He was a crusader, not an administrator. He always "sailed close to the wind" financially. Under constant financial stress, he found the lack of response to his appeals distressing. From the Dominion government, in the person of the Minister of Labour, W. L. Mackenzie King, he received only platitudes. King was "greatly interested" in work which was "most beneficial and far-reaching in its influence,"[36] but when Fitzpatrick asked the Dominion government to do "its duty" he was "slapped . . . over the back with the British North America Act and referred . . . back to the Provinces."[37] The provinces, while donating funds to Frontier College, recognized no responsibility for Canadianization, and adult education programs, at least for campmen, were simply not acknowledged at that time.

Failing to evoke any response from government to his ideal of education as the right of all, Fitzpatrick in his book, *The University in Overalls, A Plea for Part-time Study,* then called upon the universities to don overalls, both literally and symbolically. Building on his idea of the whole man, who had the opportunity to develop all his physical, intellectual, and spiritual qualities, and of humane societies, which aspired to marry mental and physical labor and to bridge the gap between civilization and the frontier, Fitzpatrick looked to the universities to redeem labor from its disrepute by expanding their curricula so as to make physical labor a degree requirement for all students. At the same time, the universities would serve all the people by awarding credits to those workers who had successfully mastered laboring skills and who now wanted to learn more in the way of academic skills. If this seemed too radical a role for the university, surely, Fitzpatrick reposted, it was a simple matter to recognize that the felling of a tree required as much mental skill and discipline as any academic endeavor. Without labor there could be no university, or any other cultural institution for that matter. It was now up to the universities to extend his dream of bringing education to the man not the man to education, by committing half their students and staff to a two-year extramural stint in the camps, homesteads, and factories of Canada, engaging in part-time labor, part-time learning, and part-time teaching. With working, learning, and service to others thus united, students would have a well-rounded education, while education would be diffused to all the people.

That "the medium is the resident instructor" in the camps, homesteads, and factories, Fitzpatrick had long been saying.[38] However, the universities, faced with severe practical constraints, could not accept his challenge. Moreover, he had seen some of his own laborer-teachers fail to meet the challenge of the camps. Because of his difficulty in finding suitable laborer-teachers, he had decided by 1909 that he would have to train them himself to become that special kind of educator who would be able to work, learn, and teach at the same time. To train its own special breed of instructors, Frontier College required degree-granting rights. To serve camps along a

Dominion-wide frontier, Frontier College required a Dominion charter, which would enable a campman or any worker anywhere in Canada to avail himself of his right to education, even to university level, while earning his daily bread. He was determined to make the dream a reality.

In 1919, Frontier College received letters of patent from the Province of Ontario. In 1922, now with the personal support of Mackenzie King, Fitzpatrick won his Dominion charter containing degree-granting rights. He then brought together some of the most prominent scholars in Canada to establish a curriculum and examining boards in each discipline. In time, the provinces awakened to their constitutional powers in the field of adult education, so that by 1931 Frontier College had to relinquish its right to grant degrees, but not before one hundred and twenty-one had applied for admission, nine had written examinations, and three had completed degrees. Inevitably, there had been much dissension in the College, but the original commitment to basic adult education won out. Clinging to his ideal of making all education available to all men, Fitzpatrick resigned in protest in 1931. He died a disappointed man four years later.

Under the direction of Edmund Bradwin until 1954, Frontier College was thereafter to devote its efforts to basic adult education in the camps. During the depression years the College was to reach the peak of its service when volunteers by the hundreds provided the only educational and recreational facilities available in the unemployment relief camps. The Second World War brought rapid technological change and with its end another massive movement of non-Anglo-Saxon immigrants into Canada's frontier industries and another challenge to Frontier College.

In its university phase, Frontier College was a constitutional anomaly. It was, however, an educational trailblazer, as it had been since its inception. Expecting the state to do its duty, Fitzpatrick had always protested that Frontier College had no ambitions towards permanency. He had begun his work because he had seen practical human problems in the camps which could not be dealt with by missionaries. The Reading Camp Association was established merely to demonstrate to the state and others the feasibility of camp education programs as a means of dealing with camp conditions. Frontier College was a living experiment designed to demonstrate what could be done in a practical way to bring education to the campmen. When the Canadian universities had organized themselves to provide university extension programs for Canada's servicemen overseas, Frontier College had withdrawn. When the provincial governments organized themselves to do their duty in tackling the frontier problems, the College would have "accomplished its object so far as Canada is concerned" and would pass from the scene. However, so far as frontier education was concerned, Fitzpatrick wrote in 1917, Frontier College had been "a voice crying in the wilderness."[39]

Frontier College was obliged to become a permanent institution. The Dominion charter, an event unique in Canada's educational and constitutional history, represented the logical development of Fitzpatrick's previous crusading, the ultimate development of the laborer-teacher approach, and a new phase in Fitzpatrick's crusade on behalf of Canada's quarter of a million campmen. Here, at least, the teacher would work with his students.

Footnotes

1. Alfred Fitzpatrick, "An Experiment in the Canadian Lumber Industry," *National Conference on Social Welfare: The Social Welfare Forum,* Official Proceedings . . . 1924 (Chicago: 1924), p. 351.

2. Alfred Fitzpatrick, *A Corner in Education,* with Tenth Annual Report (Reading Camp Association, Toronto, 1910), p. 42. Each year Fitzpatrick would incorporate a pamphlet with the Annual Report. Hereafter, the title of the pamphlet will be provided with the year of the Annual Report on first citation, but thereafter only the year of the Annual Report will be referred to, that is: Tenth (1910). All annual reports are found in the Frontier College Papers, Public Archives of Canada.

3. *Toronto Star Weekly,* 27 September 1919.

4. Alfred Fitzpatrick, "The Neglected Citizen in the Camps," *The Canadian Magazine,* XXV (May 1905), p. 45.

5. *Camp Education,* with Seventh Annual Report (1906-1907), p. 3.

6. *The Education of the Frontier Laborer,* with Fifth Annual Report (1904-1905), p. 10.

7. Seventh (1906-1907), p. 13.

8. Edmund Bradwin, *The Bunkhouse Man: A Study of Work and Pay in the Camps of Canada, 1903-1914* (New York, 1928; reprinted Toronto: University of Toronto Press, 1972), pp. 8, 183.

9. Edmund Bradwin, "The Challenge of the Migratory Worker," Proceedings of the Ninth Annual Meeting of the International Association of Public Employment Services, Buffalo . . . 1921 (Washington, 1922), p. 22. No evidence exists to indicate whether or not homosexuality was widespread in the camps. Prostitutes would occasionally visit camps to offer their services.

10. Tenth (1910), p. 41.

11. Bradwin, "Migratory Worker," p. 15.

12. *The Diffusion of Education,* with Eleven†ʰ

13. Bradwin, "Migratory Worker."

14. *Camp Education by C⌐*

15. Joseph Wearir⌐
    (Januar⌐ ͺ

16   ⌐

19. Third (1902-1903), p. 8.

20. Alfred Fitzpatrick, *The University in Overalls: A Plea for Part-time Study* (Toronto: Frontier College Press, 1920), p. 107.

21. *The Frontier College,* with Thirteenth Annual Report (1913), Frontispiece, quoting Maria Montessori's "Pedagogical Anthropology."

22. *The Instructor and the Red,* with Nineteenth Annual Report (1919).

23. Jessie Lucas, "The Financial History of Frontier College" (1957), typed mss., p. 1. Miss Lucas was Fitzpatrick's secretary from 1920 until his retirement in 1932, and remained secretary to his successors until her own retirement in 1963.

24. Seventh (1906-1907), p. 10.

25. Fitzpatrick to A. J. Matheson, Provincial Treasurer of Ontario, 29 June 1910, in E. W. Robinson, *"The History of Frontier College"*, unpublished M.A. thesis, McGill University, 1960, p. 24.

26. *Library Extension in Ontario: Reading Camps and Club Houses,* with Second Annual Report (1901-1902), p. 16. The first professional teacher hired by Fitzpatrick in this manner was A. O. Patterson, whose paper, "Camp Schools," which was read before the Ontario Educational Association, is in the Third Annual Report (1902-1903), pp. 13-19. In 1901-1902, of seven instructors, two were women.

27. Bradwin to Fitzpatrick, July 1906, in Robinson, "History," p. 83.

28. Report of instructor E. H. Clarke, Ninth (1909), p. 23.

29. H. N. Bethune to Fitzpatrick, 12 November and 13 December 1911, in Roderick Stewart, *Bethune* (Toronto, 1973), pp. 5-6.

30. J. R. Mutchmor, *Mutchmor: The Memoirs of James Ralph Mutchmor* (Toronto, 1965), pp, 35-45.

31. *Canadianizing the Foreigner,* with Fifteenth Annual Report (1915).

32. *Frontier Camp Schools,* with Fourteenth Annual Report (1914), p. 4.

33. Fourteenth (1914), p. 5.

34. *The Frontier College 'Coming of Age', Annual Report* (1921), pp. 3, 11. On the development of radical movements in the camps and of Fitzpatrick's response, see a perceptive study by Marjorie E. Zavitz, "The Frontier College and 'Bolshevism' in the camps of Canada, 1919-1925," unpublished M.A. thesis, University of Windsor, 1974.

35. Nineteenth (1919).

36. King to Fitzpatrick, 3 May 1905 and 15 May 1911, in Zavitz, "Frontier College and 'Bolshevism'," pp. 28-29.

37. Fitzpatrick to R. H. Grant, Minister of Education of Ontario, in D. Avery, "Canadian Immigration Policy and the Foreign Navvy," Canadian Historical Association, *Historical Papers* (Ottawa, 1972), p. 148.

38. *University in Overalls,* p. 119.

39. *The Diffusion of Education,* with Seventeenth Annual Report (1917), p. 7.

"Housekeepers of the Community": The British Columbia Women's Institutes, 1909-46

Carol J. Dennison

The formation of the British Columbia Women's Institutes (BCWI) came as a direct result of the British Columbia Farmer's Institutes' efforts to provide speakers on topics of interest to their members' wives. These talks were so popular with the women that the provincial government invited Miss Laura Rose, a dairying instructor at the Ontario Agricultural College, to organize Women's Institutes throughout the province. By the end of 1909 sixteen Institutes had been organized.[1] They were so well received that the government passed legislation in 1911 giving them statutory authority and providing for financial grants.[2]

Why were the Women's Institutes so easily organized and so successful? The obvious answer — that they meet a need — begs the question, what need? To answer this, one must look at the unique situation of agriculture and of farmers in British Columbia. Unlike other areas in Canada, British Columbia had never been a predominantly agricultural province.[3] Less than 5 percent of its land surface was arable, and this land was scattered throughout the province in distinct pockets divided from each other by mountains and water. Each area was suited to a different type of agriculture.[4] In many areas the land was either hard to clear or needed irrigation and drainage to make it useful. Thus, farmers in British Columbia were divided by geography, by types of agriculture, and by differing marketing practices. In the early part of the twentieth century, the isolation of the agricultural areas from each other was matched by the isolation of the farms and small communities themselves, for roads and railroads were expensive and difficult to build in most areas of the province. Communication between and within farming areas was therefore difficult. To organize groups of farmers or their wives into province-wide associations was no mean feat.[5] Only the resources of government allowed such efforts to be successful at that time.

The isolation of farm areas and communities was one of the prime factors in attracting women to the Women's Institutes. Women often saw no one except their immediate family for weeks on end. Nor did they have much time to relax since the multitude of chores which they were required to perform left little time for leisure. Trips to town were infrequent and neighbors were too far apart for easy visiting.[6] A pioneer woman in the Lumby area of the Okanagan remembered:

> I always got a sore throat during these visits to Lumby. The women there used to think I was the greatest talker on Earth. They overlooked the fact that for months on end, I had no woman to talk to, and that my husband had no time to even listen.[7]

Isolation and loneliness were less acute in the small towns.[8] Nevertheless, the burden of housework was great and, even for those who had servants, the jobs of overseeing the running of the household and of caring for children were sufficient to occupy them most of the time.[9] The opportunity to get out of the house and to meet with other women was as attractive to them as to their more isolated farm sisters.

Another attraction of these early Women's Institutes was their program of lectures and demonstrations in cooking, sewing, and other household arts. Many rural women originally came from cities and towns in more settled areas and were unfamiliar with farm work, housework and cooking in the less modern conditions of the British Columbia frontier. One such woman, Nan Bourgon, recalled: ". . . I had never been where I had to cook a meal, and things were so primitive here in this new country."[10] Opportunities to discuss their problems with other women and to receive help and advice in a congenial setting were very effective lures.

These needs were paramount in making the Women's Institutes an attractive option. However, the social climate for women was also a factor. From the 1880s onward in Canada, the United States, and elsewhere, women were becoming actively involved in the world beyond their homes. One of the leading suffrage activists in British Columbia, Mrs Gordon Grant, explained this phenomenon in 1913:

> Today the womanhood of not only B.C., but of all the world, is being awakened, and we feel that we must have an opinion on a great many of the questions of the day. . . . As a result of this awakening of the women, there have come the Women's Institutes of B.C. and of Canada. There has come the organization of the Canadian Club, the Daughters of the Empire, and the various moral and philanthropic organizations all through the world.[11]

This awakening public consciousness of women was accompanied by a renewed and expanded view of the family as the important unit of society and of the paramount importance of the mother in raising children.[12] A corollary of these views was the notion that the woman's sphere was the home. Alice Ravenhill, a prominent figure in the early Institutes and in the field of public health, observed:

> . . . a broad line of demarcation nevertheless existed between the activities of men and women. Public opinion accepted domestic duties as constituting the one correct sphere for women. . . .[13]

To justify their greater participation in public affairs, women concentrated on issues related to their role as housewives.[14] Politically powerless, women grasped at club membership as an opportunity to exercise some control and power over community decisions.[15] Rural women saw in the Women's Institutes an opportunity not only to take part in new activities but also as a way to gain recognition by using their housewifely skills. Best of all, because their actions were merely extensions of their role as housewives, society was able to accept women's presence in community affairs.

Did Institute members recognize what they were doing and why? Most of them certainly were aware of *what* they were doing. Mrs J. D. McBride of Cranbrook noted that a woman "must not only be a housekeeper to her individual home, but a wholesale housekeeper of her community as well."[16] Miss Ravenhill and Mrs Davies, members of the Advisory Board, also refer to this "larger housekeeping."[17] Others couched this same view in terms of motherhood, but their actions and writings reveal that they, too, were referring to all aspects of housekeeping not just to childcare. Few, if any, of the members explicitly expressed the real reasons for this ideology. To do so would have entailed rejection of the prevailing belief in the moral superiority of women[18] and would have required embracing a much broader conception of womanhood than was possible in the milieu of the time.

Women shared the prevailing viewpoints that humanity was progressing and that all of the society's problems could be solved by educating people to the need for a change. Reason, efficiency, and science would bring about a more perfect society in the future.[19] These attitudes, their awakening public consciousness, and their housewives' ideology were all contributing factors in rural women's acceptance of the Women's Institutes.

Women joined the fledgling Women's Institutes to satisfy their needs for companionship, education, power, and recognition. But why did the provincial government want to organize a club for rural women? The answer to this question is contained in a complex network of circumstances. Throughout Canada, rapid urbanization, with its attendant problems, made many people long for the "good old days." Rural life was idealized as pure, uplifting, and vital to the nation's well-being.[20] Across the country governments were anxious to reverse the rural to urban population drain by making farm life easier, more profitable, and more attractive.[21] Thus, they sponsored the Farmers' Institutes to educate farmers so their labors would be easier and more productive. Because "(m)any men leave farms for city life because their wives . . . are discontented with the conditions of rural life,"[22] governments began to give attention to the living conditions on farms.

Governments were also motivated by a belief in the importance of the family. They shared the belief that: "Agriculture is the basic industry of our country, the child the greatest asset, and the status of womanhood its standard of civilization. . . . The country home is the foundation."[23] By organizing the Women's Institutes, the provincial government could promote its agricultural policy, educate women in ways of making the farm home more inviting, and enlist the women's aid in making agriculture more appealing to their children.[24] Educating women in their traditional agricultural fields of poultry, dairying, and gardening would also help increase the productivity of British Columbia farms — an important factor in a province where much of the food had to be imported at high prices.[25]

Did the government have political motives for organizing the Women's Institutes? Certainly it is possible that they saw the Institutes as a means of creating a docile, stable, agricultural work force.[26] The Patrons of Industry, the United Farm Women of Alberta, and the Women's Grain Growers' Association accused the governments of Ontario and the Prairie Provinces of using the Women's and Farmers' Institutes "to channel and quell rural discontent."[27] However, this seems unlikely in British Columbia. There were no other province-side agricultural organizations in the province when either the Farmers' or Women's Institutes were formed. Neither was there any widespread discontent among British Columbia's agricultural population. Even when the United Farmers (UFBC) did organize in British Columbia in 1917 they did not attract much support. Some historians feel the Farmers' Institutes hindered the growth of the UFBC, but, except for the fact that Farmers' Institutes were well established, it seems more plausible that the real reason was a general satisfaction with provincial government policy. Even at its peak the Progressive Party elected only two candidates from British Columbia to the federal Parliament. Their commitment to the Progressive movement was weak and they were both defeated in the 1925 federal election.[28] With a sympathetic farmer-premier after 1918, the British Columbia government, in fact, met most of the farmers' demands, and this success, in effect, meant that little more was needed.[29] This does not, however, negate the possibility of the government using the Institutes to stabilize the agricultural work force. This is stated explicitly as one of the goals of the Women's Institutes.[30]

Another area of politics which may have influenced the provincial government's willingness to organize Women's Institutes was the issue of female suffrage. Like most other governments in Canada before the First World War, the British Columbia government opposed giving women the vote. It is possible that the government, seeing such suffrage as inevitable, organized Women's Institutes in order either to delay or to gain their support for government policies if suffrage became a reality. Most people, including women, assumed that women would vote together as a block on all issues. As late as 1924 the Provincial Officer of Health saw the BCWI as "the leaders of the feminine vote,"[31] despite the fact that the women in the Institutes already recognized the absurdity of the view. A writer in *The Agricultural Journal* observed: ". . . scarcely two [I]nstitutes had the same opinions, and yet one of the objections to women becoming citizens was that they would go in a mass on any important issue."[32] However, the government did attempt to discourage Women's Institutes from considering suffrage in their programs and activities.[33] This indicates that the government was perplexed by the emergence of feminism and saw the Institutes as one way in which the "new woman" of the twentieth century might be effectively controlled.

The use of the Women's Institutes as propagandists for the provincial government also suggests political considerations. The government quite openly and repeatedly stated this purpose. The Provincial Officer of Health thanked the Institutes "for the splendid propaganda work done"[34] and many other officials refer to them as moulders of public opinion on behalf of the government.[35] However, this was not propaganda on behalf of any political party since the Institutes remained staunchly non-partisan. Rather, its regular activities on behalf of government were usually in the fields of agricultural extension work, health, and educational policy — all activities which fitted in with the "housewifely" activities of the Institutes.

The organization of the Women's Institutes in British Columbia was a complex response to the needs of women, the requirements of government policy, and the prevailing social climate. Opportunities for social life, education, and participation in public life, which increased agricultural production and stemmed the rural to urban population flow, played decisive roles in making the Institutes desirable and successful. The housewives' ideology made it a "safe" women's group to those in authority and its program attractive to women. Nonetheless, women made use of the Institutes for their own and their communities' purposes, effectively linking self and community development.

One of the major areas of Women's Institute work was adult education, and the Department of Agriculture regarded the Institutes as "the logical educational agency between the Government and the people . . ."[36] Lady Tweedsmuir, wife of one of Canada's Governors-General, remarked in 1939 that the Women's Institutes were "perhaps the greatest adult education movement in the world."[37] Women's Institutes' actions in adult education were concentrated into five main subject areas: Institute work and methods, legislation, home economics, agriculture, and health. The following examples of their efforts in the first three topics will serve to illustrate the methods used.

One of the first areas in which Institute members needed instruction was organizational methods, including parliamentary procedure. Universal free education was a fairly recent development in Canada — the 1870s in British Columbia.[38] Attendance was not compulsory in British Columbia's elementary schools until 1921.[39] High schools were few in number and catered to a small group.[40] It is little wonder that the majority of adults had relatively little formal education.[41] Women had only recently begun to take part in public life to any degree. This, along with their lack of education, made many very unsure of themselves. Rural women, used to working alone or in family groups, were even more uncertain of their capabilities.[42] One lecturer in 1913 noted that many members were "afraid of the sound of their own voices"[43] and as late as 1936 the Superintendent of Women's Institutes, Mrs MacLachlan, noted that a "good many members are lacking in self-confidence."[44] This lack of confidence revealed itself in their conduct of business. Mrs Watt, a member of the first Advisory Board, noted: "We start out to reform the world and very often we cannot conduct a meeting or even hold an Institute together."[45] Such a state of affairs needed immediate remediation if the Institutes were to progress.

The Advisory Board and Superintendent gave personal assistance on visits to the Institutes. The minute books provided to the Institutes by the Department of Agriculture contained detailed instructions for use, forms to follow, and copies of the rules and regulations. More knowledgeable women and those willing to do the research presented papers on parliamentary procedures, making reports, and the duties of officers. The most outstanding papers were published in the *Women's Institute Quarterly, Agricultural Journal,* and other Institute publications. Institutes were urged to have a brief parliamentary drill and reading of the rules and regulations at each meeting. However, these measures did not completely satisfy the need.

A more intensive effort began in 1922. The Advisory Board started an experimental project, an Institute school, with the co-operation of the Esquimalt Women's Institute. Their purpose was "to provide practical training in the rules of order and instruction on the various lines of institute activities."[46] The first part of each lesson taught some rule of order or the way to make motions and amendments to motions. Different persons acted as chairperson and secretary for each lesson. This gave everyone an opportunity to receive officer training. There was then an address on the work of one of the standing committees followed by a discussion. The school was so well received that an outline of the ten lessons was filed with the office of the province's organizer of technical education. Institutes were encouraged to arrange classes through his office. Mrs J. D. Gordon, supervisor of women's work for the Soldier Settlement Board, was made available to instruct. Many Institutes did hold such schools but the exact numbers are not available.[47]

Another method used was the model meeting, the first of which was held at the Vancouver Island District conference in 1922. It was a demonstration of a model Institute meeting on industries which covered four points in the rules of order. It was such a success that several nearby districts asked to have it repeated in their local Institutes.[48]

Short articles, question-box columns, and, after 1942, radio broadcasts were all used to give further instruction. These gave explanations of specific rules, model reports, duties of officers, and answers to procedural questions. This type of information continued to be needed as new settlers and immigrants entered the organization. The latter were more open and eager to learn and they often achieved better results than their more educated and settled neighbors! Mrs MacLachlan noted this at a 1939 Peace River District conference:

> . . . this unusual quality [concise reports] had been developed in secretaries, many of whom are foreign-born or of limited educational advantages. As much work was transacted in one day at Rolla as many conferences achieve in two or three days.[49]

This illustrates graphically the truism that the attitude of the learner is as important as the skill of the instructor in ensuring the success of any educational program.

As the Institutes began to make and pass resolutions a new difficulty arose. The Superintendent noted that:

> . . . resolutions have been submitted to the various Government departments, many of them showing a lamentable lack of knowledge of the Statutes already in force in the Province. . . . succintly [sic] described . . . as 'ill-considered, ill-advised resolutions'.[50]

The same criticism applied to knowledge of federal and municipal laws and regulations.[51] This lack of knowledge was partially due to women's lack of participation in the political process prior to 1916. Women were encouraged to think of law and politics as the male sphere. Another reason was the widely held belief of most lay persons that laws were not important to them in their everyday life.[52] Educational efforts had to combat both of these false premises.

The suffrage movement of the early twentieth century went far to remove these ideas. As speakers and lecturers spoke on British Columbia's laws in relation to women and children, women began to see and feel their powerlessness before the law. Mrs Gordon Grant's words at a 1913 Women's Institute convention give some idea of the picture painted:

> Do you know that a man can dispose of his property during his natural life without consulting his wife, and by his will can at his death leave her and his family without a farthing . . . Do you know that the father is the sole guardian and has sole control of the children?. . .Do you know that although women were last year able to sit as members of the School

Board in rural districts, that privilege has now been taken away from them, and they can no longer sit on school boards unless property owners? That they have no voice in the education of their children?[53]

Women's Institutes heard many similar speeches before 1916. Besides encouraging individual members and possibly some Institutes to support suffrage, they fired the Institutes with the determination to see that such laws were changed for the better. Many resolutions and delegations protested against and asked for such changes. Many of these changes demanded by all women's groups were implemented.

With the advent of women's suffrage in 1916, some of the impetus for the study of legislation was gone. Despite being urged to study recent legislation, to contact their MPs and MLAs, and to study the reports of the various government departments, the Women's Institutes' interest was at best lukewarm. Like most people even today they were difficult to interest in laws which did not directly touch their own well-being. Only when specific cases of injustice arose could they be aroused to protest and petition governments for change.[54] Even the offer of a new 1939 edition of Dr MacGill's booklet on British Columbia's laws for women and children failed to interest them. The author had difficulty securing sufficient orders to justify its publication even though it was sponsored by the Women's Institutes and the local Councils of Women.[55] Educating themselves on content was about as far as most Institutes ever went.

Home Economics was another field of study for Women's Institutes. This is hardly surprising since their founder, Adelaide Hoodless, was one of Canada's foremost promoters of home economics education. Their own lack of skill and information on home-making in frontier conditions were major problems for most W.I. members. Many joined the Women's Institutes specifically because of their home economics education program. Prevailing social attitudes supported the view that woman's role was that of wife, mother, and homemaker. As one member stated:

First of all, a woman's duty, when she is the head of a home, is the care of that home, the care of her house, the preparation of proper food, and the provision of clothing for her family. Not less important is the most sacred duty of all — the duty of properly bearing and bringing up children.[56]

The promoters of education in home economics sought to raise this role to one of equal status with that of men by treating home-making as a science.[57] Women's Institute members actively supported this view and their educational efforts in this area were substantial.

Sewing and cooking were the main areas of instruction before the 1920s. Lectures, demonstrations, and papers were regular features of monthly meetings. The Department of Agriculture lecture tours were predominantly concerned with these areas as well. Canning of meats, fruits, and vegetables, food values, millinery, and baking were favorite topics. The First World War saw a special emphasis on conserving food and practical sewing, including the remaking of old clothes. These topics reflect wartime shortages and rationing. The 1920s and 1930s saw a sharp decline in interest in such basic subjects. During the Second World War this interest was renewed and the preservation of foods by drying became a favorite topic as sugar rationing limited the amount of canning which could be done.

The interwar years saw a surge of interest in the appreciation of handicrafts. These were actively promoted by the Advisory/Provincial Board as a means of assisting "rural women to augment their income. . . ."[58] At first there were some who felt that women should not have to work to supplement the family income.[59] However, the depression in the early 1920s and the Depression of the 1930s swept away such opposition. The Women's Institute members soon discovered that even if they did not wish to make handicrafts for sale they could "make them for oneself and so avoid purchasing inferior articles."[60] Handicrafts, especially those such as weaving, could produce clothing to be given to others during the Depression and during the wars. These were all factors in their popularity.

The BCWI's first loyalty was always to their local communities.[61] This emphasis was a direct consequence of their housewife ideology, which put the home first, and of the members' restricted mobility, caused by their family responsibilities. The needs of their immediate area were naturally more easily seen and usually more remediable by direct action. When the Institutes' concerns expanded into the wider neighborhood of the province and beyond, only indirect action could be taken. This diminished their effectiveness but did not make them wholly powerless.

Community and town improvements were a major part of Women's Institute's local efforts. The first order of business for many Institutes was to build, improve, or raise funds for a hall for their own and community use. Some groups quickly accomplished this aim, but others took up to ten years, especially during the Depression. A few rented or leased halls and never built one for their own use. Institute halls gave the women a place of their own to meet and to hold their fund-raising and social events without charge. Institutes also rented the halls for use as polling stations and to other organizations. Community halls required joint use scheduling but were more common in small communities where they also served as churches, dance halls, and meeting places.

Women's Institutes were "the pivot of efforts for community betterment"[62] in the area of jointly used public property and services. In smaller towns and settlements Institutes purchased land for cemeteries and took an active part in their upkeep and improvement. The acquisition of library facilities, whether travelling or permanent, was a priority of all Institutes. Town and urban groups led efforts to provide garbage disposal sites, sewer systems,

Federated Women's Institutes of Canada convention, Victoria, BC, 1925.

National Archives Canada/NA-139661

and fire halls. Rural members petitioned for better mail service and for telephone systems. Some Institutes were instrumental in preserving local historical sites. Institutes also beautified public areas by planting trees and flowers and by sponsoring clean-up days. These actions helped improve the quality of life in their communities.

Institutes sought to serve women shopping in their towns by providing restrooms. When rural women, often accompanied by young children, made their infrequent trips to town they faced a long day of walking and shopping. There was nowhere they could go to sit down, rest, feed their children, change babies, and have a drink while waiting for their husbands to finish their business. It was to this need that Institutes addressed themselves. The ideal restroom was described in 1919 as an attractive heated room with a kitchenette, a small lending library, proper and sanitary conveniences, comfortable chairs, and a table. Here women could, for a price, make themselves a drink or heat water, borrow books, eat a lunch, and purchase handicrafts. Because these facilities were seen as public conveniences, many Institutes asked for and received financial aid from local businesses, and from city or municipal councils.[63] Even as late as the 1940s money was raised to open such a restroom in Dawson Creek, and Institutes around the province responded to the need.

Improving local roads and transportation facilities was another aspect of Institute neighborhood work. They presented petitions and resolutions to local and provincial governments and to transportation companies. These requests urged the extension, repair, and improvement of railways, roads, and other transportation networks. Despite the fact that only indirect action was possible, the Institutes met with some success. For example, the Metchosin, Shirley, and Luxton-Happy Valley groups were able to obtain better road signs and improve safety on some road corners.[64] Unfortunately, many other requests were turned down or ignored.

Providing recreational facilities such as playgrounds, parks, landing docks, and tennis courts for their communities was a high priority for Women's Institutes. The Nakusp Women's Institute led efforts to develop the nearby hot springs.[65] Equipment for sports and other recreation was donated to community halls and groups. Institutes also petitioned governments to purchase beach areas for national parks and to preserve public beaches.[66] It is not known if these requests were granted.

Women's Institutes' aims included the development of community social life.[67] Monthly Institute meetings, social events, recreational activities, and general friendliness did much to relieve loneliness and to create community spirit. Most meetings had a social hour when the women gathered for a cup of tea, talk, and in some cases, special entertainment. This might include musical numbers, literary readings, or special presentations by young people. Some Institutes even made special arrangements to care for young children while their mothers attended the meeting.[68] Most of the time, however, small children came to the meeting too. A few Institutes held business and social meetings on different days. This practice enabled them to take trips to experimental farms or nearby communities. Special meetings for all the women in the district were held in a few areas. Mrs Davies reported that these women:

> . . . have very little leisure or recreation, . . . helpful speakers give addresses, a playroom is provided for the children that the [m]other must bring and a social cup of [t]ea is enjoyed at the close of the afternoon.[69]

Women's Institutes often organized, sponsored, or helped other recreational and social groups. In 1931-32, The Nelson Women's Institute established a weekly community social club which had 170 members.[70] Institutes supported Chautaugqua committees, amateur musical and dramatic groups, bands, choirs, and youth groups with time, money, and other aid. These organizations all "helped considerably to keep up the morale of the people . . ."[71] Institute social events provided fun and entertainment as well as raising funds for projects. Whole communities were invited to attend dances, picnics, card parties, movies, plays, musical evenings, and sport events arranged by the Institutes. No one could remain lonely or downhearted for long at their gatherings!

Welcoming new arrivals to the community was another part of Institute efforts. Most groups quickly visited and invited the new women to their meetings. Some went farther:

> . . . if the committee know[s] of the new settlers arrival, they have had the home in readiness, a fire prepared, a meal on the table, and some one to receive and welcome the newcomers.[72]

Sometimes special get-acquainted evenings were given. Such deeds helped new settlers to feel part of the community quickly and made it more likely they would remain.

Women's Institutes accepted social service work as an additional responsibility. Before unemployment insurance, universal Old Age Pensions, and medical care insurance, the care of the aged, unemployed, and ill was largely a family or community duty. Government aid, when available, was seldom sufficient. Institutes quickly entered this field and, according to one observer, there wasn't an Institute which hadn't "been the good Samaritan to some individual or some family in the community."[73] Their assistance went to anyone in any kind of need.

Aid to the elderly members of the community took many forms. Gifts of food, clothing, and fuel were common. Organizing homes for the aged in their own communities was another project. From 1940 onwards, the BCWI agitated to have changes made which would increase the amount of the old age pension and make it more nearly universal. Institutes did, however, want such pensions limited to residents who had been in Canada at least twenty years.[74] Their efforts were successful, but most of these results came after 1946.

Along with the elderly the Institute aided the destitute with donations of clothing, food, furniture, and money. Even in normal times most Institutes aided one or two families a year. During the Depression, the assistance needed and given rose dramatically. In 1936, The Comox Women's Institute gave assistance to eight to ten families a month. The Aldergrove Women's Institute gave a ton of foodstuffs to Scandinavians in Vancouver who did not meet residence requirements for relief.[76] They sent carloads of fruit and vegetables to Saskatchewan and provided used clothing, school supplies, and financial assistance to the needy in the Peace River District, in other areas of Canada, and other parts of the world. Institutes tried to find work for unemployed local residents and widows on limited incomes. The BCWI members gave generously in a time when many of them were also in dire straits.

Assistance to the sick and to victims of various disasters was another phase of the Women's Institutes' social service work. One Institute had a window put in to enable a bedridden woman to see people as they passed.[77] Institute halls served as places of refuge during floods and members fed the persons sheltered there.[78] After the Second World War every Institute resolved to send one food parcel a month to famine areas of the world.[79] Institutes helped people apply for mother's pensions and protested unfair rulings by the Workmen's Compensation Board.[80] In these and many other ways the BCWI's were neighbors to those in need.

Efforts to protect and extend the rights of citizens were made on behalf of women, children, and native Indians. Resolutions seeking amendments to divorce laws, equal pay for equal work, and equal guardianship were prominent after 1914.[81] Institutes asked that married women be allowed to take out their own citizenship papers and that citizens be allowed to call themselves Canadians on the census.[82] After 1944, Institutes requested full citizenship rights for native Indians in the armed forces, and improved health and educational opportunities for native people.[83] They also passed resolutions concerning ecological, pension, and international concerns. These efforts indicate a broadening view of the community.

This broader view included all those in the armed forces. They held send-off and welcome home parties for soldiers, welcomed war-brides, and were in the forefront of efforts to create war memorials. The Institutes asked the federal government to establish barracks for women soldiers or increase their living allowance.[84] Institutes also wanted women in the services to have the same dependent's allowance as men.[85] Some wanted the rights and privileges of the armed forces to be extended to those men in the Merchant Marines serving on ocean-going ships.[86] Institutes near ports or military installations helped entertain armed service personnel. One Institute member, Mrs Annie McVie of Esquimalt, entertained over ten thousand service people during the Second World War.[87] During peacetime, some Institutes aided local cadet groups by altering uniforms or making puttees.[88] By these and other actions, Women's Institutes extended a neighborly hand to the armed services of their country.

Despite the great value of their contributions, the Women's Institutes received very little recognition for them. This lack of acknowledgement was a consequence of the nature of the aid. As the Superintendent said in 1916: ". . . what has hitherto been considered everybody's business and nobody's business, the [I]nstitutes have taken up and are making their special duty."[89] Unfortunately, such duties did not inspire praise but forgetfulness on the part of all but those directly benefitted.

The Institutes may have taken comfort in "the admonition, 'Let not your left hand know what the right hand doeth',"[90] but the resulting lack of public recognition hampered their efforts to influence governments and thus limited their effectiveness outside the local community.

From their inception Women's Institutes were tied to a housewife ideology which both enhanced and limited their effectiveness. Government sponsorship cast them in a "dependent spouse" role and their activities resembled those performed by every housewife. The public's perception confirmed this ideology and, like housework, their activities seldom attracted comment. Yet their accomplishments were as vital to community well-being as the housewife's accomplishments were vital to the well-being of her husband and children. Such a dichotomy was endemic.

The various structural levels within the BCWI were bound together by their common ideology, common goals, and common membership. The provincial government, through the Department of Agriculture, was a unifying force through its supervision and direction. However, its financial support placed the Women's Institutes under obligation to promote government policies and limited their freedom of action. This lack of independence was especially noticeable in their relationships with the Federated Women's Institutes of Canada (FWIC) and the Associated Country Women of the World, since the Institutes could not endorse or carry out policy decisions made by these groups without prior approval from the provincial government. All spending at the provincial level also required such consent. Only at the local level was a large measure of freedom possible.

Activities at the local level flourished partially because of this freedom. More importantly, the local Institute constituted the only level at which most members, tied to their homes by family responsibilities, could function. Then too, local needs were more apparent, more amenable to direct action, and more immediately rewarding. Yet, even in this arena of greatest influence, the Institutes' work went largely ignored. It had "too much of the housekeeping business about it . . ."[91] to make the male-dominated power structure take notice until the tasks were done. As one Institute member in Alberta noted: "The Institute started something and then it was taken over by the people who should have done it in the first place."[92] Many BCWI members would have heartily agreed!

The lack of public recognition harmed BCWI efforts to obtain changes in laws and regulations. Only when their requests were made to the provincial departments of agriculture, education, and health did they meet with a high rate of success. These departments depended on Institute publicity work to promote their policies and so were aware of their effectiveness. Petitions to local and federal governments met with varied responses. Local successes were more likely in areas where the Institutes' membership constituted a large proportion of the adult female population. Federally, the support of other provincial Institutes through the FWIC and/or the support of other women's groups was needed to effect change.

Why did the Institutes have such a low public profile? An editorial in *Country Life in British Columbia* noted: "They do so many fine things, quietly and smoothly, that these contributions are too often disregarded or taken as a matter of course."[93] Just as no one notices housework "until it isn't done,"[94] so too the male-dominated media did not notice many of the Institutes' contributions to their communities. These actions were women's work and thus peripheral and irrelevant to the "important" issues which men faced. The fact that the majority of these contributions were made at the local level further contributed to their invisibility. Yet, the "constraints of household and family responsibilities and the strong sanctions against neglect of them [made] local involvement more acceptable for women."[95] The tendency of Institutes to turn their projects, especially at the provincial and district levels, into co-operative efforts with other groups further obscured the public's view of their contributions. While government and elected officials would praise them to their face, the wider community often remained ignorant of their work.

Why then did the BCWI continue to pursue such housewifely activities? One reason was that these were the activities they felt most comfortable and competent to do. Through the BCWI the members could "make our voices heard in the land"[96] as the only representatives of rural women. More importantly, they saw the beneficial results of their efforts in their own communities and families. This was reward enough for most of them.

The BCWI did improve all facets of rural life in British Columbia. They advanced government programs in health, education, and agriculture; they educated themselves and the public while easing the loneliness of rural life; and they improved the quality of community life. They were good housewives "for home and country."

Footnotes

1.   British Columbia, Legislative Assembly, *Sessional Papers 1909* (Victoria: King's

Printer, 1909), K7, K46; *Sessional Papers 1910* (Victoria: King's Printer, 1910), pp. 105-107.

2. British Columbia, *Statutes,* 1911, Agricultural Associations Act, p. 2.

3. Martin Robin, *The Rush for Spoils: The Company Province 1871-1933* (Toronto: McClelland and Stewart Limited, 1972), p. 35.

4. Margaret A. Ormsby, "Agricultural Development in British Columbia," *Agricultural History* 19 (January 1945), p. 14.

5. J. Schulz, *The Rise and Fall of Canadian Farm Organizations* (Winnipeg: The author, 1955), p. 108.

6. LaVonne Byron, "The Better Halves — The Way of Life and Influence of Women in the Vernon Area from Settlement to 1921," *Forty-Fifth Annual Report of the Okanagan Historical Society* (Vernon, British Columbia: The Okanagan Historical Society, 1981), p. 68; British Columbia, *Annual Report of Women's Institutes, 1914* (Victoria: King's Printer, 1915), p. 20; British Columbia, *Annual Report of Women's Institutes, 1915* (Victoria: King's Printer, 1916), p. 44, and numerous others.

7. Grace Worth, *Autobiography* (Okanagan Historical Society, Vol. 33), cited in Byron, "Better Halves," p. 68.

8. Note that in 1909, of the towns where Institutes were organized, only Nelson, Cranbrook, and Chilliwack were over 1000 in population, with Nelson being over 5000. The Nelson area received a large influx of British settlers around this time and many were unfamiliar with farming and were used to having household help. Canada, Dominion Bureau of Statistics, *Eighth Census of Canada, 1941,* Vol. II (Ottawa: King's Printer, 1944), p. 188; Evelyn A. Cameron, "British Columbia — Looking Back," in *Making History — An Anthology of British Columbia,* edited by Millicent A. Lindo (by the author, 1974), p. 48.

9. It appears that except for a few properous farmers most farm housewives did not have domestic servants. The possible exception to this would be the hiring of harvest-time help when it was available. Town dwellers of moderate means may have had a domestic servant or two. References to servants in the sources are mainly to the need of domestic help in farm homes and to the lack of finances to make it possible. Two examples are: British Columbia, Department of Agriculture, *Eighteenth Annual Report of the Department of Agriculture for the Year 1923* (Victoria: King's Printer, 1924), p. 193, and *Nineteenth Annual Report of the Department of Agriculture for the Year 1924* (Victoria: King's Printer, 1925), p. 177.

10. Nan Bourgon, *Rubber Boots for Dancing and Other Memories of Pioneer Life in the Bulkley Valley* (Smithers, British Columbia: Tona and Janet Hetherington, 1979), p. 51.

11. British Columbia, Department of Agriculture, *Handbook of Women's Institutes and Report of Advisory Board 1913 — Bulletin No. 54* (Victoria: King's Printer, 1914), p. 50.

12. Neil Sutherland, *Children in English-Canadian Society: Framing the Twentieth-*

Century Consensus (Toronto: University of Toronto Press, 1976), pp. 17, 24.

13. Alice Ravenhill, *The Memoirs of an Educational Pioneer* (Vancouver: J. M. Dent & Sons (Canada) Limited, 1951), p. 180.

14. Linda Kealey, ed., *A Not Unreasonable Claim — Women and Reform in Canada, 1880s-1920s* (Toronto: The Women's Press, 1979), pp. 7-8; British Columbia, Department of Agriculture, *The Agricultural Journal* II (December 1917), 204, and III (November 1918), 223; and Suzann Buckley, "Ladies or Midwives? Efforts to Reduce Infant and Maternal Mortality," in *A Not Unreasonable Claim*, edited by L. Kealey, p. 133.

15. Janet L. Bokemeier and John L. Tait, "Women as Power Actors: A Comparative Study of Rural Communities," *Rural Sociology 45* (summer 1980), 241.

16. Mrs. J. D. McBride, "Civics," *The Agricultural Journal*, III (November 1918), 223.

17. *Annual Report, 1914*, pp. 20, 32.

18. Veronica Strong-Boag, Introduction to *In Times Like These* by Nellie L. McClung, 1915 Reprint. *Social History of Canada* 5 (Toronto: University of Toronto Press, 1972), p. ix.

19. Sutherland, *Children in English-Canadian Society*, p. 27, and The Corrective Collective, *Never Done, Three Centuries of Women's Work in Canada* (Toronto: Women's Educational Press, 1974), p. 131.

20. Carl Berger, *The Sense of Power — Studies in the Ideas of Canadian Imperialism, 1867-1914* (Toronto: University of Toronto Press, 1970), pp. 177, 192.

21. Sutherland, *Children in English-Canadian Society*, p. 181, and *Handbook, 1913*, pp. 12, 60.

22. British Columbia, *Report of the Royal Commission on Agriculture, 1914* (Victoria: King's Printer, 1914), p. 36.

23. A Country-Woman, "As I See It." *The Agricultural Journal* IV (June 1919), p. 125.

24. "Women's Institute Work and Method," *Country Life in British Columbia* XIII (July 1925), p. 3; Carol Bacchi, "Divided Allegiances: The Response of Farm and Labour Women to Suffrage," *A Not Unreasonable Claim*, edited by L. Kealey, pp. 103-104.

25. Ormsby, *Agricultural History* 19 (January 1945), 14.

26. Barbara Ehrenreich and Deirdre English, "The Manufacture of Housework," *Socialist Revolution* 26 (October-December 1975), 14.

27. Carol Bacchi, "Divided Allegiances: The Response of Farm and Labour Women to Suffrage," *A Not Unreasonable Claim — Women and Reform in Canada, 1880s-1920s*, edited by Linda Kealey (Toronto: Women's Educational Press, 1979), p. 104.

28. W. L. Morton, *The Progressive Party in Canada* (Toronto: University of Toronto Press, 1950), pp. 129, 245, and Hugh G. Thorburn, ed., *Party Politics in Canada*, 3rd ed.(Scarborough, Ontario: Prentice-Hall, 1972), p. 247.

29. Robin, *The Rush for Spoils*, p. 39; Margaret A. Ormsby, "The United Farmers of British Columbia — An Abortive Third-Party Movement," *The British Columbia Historical Quarterly* XVII (1953), pp. 53-54, and Reginald Whitaker, introduction to *The Farmers in Politics*, by William Irvine, 1920, Reprint. The Carleton Library No. 114 (Toronto: McClelland and Stewart, 1976), p. viii.

30. British Columbia, Department of Agriculture, *Fifteenth Annual Report of the Department of Agriculture for the Year 1920* (Victoria: King's Printer, 1921), p. 1109, and Women's Institutes of British Columbia, *Year Book, 1923-24* (Victoria: British Columbia, British Columbia Women's Institutes, 1924), p. 27.

31. *Advisory Board of Women's Institutes of British Columbia Minutes, 1911-1932* (Victoria: Provincial Archives of British Columbia, ADD. MSS. 178), January 17-19, 1924.

32. *The Agricultural Journal* III (September 1918), 177.

33. *Advisory Board Minutes,* 14-16 May 1914, p. 2.

34. *Advisory Board Minutes,* 17-19 January 1924.

35. *The Agricultural Journal* VII (September 1922), 165; *Country Life in British Columbia* XIII (July 1925), 3; and British Columbia, Department of Agriculture, *Sixteenth Annual Report of the Department of Agriculture for the Year 1921* (Victoria: King's Printer, 1922), p. U115.

36. *Department of Agriculture Report, 1921,* p. U115.

37. *British Columbia Women's Institute Bulletin* (March 1929), p. 1.

38. F. Henry Johnson, *A Brief History of Canadian Education* (Toronto: McGraw-Hill, 1968), p. 80.

39. Timothy A. Dunn, "The Rise of Mass Public Schooling in British Columbia, 1900-1929," in *Schooling and Society in 20th Century British Columbia,* edited by J. Donald Wilson and David C. Jones (Calgary: Detselig Enterprises Limited, 1980), p. 33.

40. Johnson, *A Brief History of Canadian Education,* pp. 87, 100.

41. Dunn, "The Rise of Mass Public Schooling," p. 27, and Canada Dominion Bureau of Statistics, *The Canada Year Book, 1921* (Ottawa: King's Printer, 1922), pp. 124-25.

42. A Country-Woman, "Co-operation for the Betterment of the Country Home," *The Agricultural Journal* IV (May 1919), pp. 93-94, and Alice Ravenhill, *The Memoirs of an Educational Pioneer* (Vancouver: J. M. Dent and Sons (Canada) Limited, 1951), p. 180.

43. British Columbia, Department of Agriculture, *Deputy Minister Reports Received 1913* (Victoria: Provincial Archives of British Columbia, GR 402), File 004, pp. 6-7.

44. Mrs. V. S. MacLachlan, "How To Make W.I. Reports," *Country Life in British Columbia* XX (January 1936), p. 15.

45. Mrs. Alfred Watt, "Selection of Women's Institute Organization and Technique Embracing Principles, Aims, and Methods of Work of Women's Institutes" (Ottawa: Public Archives of Canada, MC28, I316, Volume 8), p. 1.

46. *The Agricultural Journal* VIII (June 1923), 95.

47. *Department of Agriculture Report, 1923,* p. I104; Women's Institute of British Columbia, *Year Book, 1923-24* (Victoria: British Columbia Women's Institutes, 1924), p. 29, and *The Agricultural Journal* VIII (June 1923), p. 95.

48. British Columbia, Department of Agriculture, *Seventeenth Annual Report of the Department of Agriculture for the Year 1922* (Victoria: King's Printer, 1923), p. W126.

49. British Columbia, Department of Agriculture, *Thirty-Fourth Annual Report of the Department of Agriculture for the Year 1939* (Victoria: King's Printer, 1940), p. B92.

50. *Department of Agriculture Report, 1922,* p. W123.

51. Charter Member, "Women As Politicians," *The Creston Review,* 1 October 1920, n.p.

52. Mrs. Gordon Grant, "The Legal Status of Women in British Columbia," *Handbook, 1913,* pp. 50-52.

53. Ibid., pp. 51-52.

54. *Department of Agriculture Report, 1923,* p. I97.

55. *British Columbia Women's Institute Bulletin,* March and May 1939, and Elsie Gregory MacGill, *My Mother the Judge* (Toronto: Peter Martin Associates Limited, 1981), p. 229.

56. *Women's Institutes Report, 1915,* p. 30.

57. The Corrective Collective, *Never Done,* p. 131.

58. Elizabeth Bailey Price, "National News Notes of the Women's Institutes," *Country Life in British Columbia,* February 1929, p. 11.

59. Harriet E. Johnson, "Women's Exchanges," *The Agricultural Journal* VIII (April 1923), p. 17.

60. "Women of B.C. Trying to Find Industries of Practical Value," *Country Life in British Columbia* (September 1935), p. 14.

61. British Columbia, Department of Agriculture, *The Agricultural Journal* III (July 1918), 127.

62. British Colombia, Department of Agriculture, *Twenty-Eight Annual Report of the Department of Agriculture for the Year 1933* (Victoria: King's Printer, 1934), p. Y66.

63. *The Agricultural Journal* III (January 1919), 272, and Elizabeth Bailey Price, "Interests of Women's Institutes," 22 February 1933, n.p., in British Columbia Women's Institutes files, Abbotsford, British Columbia, 1930s file.

64. British Columbia, Bureau of Public Information, *British Columbia Public Service Bulletin* 2, March-April 1927), 74; 2 (June 1927), 109; and 3 (April-May 1928), 18.

65. "News of the Institutes," *British Columbia Public Service Bulletin* 2 (March

1928), 208, and "History of Nakusp Women's Institute," *Arrow Lake News,* 12 November 1959, p. 3.

66. *Provincial Board Minutes,* 26 August 1936, p. 8; *Country Life* (November 1946), 34; and *British Columbia Public Service Bulletin* 2 (March 1928), 208.

67. British Columbia, Department of Agriculture, *Handbook of Women's Institutes and Report of Advisory Board, 1913,* Bulletin No. 54 (Victoria: King's Printer, 1914), p. 14.

68. British Columbia, Department of Agriculture, *Twenty-Third Annual Report of the Department of Agriculture for the Year 1928* (Victoria: King's Printer, 1929), p. 0100.

69. Mrs. Davies, "Report of the W.I. of B.C., 1909-1914," in *Advisory Board Minutes,* p. 8.

70. *Country Life in British Columbia* XVI (July 1932), 27.

71. *Department of Agriculture Report, 1933,* p. Y 67.

72. *British Columbia Public Service Bulletin* (February 1928), 188.

73. British Columbia, Department of Agriculture, *Twenty-First Annual Report of the Department of Agricultural for the Year 1926* (Victoria: King's Printer, 1927), p. N85.

74. *Provincial Board Minutes,* resolutions passed at provincial convention, 20 August 1940, p. 42; miscellaneous correspondence, p. 84A; minutes of provincial conference, 30 May 1946, p. 128; "B.C. Women's Institutes Choose Their Officers," 1940; "Sumas Session W.I. Conference 'Second to None'," 1941, in private files of Mrs. Stella Welch, West Vancouver, British Columbia; "South Fraser District Women's Institute Conference, October 15-16, 1946" and "North Fraser District Women's Institute Conference, October 17-18, 1946," in files of British Columbia Women's Institutes, Abbotsford, British Columbia, 1940s file.

75. *Country Life in British Columbia* XX (February 1936), 10.

76. Ibid. XX (March 1936), 12.

77. British Columbia, Department of Agriculture, *Thirty-Ninth Annual Report of the Department of Agriculture for the Year 1944* (Victoria: King's Printer, 1944), p. S98.

78. Elizabeth Bailey Price, "Fraser Valley W.I. Active for Last Quarter Century," *Country Life in British Columbia* XIX (July 1935), 8.

79. *Provincial Board Minutes,* minutes of provincial conference, 30 May 1946, p. 138.

80. *Kalamalka Women's Institute Minutes, 1922-1926* (Victoria Provincial Archives of British Columbia, A-949), 12 November 1924.

81. The Agricultural Journal II (November 1917), 185, and *Advisory Board Minutes* 12-14 October 1916, p. 8.

82. *The Agricultural Journal* VII (October 1922), 191; *Advisory Board Minutes,*

minutes of provincial conference May 1902-, 1927, p. 7, and *British Columbia Public Service Bulletin* 2 (May 1927), 92.

83. *Provincial Board Minutes,* minutes of provincial conference, 2 June 1944, p. 96; 21 February 1945, p. 107; and minutes of provincial conference, 30 May 1946, p. 127.

84. "Resolutions Passed at the South Vancouver Island District Conference, November 28, 1942," n.p. in *Brentwood-Women's Institute Records, 1915-1918, 1937-70* (Victoria: Provincial Archives of British Columbia, ADD. MSS.8), file folder "B.C.W.I. Correspondence, 1942-44."

85. Ibid., and *Provincial Board Minutes,* 16 November 1942, p. 81.

86. "Resolutions Passed at the South Vancouver Island District Conference, November 28, 1942," n.p.

87. Elizabeth Forbes, "Mrs. McVie's 'Good Works' Recognized," Victoria *Times,* 7 May 1977, p. 32.

88. *Chilliwack Women's Institute Minutes,* 17 May 1921.

89. British Columbia, Department of Agriculture, *Eleventh Annual Report of the Department of Agriculture for the Year 1916* (Victoria: King's Printer, 1917), p. N85.

90. *Department of Agriculture Report, 1926,* p. N85.

91. Irene Parlby, "Letter to Violet McNaughton, March 14, 1916," in *A Harvest Yet to Reap — A History of Prairie Women,* compiled by Linda Rasmussen et al. (Toronto: The Women's Press, 1976), p. 138.

92 *A Harvest Yet to Reap,* p. 142.

93. "Unsung Heroines," *Country Life in British Columbia* XXIV (October 1940), 15.

94. Ehrenreich and English, "The Manufacture of Housework," p. 6.

95. Janet L. Bohemeier and John L. Tait, "Women as Power Actors: A Comparative Study of Rural Communities," *Rural Sociology* 45 (Summer 1980), 240.

96. "Women of B.C. — Organize!," *Country Life in British Columbia* XIII (April 1925), 1.

The Struggle for Autonomous Workers' Education: The Workers' Educational Association in Ontario, 1917-51

Ian Radforth and Joan Sangster

The Canadian Workers' Educational Association (WEA) was an offshoot of its British counterpart. In Britain, the WEA was founded in 1903 by Albert Mansbridge, a clerical worker active in the co-operative movement. The WEA was meant to provide "a link between labour and learning" by making higher education available to working people.[1] Mansbridge understood that a worker's educational movement would succeed only if the workers themselves controlled the organization, delineating and fulfilling their own educational needs. Not only did workers serve on the executives of local associations, but the self-governing tutorials, taught by university professors, permitted a considerable degree of student participation.[2] Indeed, it was these characteristics that set the WEA apart from the older university extension movement which had relied on lectures.[3]

Although the foundation of a Toronto WEA was discussed in 1913, action was not taken until a few years later.[4] Throughout the winter of 1917-18, twenty enthusiastic workers met with Classics Professor W. S. Milner to discuss Aristotle's *Politics.*[5] In spring 1918, University of Toronto President Sir Robert Falconer called a meeting to establish a Toronto WEA. At that meeting, influential local businessmen, public figures, and trade unionists agreed to form an association. In the following weeks a committee of Toronto professors, trade unionists, and public representatives drafted and then adopted a constitution for a Workers' Educational Association of Toronto and District. In the fall of 1918, sixty members registered in eight evening classes held at the University of Toronto, Upper Canada College, and at some large industrial plants. The most popular subjects were economics, history, and political science.[6]

Why was the WEA successfully established in 1918? In his letter inviting influential individuals Falconer stated that the workingmen of this city had asked the University "to co-operate with them" in establishing an organization similar to the British WEA.[7] (The men were probably students in Milner's class.[8]) At the time there was a need for educational opportunities for working-class adults. The Mechanics' Institutes had long since disappeared; public libraries offered educational resources, but few classes; and the university extension programs provided only expensive courses.[9] Working-class people, however, were not the main impetus behind the founding of the WEA in Toronto. The prime movers were members of the educational élite who for the most were dedicated to the cause of strengthening Empire ties.

The foremost figure in the formation of the WEA was the Principal of Upper Canada College, W. L. Grant. He was an intellectual of the imperial school who took a keen interest in social reform.[10] When Grant held the Beit Chair in Colonial History at Oxford from 1906 to 1910, he came into contact with Mansbridge who kindled in Grant an interest in workers' education.[11] Closely associated with Grant was Arthur J. Glazebrook, an exchange broker in Toronto. As a key figure in the imperialists' Round Table Movement in Canada, Glazebrook shared many of Grant's views on Empire.[12] Of less importance were two friends of Grant and Glazebrook: W. S. Milner, the first WEA tutor, and Sir Robert Falconer. Milner, a senior member of the Classics Department at the University of Toronto, was a devout Methodist and a firm believer in the need for stronger Empire bonds.[13] Falconer greatly facilitated the university's participation in the project and willingly served as Honorary President of the Association after retiring as President of the University.[14]

R. M. MacIver was also a very important figure in the WEA. Scottish-born, MacIver was educated at Edinburgh and Oxford where he probably came into contact with the British WEA.[15] Among the Toronto Association's academic supporters MacIver was an outsider because of his anti-imperialism and, as Glazebrook put it, his "English Radicalism."[16] Similarly, he was not at home at the University of Toronto. In 1927 he eagerly accepted an offer to teach sociology at Columbia University.

The imperialism of all these men (except MacIver) served a few important purposes. First, it gave them a common aim. In a 1918 letter to British Round Table leader Lord Milner, Glazebrook wrote:

> I have to confess that I have not been altogether "pure of heart" in working so hard for this result (getting the WEA started). I have always had in mind that some channel must be established by which we could reach the working men of this country in a more intimate manner in reference to the Imperial problem. Nearly all the tutors who so far have been suggested for the first eight or ten groups are more or less on our side . . .[17]

He saw the WEA, then, as a propaganda vehicle for imperialist doctrines.

All the educators, including MacIver, also stressed that the prime purpose of workers' education was to provide "education for citizenship."[18] The late war years and immediate postwar period saw the rise of labor militancy and radicalism on an unprecedented scale. The Russian Revolution, the Winnipeg General Strike, and the One Big Union provided dramatic warnings. Meanwhile, in Ontario the enormously increased strike activity, rapid growth of trade unionism, and the expansion of labor political action startled middle-class academics. Alarmed by these developments, the intellectuals behind the WEA sought to use the Association as a means to curb the spread of radicalism. In an article publicizing the WEA, W. L. Grant opined: "Ideas without education are very dangerous fodder. Ideas without education mean the triumph of the half-baked; and the results of the triumph of the half-baked are manifest to the world in Russia today."[19] MacIver was just as blunt in the student newspaper, *The Varsity*: "The inherent policy of the WEA is averse to Bolshevism, the chief object being to give a University culture to the labour man."[20]

The academic supporters of the Association had other aims for the WEA as well. The university élite saw the WEA as a vehicle for training labor leaders for their larger role in society. Grant, for instance, believed there was a "new concordat between Capital, Labour and the State under which the working man may play his part as an owner alike in industry and in politics." But he stressed that "it must be educated Capital, educated Labour and an educated State."[21] These academics also emphasized that the WEA must provide a "liberal," "cultural," or "social" education, and not a technical one.[22] Even MacIver, a liberal who expressed some reverence for technology, contended that the First World War had shown that "science is not enough."[23]

All the educators who supported the WEA insisted that the teaching be done by university professors. "It is the University, after all," declared Glazebrook, "that contains the treasury of knowledge and the training in method that are required."[24] They also frequently maintained that knowledge and the pursuit of knowledge were free of bias: it was simply a matter of professors unlocking the "treasury of knowledge" for working-class people. The academics' openly expressed biases, of course, belie such claims. They were for the most part conservative men, anxious to enlist supporters for the Imperial cause and determined to combat radicalism. By insisting that WEA instructors be university professors, the academics were attempting to ensure that the WEA would not become a vehicle for attacking the fundamental power relations in society.

In order for these academics to establish a workers' educational movement in Ontario, they needed the active support of several workers who would serve to legitimize the organization so that other workers, and more particularly the leaders of the labor movement, would support the WEA. Naturally, the academics turned to the Toronto District Labour Council.

This was how trade unionists came to attend the April 1918 meeting at which the decision to form the association was made.[25] Four of them were elected to the provisional executive: James Richards, of the Plumbers and Steamfitters' Union, who was chosen President; James H. H. Ballantyne, a member of the Amalgamated Society of Engineers, who was made Secretary-Treasurer; James T. Gunn of the Electrical Workers' Union; and William Stockdale of the Painters and Decorators.[26]

The most important trade unionists in the WEA during the early years were Richards, Ballantyne, and Alfred MacGowan. Richards had long been an activist in the Plumbers' Union, the Independent Labour Party, and the Toronto District Labour Council.[27] Ballantyne was a well-known union figure who continued to serve as a competent Secretary-Treasurer of the WEA until he felt compelled to resign from the executive in 1921 upon his appointment as Deputy Minister of the recently formed Department of Labour of Ontario. The position of Secretary-Treasurer was then filled by Alf MacGowan, an activist in the Toronto local of the International Typographical Union, who proved to be the dynamic working-class figure in the WEA for most of the 1920s. He was a jovial, appealing Irishman, well suited for the promotional work which he undertook. "Mac" and W. L. Grant established a warm friendship; together they did much to build the Association during the twenties.[28]

What was it that led some workers to become active in the Association in the early years? Several worker activists were British-born. A few had attended WEA classes in the Old Country, and it was natural for them to become involved in a familiar institution.[29] But broader motivations were also at work among Canadian and British-born members. Co-operation between the workers and academics was possible because both groups shared some common ideas. First, academics and workers active in the WEA were, to some degree at least, critics of their society. None was a revolutionary. They believed that workers with more knowledge would help to improve the existing political and social system. They were disillusioned with political democracy as it was functioning. They hoped it would be improved through a workers' educational movement that increased workers' understanding of political and social issues. Worker activists shared the academics' faith that truth could be pursued in an unbiased way. And finally, they were all agreed that a technical education was not enough, that a liberal education would broaden workers' understanding, augment their pleasures, and inspire in them higher ideals.

Although some of the aims of the workers differed from the academics' goals, they did not clash with them. Many working people who attended WEA classes were very keen to gain an education denied them in their youth. The great majority of working-class people at the time had been forced to leave school and earn wages at least by the age of fourteen. A university education was regarded as a privilege of the wealthy. Alf MacGowan, a man who had been unable to go far in school, showed his strong thirst for knowledge when he wrote Grant in 1919:

During our talks last winter you said you would like to get a few chaps
together from summer study of economics or some such subject. It has
never left my mind. I am still thirsting after knowledge . . . Education
— Education — is ever uppermost in my mind . . .[30]

Naturally, Grant was delighted with MacGowan's enthusiasm.

Some working people saw workers' education as a contribution to both
personal growth and the development of the labor movement. In a student
essay published in the Toronto labor paper, the *Industrial Banner,* a WEA
member stated:

. . . anything done to educate and develop the mind is never lost to the
individual or the community as a whole. . . . We need education to help
increase our interest in the product of our labour. By increasing our intellectual powers, we give a broader, more intelligent outlook on life.[31]

A liberal education for workers was also seen by some labor people as an
antidote to mechanization's bad effects on the intellectual and emotional health
of workers. In a statement in 1923 the Toronto District Labour Council called for changes in the educational system so that workers in mechanized trades
could "retain their mental discipline and their status as reasoning beings."[32]
The Council acknowledged that the WEA was partly satisfying the needs
of such workers.

Significantly, however, some of the aims of the workers differed substantially from those of the academics. While both groups talked about the Association's contribution to democracy, workers emphasized the need for social
justice and attacked the limits of education in a class society. MacGowan
claimed that "workers suffered most today from the obstacles which restrict
(university education) to a limited class." Therefore, he continued, workers
must "assert the right of the whole people to have access to the best that
the educational system of the country can offer [and] democratize education."[33] Workers criticized the class bias of the university and organs of public
opinion. MacGowan argued that since public opinion was moulded by a daily
press "biased against labour," workers "should be taught to do their own
thinking."[34] Another labor man, who was a member of the journalism class
in Hamilton in 1928, wrote that "workers must develop their own point of
view, drag to light aspects of history — the history, for example, of the life
of the people — which have hitherto been far too much neglected."[35]

Some labor activists in the WEA believed workers' education had a social
and collective purpose. Unfortunately, however, the written records of the
WEA provide but few examples of this. The Association was ever cautious,
determined to maintain broad support from the university, the government,
and the public. In the mid-1930s, one working-class member who had been
active in the WEA since the mid-twenties did emphatically state:

Education is not for the maintenance of the "status quo". While there are injustices and inequalities in society, there is a dynamic purpose in Workers' Education. The sufferer will naturally be discontented in his lot, and the duty of education is not to stifle this discontent while the cause still exists, but to replace irrational condemnation by constructive criticism and to enable working men and women to refashion society according to their ideals.[36]

Although the WEA was "non-partisan," some of its prominent leaders were socialists. They supported workers' education because they believed that a thorough and scientific study of society would inevitably lead one to a socialist position.

Thus, common language such as "education for citizenship" masked some very significant differences between the aims of the educationalists and those of the labor activists. The class differences of the two groups do much to explain the divergent meanings behind their words. On the one hand, the educationalists saw the WEA as, in part, an experiment in social control. They sought to use their positions as academics and intellectuals to maintain existing power relations in society. On the other hand, the labor activists hoped to further the cause of labor and to help redress the imbalance of power in society. These fundamental differences existed within the Association from the start. Inevitably, as time progressed, the underlying tensions would surface.

During the WEA's first decade, WEA members were justifiably disappointed with the extent of trade-union support for the Association. In part, the problem was that the WEA, as a new organization, had to prove itself of benefit to existing labor bodies. Any new organization would have had difficulties enlisting support during the 1920s because the labor movement was weak.[37] It lacked the financial resources and the determination to aid the WEA, despite resolutions of support passed at annual conventions of the Trades and Labour Congress (TLC). Union support was also made difficult because the international unions sent money to American headquarters for education services. Supporting the WEA, therefore, raised embarrassing questions about the imbalance of Canadian dues sent abroad and the few services provided for Canadian locals.[38] Furthermore, many trade unionists were deeply suspicious of the WEA's connection with the university. W. L. Grant once noted: "The class consciousness of the working man [is] intense enough to make him very suspicious of any movement not controlled by himself. We have distinct difficulties here in getting them to come even under the nominal control of the University."[39]

The WEA also found it difficult to persuade very many unorganized workers, the great majority of the Ontario workforce during the 1920s, to join the Association. Undoubtedly the unorganized tended to share the unionists' suspicions of education and social mores imposed from above. Moreover, because the WEA appealed for members chiefly by personal contact through trade unions, most unorganized workers remained beyond the reach of the Association. Furthermore, the liberal educational offerings of the WEA, and its overwhelmingly Anglo-Celtic membership, offered few attractions for many Ontario workers. An Italian-speaking laborer, toiling long hours on a construction site, hardly had much interest in a class called "Empire Relations."

Despite the limited enthusiasm of labor leaders and workers in general, in less than a decade membership had grown to over eight hundred. Nearly all belonged to the Toronto and Hamilton Associations, which had 435 and 280 members respectively in 1925-26, and the remainder belonged to small Associations in Galt, Brantford, and Windsor.[40] The core of the WEA was its trade-union membership. But significant numbers were not trade unionists: many were clerks, stenographers, sales persons, and even some business and professional people took WEA classes. To reach beyond the unions, the WEA appealed to workers through the press, the "welfare officers" of some large industrial plants, public libraries, and at public events such as the Canadian National Exhibition. In Toronto, the WEA even held classes in suburban areas such as the Scarborough Bluffs and Earlscourt for convenience sake. Efforts were also made to diversify the curriculum. Courses were offered in such subjects as Cooperation, Trade-Union Law, and there was one class in a technical subject, Metallurgy.[41]

Women comprised a significant proportion of those attending classes. In Toronto, female membership ranged from about 25 to 50 percent in 1927-28; and 75 percent in Hamilton. Female students tended to prefer courses in English Literature, Composition, and Psychology, whereas men preferred Economics, Public Speaking, and Current Events. Special courses in Hygiene and Household Economics were offered for women. Some of these female students were in the workforce, but many were housewives. One of the WEA's attractions for housewives was described by a female member of the journalism class who wrote a fictional account about two middle-aged women discussing their desire for education. They found that their children were growing up, going on in school, and leaving their mothers "behind." "Oh, mother, you're a back number!" was a comment too frequently heard. The solution to their problem was, of course, to attend WEA classes.[42] Some of the women who became involved in the WEA learned about labor matters, and friendships formed may have helped, in however small a way, to build working-class solidarity. For most women members, the WEA at least provided an opportunity to get out of the house and meet with, and learn from, others.

The core of the WEA program was the tutorial class. At an evening class the professor usually spoke for the first hour and then the students discussed the topic during the second hour. Often, lively debates would ensue. "I remember last year," recalled a middle-aged man registering for a class in 1925, "a speaker who would insist on talking about gardening every time he got on the floor. Just as likely he would be followed by a disciple of Lenine [*sic*] who would make some Conservative hot under the collar. . . ."[43]

In addition to tutorial classes the WEA offered other programs. Journalism students produced their own newspaper which then served as promotional material for the WEA. Public debates and nature study walks were popular events. Coffee socials, Hart House theatre nights, and Island picnics fostered a sense of community among members. An article in the journalism class's newspaper of 1924 describes a class banquet at the Inglenook Tea Rooms. It gives an indication of what these social activities were like:

> After dinner, when the guests had arranged themselves around the open fireplaces in the spacious dining room, Mr. A. Key started the programme with a song, "Son of Mine" which he sang to his own accompaniment. Mr. Rossie [an editorial writer at the *Globe*] then gave an interesting and illuminating address on editorial writing, after which he answered questions put to him on the subject. Mr. Alfred MacGowan, the Secretary of the Workers' Educational Association, was persuaded to sing a very popular old Irish Folk Song, which he sang with much feeling. This was followed by a short, interesting address by Mr. James Cunningham, President of the Workers' Educational Association.[44]

Here were people spending their leisure time very much in the tradition of nineteenth-century artisans.

The diversification of the WEA's offerings, the Association's fairly rapid growth, and the leadership provided by class-conscious labor men combined to antagonize some members of the University. Both Milner and Glazebrook left the WEA in the early 1920s. Although the reasons for Glazebrook's departure are not clear, Milner withdrew because he feared the labor element within the WEA had become too radical. In a letter to Grant in 1921, Milner deplored the declining influence of academics in the Association and objected to a course in Marxist economics (not taught by a University professor, but by a trade unionist, James Ballantyne) and two courses in trade-union law which, he said, "form no part of our ideal."[45]

The most serious threat to the WEA came not from the academics, but from the University administration. In 1927 the WEA was attacked by the head of the University of Toronto's Department of Extension, the ambitious W. J. Dunlop. He "deplored the existence of class consciousness in this country," and was unsympathetic to the idea of adult education provided especially for workers.[46] Dunlop determined to reduce the size and influence of the WEA. At the WEA general meeting in 1927 Dunlop proposed a plan to limit membership to trade unionists and those in unionized occupations. Although some WEA members agreed that a few professionals were "just using the WEA as a means of getting ahead,"[47] the membership recognized the devastating impact Dunlop's proposals would have on enrollments. Reluctantly, they agreed to Dunlop's changes mainly because the University of Toronto held the purse strings.

More trouble arose in the fall of 1927 when advertisements for the Extension Department's program seemed to indicate that Dunlop had unilaterally merged the Department of Extension's tutorial classes with the WEA. For Dunlop, the WEA was primarily designed for "the ambitious working man" wishing to get ahead.[48] Condemning Dunlop for his dictatorial methods, an angered MacGowan refused to become a Canadian "John Burns"[49] and resigned as Association secretary. Despite some labor protest, the Association had lost a crucial battle with the Department of Extension and a devoted working-class leader. Moreover, membership in the Toronto Association plummeted from over 400 to just 135.[50] The WEA had to begin to rebuild from a smaller pool of potential students and, before long, in a very different environment as the worse depression in history descended on the province.

Initially the WEA executive feared that the Depression would cause "harmful effects . . . on our registration."[51] In fact, WEA membership grew substantially in the 1930s. By 1937-38 it had reached 2194 in twenty-nine districts from Halifax to Vancouver.[52] This growth was due to several developments. During the Depression the public seemed more receptive to the idea of workers' education. As a WEA executive member later recalled, "working people were seeking an understanding of their difficulties and the possibility of a solution."[53] In addition, many unemployed were attracted to WEA classes and special programs designed for them. They had both the incentive to examine their plight and the leisure time in which to study.

The WEA became more attractive as the nature of support from the faculty changed. Several faculty members who became especially active in the WEA were left-wing liberals and social democrats. Some members of the League for Social Reconstruction, the so-called "brains trust" of the Co-operative Commonwealth Federation (CCF), taught WEA classes just as their British Fabian counterparts had done. Jarvis McCurdy and Harry Cassidy, who were quite active in the Toronto Association, sought to introduce a more leftist perspective to the WEA's academic program. Political scientist Lorne T. Morgan was an ardent anti-fascist and outspoken critic of many aspects of capitalism. His writings, some of which were published by the WEA, in part were designed to raise the political consciousness of WEA students.[54] Other tutors such as Harold Logan, Bora Laskin, and H. R. Kemp were known for their sympathetic attitude towards organized labor. One professor summarized a common aim of many of his fellow academics when he stated: "Workers' education should be geared to helping the workers' movement."[55] The working-class leaders of the WEA had now found partners rather than patrons within the universities.

The leadership of the WEA was greatly strengthened in 1930 when the Association received a grant of $5000 from the Carnegie Corporation and Drummond Wren was hired as full-time organizer. A Scottish immigrant and First World War veteran, Wren began taking WEA courses in the early 1920s. Wren's daily reading, and his WEA classes, led him to question much about the social, economic, and political system. Although Wren was not a union member — there was no union for him to join — he became interested in the labor movement and often attended evening meetings at the Labour Temple. In 1927, Wren was elected general secretary following MacGowan's resignation. He initiated the request for funding from the Carnegie Corporation, and as soon as the first grant arrived, he became the Association's first paid organizer. On 1 January 1930 Wren began a career with the WEA which was to span two decades.[56]

Continuity of leadership was also provided by George Sangster, a Scottish immigrant Iron Moulder who served as a dedicated executive officer of the WEA for nearly forty years. Sangster, who had taken a WEA course in the "Old Country," was a passionate advocate of workers' education as a means of advancing the cause of the working class. Termed a "Kier Hardie socialist" by labor historian Harold Logan,[57] Sangster firmly believed that workers' education must be fought for as a right of the oppressed classes and should be used as a stimulant to working-class radicalization.[58]

The Association also benefitted from the long years of service given by Jimmie Cunningham, a patient and kindly Scot, and by two other Scottish immigrants, Bill Dunn and Jimmie Rogers. Dunn was a prominent trade unionist (a member of the Carpenters' and Joiners' union) who helped to build the WEA's ties with the union movement. Rogers was a committed socialist and member of the CCF. Because he was a civil servant who worked for the Post Office, Rogers avoided partisan political work and instead sought to serve labor's cause through the WEA.[59] These leaders co-operated effectively to build the WEA, but it was Wren's imaginative and energetic work which did most to strengthen the Association.

Upon assuming his responsibilities as general secretary in 1930, Drummond Wren's major priority was to expand the WEA's membership by persuading trade-union officers to encourage their members to join. Wren and the WEA executive continually solicited the support of union leaders and appealed directly to union members by visiting union meetings at the Labour Temple. Their efforts brought encouraging results. In 1927-28, there were only 26 trade unionists in the Toronto Association. By 1931-32, the number had increased to 225, or over 40 percent of the membership. Nevertheless, Wren believed that union officials were apathetic, suspicious of an organization they did not control, or fearful of a better informed and more critical membership.[60]

During the Depression, the Association gave special attention to the vast numbers of unemployed. The WEA waived tuition fees and held special public meetings at the Labour Temple on subjects which interested unemployed workers. For instance, Harry Cassidy, who was an authority on unemployment, spoke to an overflowing crowd on that subject. After it was determined that many of the unemployed lacked basic schooling, the Unemployment Educational Association, a semi-autonomous organization, was founded in 1931. WEA members and instructors as well as Ontario College of Educa-

Drummond Wren welcomes students to the WEA's summer school.

Ontario Archives, Toronto

tion students served as volunteer instructors in the "three Rs." Wren and Arthur Lismer, the famous landscape artist and educator at the Toronto Art Gallery, collaborated in a program to provide art classes for the jobless. Dozens of workers attended free art classes at the Art Gallery and at a Board of Education building which volunteers refurbished for that purpose.[61]

In the 1930s, the WEA grew from its Toronto and Hamilton base to become a nation-wide organization. For the first time, the WEA had the financial resources and the organizational talent, in the person of Drummond Wren, to begin a national organizing drive. By the end of the decade, the WEA boasted twenty-four district associations in Ontario and fifteen in the rest of Canada.

Local associations enjoyed a considerable degree of autonomy and took on their own distinct characteristics. For instance, in Brantford, George Keen, a prominent co-operative organizer, dominated the association and drew on his support from rural co-operators.[62] Each association was meant to be self-supporting and was responsible for attracting students, deciding on subjects, and arranging for additional activities.

It is difficult to generalize about the composition of the WEA throughout Ontario. A sample of some 1533 enrolled in classes across Ontario in the mid-thirties shows that about 80 percent were men. Of these, over 70 percent were blue-collar, and another 7 percent called themselves "labourers." One-fifth of the total enrolled was female, over half homemakers. Of the women, 26.3 percent were in white-collar occupations and 11.8 percent were in blue-collar jobs.[63]

Despite the Association's growth, WEA leaders were convinced that much more could be done to make the WEA an even more vital institution. The late 1930s proved to be crucial for the Association just as they were for the labor movement as a whole. The union movement began its transformation from a lethargic craft-based movement to a much larger and more militant industrial union movement. All these new union members, including the leaders and shop stewards, needed to learn about picketing, grievance procedures, industrial law, administering collective agreements, and a host of other matters. Drummond Wren urged the Association to provide courses of practical use for these trade unionists.

To this end, the WEA renewed its efforts to attract trade-union support by offering to develop educational services in consultation with union leaders. Two large, long-established industrial unions, the International Ladies Garment Workers Union and the United Mine Workers of America, responded to the WEA's invitations in 1937. At the same time, two of the new, rapidly expanding Congress of Industrial Organizations (CIO) unions, the United Auto Workers (UAW) and the United Rubber Workers, began to use WEA services. Special programs provided instruction in trade-union issues and leadership training. Plans were also laid to permit greater participation of union affiliates on the executive of the WEA.[64]

At the same time as the WEA was developing services of practical benefit to unions, it was experimenting with ways to reach a wider audience. A few large companies permitted the WEA to provide classes for their employees. However, progress was slow because managers tended to be suspicious of the Association, fearing its commitment to labor might endanger management's control of employees.[65] Much more successful was WEA pioneering attempts to provide visual aids and radio that would serve thousands of people who would never have attended classes. Because there were few Canadian film strips available at the time, the WEA, with the aid of a special Carnegie grant, commissioned film strips on such topics as "Canadian Labour History," "Canadian Social History," "Parliamentary Procedure", and "The Distribution of Wealth."[66] Similarly, the WEA began using the radio to teach workers and farmers. By 1937 it was broadcasting weekly on the Canadian Broadcasting Corporation (CBC) national network.[67] As a result of these activities, the Association increased its public profile and awakened the labor movement to the educational possibilities of the new media.

In the late 1930s, then, the WEA had undergone an important transformation, becoming much larger and providing a wider range of services for unions. Not surprisingly, as the Association gained a prominent image as a pro-labor institution, its relations with the University of Toronto administration came into question. William Dunlop was alarmed by the WEA's transformation and grew ever more determined to assert control over it. Dunlop objected to the WEA's pro-labor stance and criticized some of its services for farmers and unions. He even demanded to open all the Association's mail. And finally, Dunlop charged that Wren and the officers of the WEA were Communists.[68] This was not the last time Wren would have to answer such an accusation. His dedication to furthering the cause of labor, his fiercely independent stand in politics, and his willingness at times to co-operate with Communists left him open to attacks from anti-Communists. Wren, however, was never a Communist party member, nor did he follow any party's line.

In 1937, Wren and Dunlop's differences were papered over by a special investigating committee.[69] But before long the differences reappeared. In 1939, when the University's budget was cut by 10 percent, Dunlop used this as a pretext for slashing the WEA's grant from $8000 to $2000, a cut of 75 percent. Naturally, the WEA protested vehemently, but to no avail.[70]

Despite continuing tensions between the WEA and the Department of Extension, the Workers' Educational Association had reason to greet the 1940s with optimism. With twenty-four associations in Ontario, a strong Toronto centre, and a federal grant to expand in the rest of Canada,[71] the WEA had a firm base on which to build. During the Second World War, the Association further diversified its educational offerings and solidified its contacts with organized labor. As it turned out, the WEA peaked in terms of size and influence in the war period. Throughout the 1940s, however, the WEA's problems were also greatly increasing so that, by the end of the decade, it was apparent that the Association was in serious trouble.

Wartime conditions offered unprecedented opportunities for the WEA.

Unions, and especially the industrial unions, were making great strides at a time when the labor supply was tight and employers and governments were committed to fulfilling enormous production demands. The increased size, prosperity, and confidence of the union movement meant labor educational facilities were greatly needed. At the same time, some government officials realized that the WEA could play a useful role in mobilizing labor for the war effort.[72]

During the war, the WEA increased its involvement in radio and visual education. In 1941, the CBC agreed to a new format for a Saturday evening radio series, the "National Labour Forum," with the WEA as the main script writers and participants. This radio program was a source of pride for Wren and the Association, especially since the two, often estranged, labor congresses would speak together on the broadcasts.[73] Wren believed that this showed how a neutral educational body could work to unify and strengthen the labor movement. In co-operation with the National Film Board (NFB), the WEA made films and projectors available to trade unions and other groups.[74] Support from the CBC and NFB was especially forthcoming because these WEA activities were regarded as aiding the war effort.

The WEA's research department also expanded considerably in the early 1940s. Unionists needed information about the many new regulations and acts affecting labor, so, with the aid of a Carnegie grant, a full-time researcher was hired by the WEA. By the mid-1940s, the department was publishing information in the weekly WEA bulletin, *Labour Forum*, and providing unions with wage briefs and knowledgeable people for conciliation hearings.

During the war period, the WEA and the University administration experienced further conflicts, despite the efforts of a new University WEA Committee, and especially Professor Harold Innis, to ease the situation. The committee's strong support for the WEA resulted in a slight increase in the 1941 provincial grant. But the next year, the Association suddenly found itself entirely cut out of the University's budget estimates. With an abrupt telephone call on 3 June 1942 the Extension Department informed the WEA typist she was no longer on the payroll.

Outraged WEA members believed the cut had been instigated by Dunlop whose antipathy to the WEA was very apparent, but it was probably triggered by pressure from industry. H. R. Kemp, at that time with the Wartime Prices and Trade Board, confidentially informed Innis that "a number of industrialists are very annoyed" with material published by the WEA. Kemp believed Dunlop was aware of their views, and they had encouraged him to cut the WEA's grant.[75]

At a special meeting of the WEA executive, Sangster persuaded the officers to mount a public campaign in the media to expose how "Workers' rights" had been "taken away."[76] On 31 July 1942 the Toronto *Daily Star* published an article on "labour's lockout from education" along with an editorial strongly praising the work of the WEA. Politicians, educators, and unions sent the Premier dozens of letters protesting the University's action. Seemingly, the publicity paid off. Premier Mitch Hepburn, on the recommendation of his Minister of Education, not only restored the grant, but, for the first time, paid it directly to the WEA. The Association had finally won an important degree of autonomy from the University.

In the following years, the University WEA Committee, made up of tutors and members of the WEA executive, continued to plan the Association's program. However, by the war's end, it was clear that the WEA had asserted its independence and allied itself more closely with labor. This had always been the WEA's goal, but in the context of the postwar years, the Association faced especially dangerous threats to its survival.

A series of crises in the late 1940s and early 1950s proved disastrous for the Association. Financial uncertainty undermined the stability of the WEA. The grant from the provincial government that the Association expected in 1947 was not paid until April 1948; no government funds were received for the 1948-49 season; the grant arrived on time in April 1949. However, nothing was obtained from the Ontario government the following year. These difficulties arose because the Association found itself attacked by influential labor leaders who were armed with the mighty weapon of anti-Communism in a country which was becoming increasingly embroiled in the Cold War.

When Wren learned that the provincial grant had been help up in 1948, he asked the Adult Educational Board, a creation of the Conservative government, to explain the situation. The general secretary was informed that the Board's Chairman, none other than William Dunlop, had "failed to recommend continuance of the grant," apparently because of charges of Communism levelled at the WEA by some leaders of the Ontario Federation of Labour–Canadian Congress of Labour (OFL-CCL).[77] Wren was certain that these charges had been spearheaded by Charles Millard, head of the Steelworkers, who was influential in both the CCL and the CCF and an adamant Cold Warrior.[78]

Naturally, Wren vehemently maintained that the WEA still had labor's confidence; department officials asked him to prove it. Within a few days the WEA had strong letters of support from unionists representing over 80 percent of organized labor in Ontario. This overwhelming show of confidence had been given despite a letter from the OFL-CCL to all its affiliates requesting they refrain from lending support because policy concerning the Association was under review. Apparently impressed by the deluge of supporting letters, the Minister of Education, George Drew, personally informed Wren that the WEA would get its $4000 grant.[79]

About the same time, charges of Communism in connection with the WEA arose elsewhere. Charles Stevenson, the Progressive Conservative MP for Durham, gained a great deal of publicity when he declared that Communism was being taught at the WEA summer school in his constituency, as the Labour Youth Federation, a Communist "front group," had rented the summer school.[80] Another challenge came from a group within the UAW who questioned the political orientation of the WEA. After a thorough investigation, however, they withdrew their remarks and voiced full confidence in the Association.[81]

Since these allegations were a serious threat to the Association, a special WEA Investigation Committee was formed to inquire into the causes of the charges. The Committee found that certain specific charges made by the OFL-CCL regarding the WEA publication *Labour News* were partly correct. These pertained to inaccuracies in some articles (discovered by the ever-vigilant CCL Research Director, Eugene Forsey), and, most seriously, an almost exact reprinting of an article from the Communists' *Canadian Tribune*. Consequently, the man at fault, Harold Beveridge, was dismissed for "flagrant disloyalty to his trust as a WEA officer."[82] Wren and the other leaders realized that greater care would be required to ensure that staff members did not mix politics with work. They also decided to be much more careful when renting the summer school. In the atmosphere of the Cold War the Association had to be extremely cautious. Sangster noted in 1949:

> The Cold War has brought intolerance. We could at one time discuss anything with academic impunity. This free and easy situation no longer exists. The tense world situation is reflected in the Association . . . a major cause of our financial and housing situation is the branding of the WEA with Communism.[83]

In the late 1940s, Millard and a few others were only too ready to use red scare tactics. Apparently they thought such an approach would help them gain control of the WEA so that it would be used to further their own goals, one of which was to gain support for the CCF. Certainly this is what Wren believed. "The representatives of the CCF unions," wrote Wren privately, "are not interested in stopping Communist domination (because the WEA is not CP dominated), but in taking control of another labour group."[84] Wren's personal position was especially vulnerable. During the Second World War, Wren had become Education Director for the UAW, in addition to his WEA duties. Consequently he was closely associated with Canadian UAW Chief George Burt. Millard, however, bitterly disagreed with Burt, especially since Burt tried to avoid allying with any political party. In a personal letter to Sangster, Wren explained that his own contact in the OFL-CCL informed him, "it boils down to Millard being after my skin because I am closely associated with Burt and the UAW."[85]

After the 1947 crisis, the WEA continued to experience many problems. The most serious crisis in the WEA's history began in the summer of 1950 and reached a dramatic climax at a two-day meeting of the WEA Board which began on 31 March 1951. Wren reported that at the Toronto Business Agents' School held at the Port Hope summer school in August 1951 he had had a meeting with OFL-TLC officials Russell Harvey and A. F. MacArthur to discuss a proposal for a closer relationship between the labor movement and the WEA. Harvey had insisted that the first step required was a public statement from Wren declaring he and the Association were opposed to Communism. Wren resented the request, preferring to let his record speak for itself and voicing his opposition to singling out any one political party for condemnation. Reluctantly, however, he had prepared a statement. But Harvey had decided it did not go far enough, and had used this as evidence of Wren's failure to co-operate and Communist leanings. Wren also charged that Harvey had cultivated fears within the labor movement regarding the WEA and Communism. Furthermore, Wren added, Harvey had been behind a move at the Toronto District Labour Council to reconsider its support for the Association.[86]

Wren believed that the more success the WEA enjoyed in teaching trade unionists about union matters, the more some labor leaders feared the WEA and resented the Association's "interference." Russell Harvey, in Wren's analysis, was "the spearhead of a group within the labor movement who is seeking to acquire the WEA, and failing to do so, to destroy it."[87] In other words, fearing a more informed rank and file, these leaders wanted to gain control over the WEA and turn it into their own educational organization in a way not unlike the efforts of some CCL union leaders in 1947.

Russell Harvey, as a union representative on the WEA Board, attended the meeting when Wren made his report. Harvey was outraged, labelling parts of the report "nothing but mental bilge."[88] He did admit, however, that he had contributed to the Minister of Education's uncertainty about the WEA by refusing to reassure him of labor's confidence in the Association.

Jimmy Rogers responded to the charges and counter-charges by stating that "nothing more dastardly" had ever been done against the Association than Harvey's request that the Toronto District Labour Council reconsider affiliation with the WEA. This had "plastered all over the Province the word 'Communism' in regard to the WEA." Rogers agreed that the American Federation of Labor (AFL) had decided in the summer that the "WEA had to be trimmed to suit the needs of the AFL movement," and this meant getting rid of Wren.[89] Sangster concurred, adding that the AFL leaders' failure to reassure the Minister of Education regarding the WEA had been very unfair and might have been part of a plan to let the Association accumulate a large debt so that it would be in a more "pliable condition."[90]

The final moments of the spring meeting were packed with emotion as Drummond Wren, who had been the creative and organizational force behind the WEA for more than two decades, announced his resignation from the Association. With much regret and a little bitterness, Wren told the WEA that he was resigning due to "frustration" arising from charges levelled against him that were "entirely unfounded."[91] He emphasized that he had fought hard for an independent, responsive WEA, but some important union leaders had moved against him and his conception of the WEA, and so he had to leave. He concluded by saying he had been militant, but since certain union leaders "couldn't use the charge of militancy and aggressiveness," because it "would never have stuck in the public mind," they used the charge of communism.[92] George Sangster listened with tears in his eyes.[93] He realized what a loss Wren's resignation would be to the Association. In the years ahead, the WEA would try to adapt to the demands of the labor movement and move with the times. It would not succeed. Armed with the mighty Cold War weapon, the red slur, Russell Harvey and a few associates in the AFL unions had disposed of Wren. Their victory, however, was hollow, for without Drummond Wren, the WEA was a prize which the labor movement no longer really wanted.

After 1951, the WEA was a mere shadow of its former self.[94] The Association failed to compete with the ever-expanding adult education programs of the universities and a host of other institutions. "In 1917," declared Sangster in 1960, "the WEA was the forerunner in adult education . . . now, there are 52 such agencies."[95] Television, too, increased the problem of attracting students.

The WEA's greatest problem, however, was its failure to become the educational arm of the labor movement. Russell Harvey's view of workers' education prevailed. It is impossible to dismiss his democratic argument that workers' education should be controlled directly by the elected members of the labor movement. The danger is that propaganda might replace education. In the absence of a vigilant membership, union leaders might resort to indoctrinating students, teaching policies and positions of benefit to the leaders, but not to the rank and file. Instead of creative, critical members, such a system would tend to foster complacency and conservatism. In any case, the growth of large industrial unions in the 1940s and 1950s paved the way for the demise of the WEA. These unions had the incentive and means to create their own educational departments. Their huge memberships of workers with various skills made it necessary to cultivate union loyalty: their huge treasuries enabled them to provide educational services.[96]

There is much to admire about Wren's commitment to an autonomous educational body dedicated to teaching workers how to think critically. Such a system not only can enrich the student, it can also create a more active and critical union membership, ever ready to review union policies. Wren's intellectual weakness was in placing too much faith in the university professors, in assuming their teaching would be quite free of bias and that they, too, were deeply committed to developing the critical abilities of their students. His political weakness was his inability to secure the co-operation of labor leaders who felt threatened by the Association's autonomy and who had the financial means to provide their own educational facilities which they could control.

Although the Workers' Educational Association declined in importance after the 1950s, it had enjoyed a period of some influence on the Ontario labor scene. Begun partly as an experiment in social control by the province's educational élite, the WEA soon became a workers' organization, largely controlled by its working-class members. It offered many liberal arts courses for workers, and later, after the tremendous growth of industrial unionism in the late 1930s and 1940s, the WEA developed an innovative labor education program. Although the Association was continually threatened by the University of Toronto administration, the chief cause of the WEA's decline in the early 1950s came from within the labor movement. Certain labor leaders, using Cold War tactics, launched attacks on the WEA because they opposed a labor educational institution which they could not control. Despite the WEA's eventual demise, however, the Association left its mark on the labor movement. The WEA's pathbreaking efforts in labor education and research served as useful models for future trade-union educational programs.

Footnotes

1. Albert Mansbridge, *The Kingdom of the Mind* (London: J. M. Dent, 1944); Albert Mansbridge, *Adventure in Adult Education* (London: J. M. Dent, 1935).

2. Thomas Kelly, *A History of Adult Education in Great Britain* (Liverpool: Liverpool University Press, 1970), pp. 251-56.

3. J. F. C. Harrison, *Learning and Living, 1790-1960: A Study in the History of the English Adult Education Movement* (Toronto: University of Toronto Press, 1961).

4. *Daily News*, Toronto, 23 December 1913, in Clippings Files A-73-052, University of Toronto Archives (henceforth UTA); Edward Kylie, "The Workers' Educational Association," *University Magazine*, Toronto, December 1913.

5. W. S. Milner, "The Workers' Educational Association," *University of Toronto Monthly*, January 1922.

6. WEA of Toronto, *Annual Report, 1918-19,* Records of the Workers' Educational Association (henceforth WEA), Series A, Box 1, Ontario Archives (henceforth OA).

7. Falconer to S. R. Parsons, 24 April 1918, Sir Robert Falconer Papers, Box 50, UTA. The letter was sent to some other prominent figures such as H. J. Cody, C. V. Massey, and Sir John Willison, as well as to executives of such companies as Goodyear, Dunlop Tire, Eaton's, and Imperial Varnish.

8. This was Glazebrook's belief as stated in his brief to the Royal Commission on University Finances. See Ontario Royal Commission on University Finances, *Report*, App. IX, "Statement of the Workers' Educational Association," presented by A. J. Glazebrook. Glazebrook's authorship of this is confirmed in Glazebrook to Grant, 7 January 1921, W. L. Grant Papers MG-30-D-59, Box 11, Public Archives of Canada (henceforth PAC).

9. On Mechanics' Institutes in Ontario, see Foster Vernon, "The Development of Adult Education in Ontario, 1790-1900," unpublished Ph.D. thesis, University

of Toronto, 1969; James Eadie, "The Napanee Mechanics Institute: The Nine-teenth Century Ontario Mechanics Institutes in Microcosm," *Ontario History,* 68 (1976); and Bryan D. Palmer, *A Culture in Conflict: Skilled Workers and Industrial Capitalism in Hamilton, Ontario, 1860-1914* (Montreal: McGill-Queen's University Press, 1979), pp. 49-52.

10. Carl Berger, *The Sense of Power: Studies in the Ideas of Canadian Imperialism, 1867-1914* (Toronto: University of Toronto Press, 1970), pp. 196-97.

11. Grant to Mansbridge, 30 August 1934, Grant Papers, Box 11, PAC.

12. H. A. Innis, "A. J. Glazebrook: Obituary," *Canadian Journal of Economics and Political Science* 7 (1941), pp. 72-74; "Reports" prepared by Glazebrook, Box 11, Grant Papers, PAC; on the Round Table movement, see John E. Kendle, *The Round Table Movement and Imperial Union* (Toronto: University of Toronto Press, 1975).

13. C. N. Cochrane, "Head of Department Retires," *University of Toronto Monthly* 19 (June 1929), pp. 342-43; "William S. Milner," Biographical Files, UTA.

14. On Falconer and the Round Table, see Glazebrook to Lord Milner, 5 June 1916 and 2 December 1918, Glazebrook papers, PAC. On Falconer and adult educa-tion, see his "Leaders Can See Things Whole," in J. R. Kidd, *Adult Education in Canada* (Toronto: Canadian Association for Adult Education, 1950), pp. 29-31, and his "The Workers' Opportunity," *The Link*, Toronto, April 1930, copy in Wren Files, 70.1.4, WEA, OA.

15. R. M. MacIver, *As a Tale That Is Told* (Chicago, 1968), 44. See also his *Labor in the Changing World* (New York: Dutton, 1919).

16. Glazebrook to Lord Milner, 21 May 1918, Glazebrook Papers, MG-30-A-43, PAC. On MacIver, see also "R. M. MacIver," Biographical File, UTA; "Workers' Educational Association," Clippings File, UTA; Carl Berger, *The Writing of Canadian History* (Toronto: Oxford University Press, 1976), pp. 154-55.

17. Glazebook to Lord Milner, 21 May 1918, Glazebrook papers, PAC.

18. See the WEA constitution in the *Annual Report, 1918-19.*

19. W. L. Grant, "The Education of the Workingman," *Queen's Quarterly* 27 (December 1919), p. 160.

20. *The Varsity*, Toronto, 2 December 1918.

21. Grant, "Education on the Workingman," p. 161.

22. See, for example, Glazebrook, "Statement."

23. MacIver, *Labor in the Changing World*, pp. 217-18.

24. Glazebrook, "Statement."

25. Toronto District Labour Council Minutes, April 1918, Metro Toronto Council Collection, MG-28-I-44, PAC.

26. *Annual Report*, 1918-19.

27. Wayne Roberts, "Artisan, Aristocrats, and Handymen: Politics and Unions

Among Toronto Skilled Building Trades Workers, 1896-1914," *Labour/Le Travailleur, 1* (1976), pp. 105-107.

28. For evidence of MacGowan's friendship with Grant, see their correspondence in Grant Papers, Box 11, PAC.

29. The Britishness of the WEA is discussed (and probably exaggerated) by J. A. Blyth in *A Founding at Varsity: A History of the Division of University Extension, University of Toronto* (Toronto: School of Continuing Studies, University of Toronto, 1976), pp. 28-33.

30. MacGowan to Grant, 27 May 1919, Grant Paper, Box 11, PAC.

31. *The Industrial Banner,* Toronto, 9 April 1920.

32. "Memo to the University Committee," Toronto District Labour Council Minutes, 15 February 1923, Metro Toronto Labour Council Collection, PAC.

33. Alfred MacGowan, "The Workers' Educational Association of Ontario: What It Is, Does and Needs," *Canadian Congress Journal,* Ottawa, February 1926, p. 6.

34. Ibid., p. 13.

35. J. O'Hanley, "WEA," in *WEA Reporter,* Toronto, 29 March 1928 (copy in Wren Files, Box 1, OA).

36. George Sangster, "Editorial," *The Link,* October-November 1936 (copy in Wren Files, Box 1, OA).

37. Ian Radforth, "Organized Labour in Ontario during the 1920s," M.A. research paper, York University, 1976.

38. WEA Minutes, 18 December 1923, 10 January 1929, WEA, OA; Trades and Labour Congress of Canada, Executive Council Minutes, 30 November 1923, Canadian Labour Congress Collection MG-28-I-103, PAC; Trades and Labour Congress of Canada Convention *Proceedings,* 1925, 106, and 1928, 1452.

39. Grant to J. Gustave White, 8 March 1921, Grant Papers, PAC. Toronto Labor activist Jimmie Simpson had questioned the University's involvement in the WEA at one of the first WEA meetings in 1918. See Toronto *Daily Star,* 8 June 1918.

40. University of Toronto, *Annual Report,* 1925-26, p. 69.

41. WEA Minutes and *Annual Report,* 1920-28, WEA, OA.

42. Constance Lea, "Keeping Pace With the Children," *WEA Bulletin,* Programme Edition, 1928-29 (copy in Wren Files, Box 43, OA).

43. *Daily Star,* Toronto, 23 October 1925. Although left-wingers attended some WEA classes, the Communist party of Canada took only a brief interest in the WEA in spring 1923 when two Toronto Communists, Annie Buller and William Moriarty, became active in the WEA for a few weeks. There is no record indicating they were welcome; they seem to have soon lost interest.

44. "Social and Personal," *Queen City Gazette,* Toronto, 11 February 1924 (copy in Wren Files, Box 43, OA).

45. Milner to Grant, 13 October 1921, Grant Papers, Box 11, PAC.

46. W. J. Dunlop, "Class Consciousness as a Factor in Adult Education," National Conference of Canadian Universities, *Proceedings*, 1929, App. L. 84.

47. WEA Minutes, 18 March 1927, WEA, OA.

48. Copy of circular in Grant Papers, Box 11, PAC.

49. MacGowan to Grant, 12 August 1927, Grant Papers, Box 11, PAC.

50. In 1925-26 the WEA of Toronto and District had an enrollment of 435, by 1927-28, enrollment had dropped to 135. Districts outside Toronto were not affected by Dunlop's new policy. (*Annual Reports,* 1925-26 and 1927-28, WEA, OA).

51. WEA Minutes, Annual Meeting, 1931-32, WEA, OA.

52. *Annual Reports,* 1934-35 and 1937-38. In that year the Ontario centres were: Brantford, Fergus, Guelph, Hamilton, Kingston, Sault Ste. Marie, Stratford, Toronto and suburbs, Windsor, and Woodstock. There were study circles in Fort William, Galt, Sudbury, and Timmons (Annual Report, 1937-38).

53. Drummond Wren, "Address to the President and Board Members of the WEA of Canada," presented 31 March 1951, p. 25. (Copy in "Education and Labour, Canadian Publications, 1951-71," Industrial Relations Centre Library, University of Toronto, henceforth Wren's Address, 1951.)

54. Lorne T. Morgan, *Fascism* (Toronto, 1942) and his *Homo the Sap* (Toronto, 1943). On Morgan's left-wing views, see Michiel Horn, "The League for Social Reconstruction: Socialism and Nationalism in Canada, 1931-45," unpublished Ph.D. thesis, University of Toronto, 1969, pp. 232-35.

55. WEA Toronto Minutes, 4 May 1931, WEA, OA. The WEA also provided a non-partisan outlet for socialists at a time when academic freedom outside the classroom was severely limited. On academic freedom, see Peter Oliver, *G. Howard Ferguson: Ontario Tory* (Toronto: University of Toronto Press, 1977), pp. 242-43, and Carl Berger, *Writing of Canadian History,* pp. 80-84.

56. Wren's Address, 1951, pp. 1-6; taped interview with Drummond Wren, 29 September 1976, Special Collections, McMaster University.

57. Harold Logan, *Trade Unions in Canada* (Toronto: Macmillan, 1948), p. 607.

58. Personal information of author Joan Sangster; George Sangster notebook, in possession of Ed Philip, Etobicoke; Ed Philip, "A Few Perspectives on the Workers' Educational Association," in WEA, *History, 1917-77,* p. 27.

59. Tape of interview with James Rogers, 25 May 1972, in possession of Professor Richard Allen, McMaster University.

60. WEA Minutes of Annual Meetings, 1928-29, 1929-30, 1930-31, WEA, OA.

61. Wren's Address 1951, pp. 19-21; *Annual Report,* 1937-38; Wren interview, McMaster University.

62. On the WEA's contact with the co-operative movement, see Ian MacPherson, *Each For All: A History of the Co-operative Movement in English Canada, 1900-45* (Toronto: Macmillan, 1979), pp. 112, 182.

64. *Annual Report,* 1937-38; WEA Canada Minutes, 24 April 1937, 18 December 1937, WEA, OA.

65. WEA Canada Minutes, 27 February 1937 and 24 April 1937, WEA, OA.

66. Wren's Address, 1951, pp. 16-18; *Annual Report,* 1937-38; Wren interview, McMaster University.

67. Ibid.; Peter Sandiford, ed., *Adult Education in Canada* (Toronto: University of Toronto Press, 1935), Ch. 4, pp. 4-6; "WEA Radio Forum," *Adult Learning* 4 (November 1939), pp. 23-24.

68. WEA Canada Minutes, 27 February 1937 and 24 April 1937, WEA, OA; Wren Memo, n.d., Wren Files, 70.1.1 and Dunlop to Dunn, 11 March 1937, Wren Files, WEA, OA.

69. WEA Canada Minutes, 24 April 1937, WEA, OA.

70. Minutes of ? [information source incomplete] and App. 11, November 1939, Wren Files 70.1.3, WEA, OA.

71. During the 1937-38 session, the Federal Minister of Labour, Norman Rogers, granted the WEA $5000 for the support of its work among young adults throughout Canada. (*Annual Report,* 1937-38). Rogers had been a supporter and WEA tutor in Kingston before joining the government.

72. W. R. Young, "Academics and Social Scientists Versus the Press: The Policies of the Bureau of Public Information and the Wartime Information Board, 1939-45," Canadian Historical Association, *Historical Papers,* 1978, pp. 217-40.

73. Wren's Address, 1951, pp. 16-18; Box 209, Canadian Labour Congress Collection, PAC.

74. Ibid., pp. 19-21; National Film Board of Canada, *Annual Report,* 1945-46, p. 16; WEA Canada Minutes, 7 November 1948.

75. Kemp to Innis, 19 July 1942, H.A. Innis Papers, UTA.

76. WEA Canada Minutes, 7 July 1942, WEA, OA.

77. Ibid., 15 February 1948.

78. Ibid.; Irving Abella, *Nationalism, Communism and Canadian Labour* (Toronto: University of Toronto Press, 1973).

79. WEA Canada Minutes, 15 February 1948 and 7 November 1948, WEA, OA. See also "Proceedings of a Meeting of the WEA, Toronto 31 March, 1 April, 1951," verbatim transcript in possession of the authors. (Henceforth Proceedings, 1951.)

80. WEA Canada Minutes, 2 November 1947.

81. Wren's Address, 1951, p. 48.

82. WEA Canada Minutes, 7 November 1948; see also Box 209, Canadian Labour Congress Collection, PAC.

83. *Annual Report,* 1949.

84. Wren to Sangster, 26 September 1947, Sangster Papers, in possession of Ed Philip, Etobicoke.

85. Ibid.

86. Wren's Address, 1951, p. 43.

87. Ibid.

88. *Proceedings,* 1951, p. 3.

89. Ibid., pp. 10-12.

90. Ibid., pp. 21-22.

91. Ibid., pp. 65.

92. Ibid., pp. 65-66.

93. Ibid.

94. WEA Minutes and *Annual Reports,* 1951-58.

95. Annual Report, 1960.

96. See Canadian Labour Congress — Canadian Association for Adult Education, *Conference Report: Labour — University Co-operation on Education* (Ottawa, 1956), 11, and Manitoba, Royal Commission on Adult Education, *Report* (Winnipeg, 1947), p. 133.

[We would like to thank Ed Philip for allowing us to use the George Sangster papers in his possession. We benefitted greatly from discussions with former WEA members Drummond Wren, Syd Robinson, and the late George Sangster, grandfather of author Joan Sangster.]

"Knowledge for the People": The Origins and Development of the Antigonish Movement

Jim Lotz and Michael R. Welton

The Antigonish Movement is universally recognized as a significant Canadian contribution to the theory and practice of social change. It was a program of adult education, self-help, and co-operative development that arose in Eastern Nova Scotia in the 1920s, flowered in the 1930s, and became part of the social and economic fabric of the whole of the Maritimes in the 1940s and 1950s. It was based at the Extension Department of St Francis Xavier University in Antigonish, Nova Scotia. It eventually became world famous, and is often cited as an example of successful grassroots social action.[1]

A great deal of attention has been paid to the philosophy, achievements, and techniques of the Movement, but little to its historical and social context.[2] Outside observers have often made grandiose claims for the Movement,[3] and insiders have used the Movement to legitimize their social practice.[4] This has hampered our critical historical understanding. The aim of this paper is to give a brief résumé of the Movement, drawing upon recent scholarship, and to try to set it into a conceptual framework.[5]

The Antigonish Movement was the creation of the thought and action of a group of strong-minded leaders and dedicated followers. It was an indigenous social movement; all the leaders came from Nova Scotia. Social movements usually appear in periods of dislocation, breakdown, and stress, and they often follow a well-defined course, from initial agitation to eventual institutionalization, eradication, or transformation. Dislocation and breakdown do not automatically produce social movements, however. A successful movement must create the social infrastructure (solidarities, cadre organizations, networks) to mobilize a defined constituency for particular ends.

The Antigonish Movement had the three typical leaders of a social movement, who appeared in succession. The prophet, Father Jimmy Tompkins, who cried out for years in the wilderness, came from the Margaree Valley in Cape Breton. The messiah was Father Moses Michael Coady, a cousin and protégé of Father Jimmy, and a man of great physical presence. The organizer was Angus B. MacDonald (''A.B.'') who did the careful planning and administrative work that every successful social movement needs if it is to succeed. And it was the mediating relationship between the community-based priests and the people which allowed the movement to take root. The Movement developed as a creative response to certain universal social trends (urbanization, industrialization, rural depopulation), as part of a social gospel movement within the Catholic Church, and as an alternative to the left-wing and right-wing ideologies and movements that arose in the 1920s.[6]

The roots of the Movement lay in the social, economic, and historical conditions of Eastern Nova Scotia. This area was settled mainly by Highland Catholic Scots who established themselves on small farms carved from the thick Acadian forest. Here they lived a subsistence life during most of the nineteenth century, secure in the ownership of their farms, and relying on a system of self-help and mutual aid in times of crisis. In some parts of the area, however, even the hardest labor returned only a meagre living. The Highland Scots had no tradition of trading. In the close-knit, self-sufficient economy, it was usually an outsider who became the merchant or the middleman. This person bought the surplus of the production, and supplied the manufactured goods. In the Acadian settlements of Chéticamp, the Jerseymen moved in after the French left, and occupied the trading niches in the economy.[7]

Eastern Nova Scotia was — and still is — a land of small, one-family farms. These farms could not provide an adequate living for the children of the original settlers, even if these young people wanted to stay. After the middle of the nineteenth century, when most of the good farming land had been occupied, extensive migration took place from Eastern Nova Scotia. The young people moved to the ''Boston States'' and to Upper Canada. They also found wage employment in the coal mines, steel mills, and the factories that were built in New Glasgow and industrial Cape Breton at the end of the nineteenth century. Many of the people of Arichat left the community when St Peter's Canal was completed in 1869 and steamships replaced the sailing vessels that once crowded Arichat Harbour. Between 1891 and 1931, the population of the seven eastern counties of Nova Scotia dropped from 131 886 to 105 279.

It was the plight of those who were left behind that engaged the attention of the reformers. They saw how farmers and fishermen were being pushed deeper into debt, poverty, and dependency. Slowly, the rural areas were moving from a subsistence-based to a market-based economy. Improvements in communications led to the centralization of population and the decline of rural communities. The small country stores began to disappear, and so did many of the services that were once located in rural areas, including doctors and lawyers. The improvement in roads, and the arrival of automobiles and trucks in the region accelerated the processes of rural decay. The sense of community declined. The ambitious and restless young kept leaving. The social and economic structure had few niches in which they could use their talents, even if they decided to stay. As Coady noted in 1945:

> The bright child who gives signs of intelligence in school is immediately picked for a different career from that into which he was born. People will mortgage their farm, and workers will contribute their savings to the last cent to see that a favoured boy or girl gets a so-called chance in life . . . in our present educational procedure — which is essentially a skimming process — we are robbing our rural and industrial population of the natural leaders.[8]

A community-based social order suddenly began to experience the demands for individual achievement, with all that this meant in the way of competition. Moreover, perhaps most significant from the Diocese of Antigonish's perspective, industrialization was undermining the old ethnic-religious identity of Scottish Catholics. The Roman Catholic Church had to find a way to synthesize the traditional religious–cultural formation with the emergent culture of modernity (reform liberalism, scientific rationality, and democratic participation).[9]

With the onset of the Depression, incomes dropped and resources became increasingly more scarce. The concern about rural depopulation was communicated to the parish priests who preached to a dwindling population of old people in their churches. Rapid urbanization created slums around Sydney. Each coal company had its own town, and here the miners lived in a state of economic dependency. The farmers and fishermen owed their souls and their livelihood to the middlemen who bought their products, extended credit, and supplied them with such little luxuries as tea and sugar. The miners owed their souls to the company stores, the infamous "pluck-mes." No matter how hard the miners worked, they saw little cash. Their earnings were checked off by purchases by their wives at the pluck-mes. The coal companies ran hospitals and health insurance plans, and owned most of the housing. Added to this was the antagonism of companies to unionization, absentee ownership, and management by outsiders. It was little wonder that the miners were radical, considering their lack of control over their own destinies.[10]

At certain times in history, individual discontent fuses into group and community action. Action — any action — seems to be preferable to living under conditions of uncertainty and deprivation, always waiting for "something" to happen. But action by the minority is usually accompanied by apathy and inertia among the majority, who wait to see if things work before jumping on the bandwagon. The genius of the organizers of the Antigonish Movement lay in the way in which they helped to channel frustration and excess energy at the grassroots level into channels that resulted in both individual and structural change.

The arrival of Father Jimmy Tompkins to teach at St Francis Xavier University in 1902 probably marks the formal beginning of the Antigonish Movement. Father Tompkins was a small, tough-minded Irishman with a Socratic approach to problems. He never ceased to question the obvious. Like his cousin Father Coady, he was a social animator who tried to make people aware of their problems. Once he made people aware, he suggested ways in which they could tackle the problems. One of his basic approaches was to make sure people got the best knowledge and information available. "Ideas," Tompkins was fond of saying, "had to have feet and hands." He saw the university as the "missing link" in development, bringing knowledge and resources to bear on the problems of the "little people" of the region, coordinating effort, pumping in new knowledge, training leaders, helping people to use the best brains inside and outside the region.

Activist priests were a common enough phenomenon in the Maritimes. In the parish of Rustico on Prince Edward Island, the Abbé Belcourt organized the first "people's bank" in North America in 1862, the Farmers Bank of Rustico. At Chéticamp, the redoubtable Père Pierre Fiset organized economic endeavors between 1875 and 1909. Both Tompkins and Coady taught school in Chéticamp before they were ordained. But the efforts of these priests began and ended with the individual. Above all, Father Tompkins stressed the importance of education in social change. Initially, he hoped to inspire students at the university to stay in the region, and to help it grow and develop. He did manage to inspire some students. But the majority passed through the university and joined the ranks of the "big wigs," Father Jimmy's term for those whom he saw as the oppressors of the little people. Or the students left the region. Father Tompkins had a magpie mind. He synthesized the bits and pieces of knowledge that he picked up on his travels and in his reading, and tried to determine their relevance to the local scene. He was influenced by the British Workers' Educational Association, by Bishop O'Dwyer's thoughts on how the university could solve the problem of rural poverty in Ireland, by the Danish Folk School concept that had sparked a rural revival in that country, and by the Swedish Discussion Circle Approach. In 1921, Father Tompkins published and distributed a pamphlet called *Knowledge for the People — A Call to St. Francis Xavier College*. He saw the university as his base for social action.

This small and rather undistinguished Catholic college was the creation of the Diocese of Antigonish. Dr Hugh MacPherson, the Dean of Engineering, had done some pioneering co-operative organizing work in the region. He started out by helping the farmers to grade and market their wool and their lambs. In 1914, the province passed the Agricultural Instruction Act, which provided for the hiring of field workers. In 1915, MacPherson, who was a priest, joined the Department of Agriculture as an Extension worker. Along with Tompkins and Coady, MacPherson should be considered as one of the major clerical leaders of the Movement. MacPherson's role has been underplayed, and little attention has been paid to the role of the Department of Agriculture in the field of rural development in Nova Scotia in the 1920s and the 1930s. Their field workers co-operated closely with the people involved in the Movement.

Coady's work with fishermen in the late 1920s, and A. B. MacDonald's extensive agricultural experience cemented bonds between Extension and government. Both men also had links with the national co-operative movement. Dr Hugh MacPherson had created strong ties between St Francis Xavier and the Provincial School of Agriculture at Truro. Leading agricultural representatives were Catholic Scots and protégés of the leadership cadre. Waldo Walsh, J. C. F. MacDonnell, S. J. MacKinnon, and R. J. MacSween became "*de facto* agents for the Extension Department while employed as civil servants."[11]

Various attempts had been made to get farmers to co-operate in marketing their produce. Co-operative creameries were established as early as 1894. In 1907, the Bedwick Fruit Company was formed as a marketing body. Alex D. MacKay did excellent work among the farmers of Pictou County, helping them to buy supplies (especially fertilizer) in bulk, and to sell their products the same way. His efforts led to the creation of a regional co-operative called the Pictou and North Shore United Farmers. In 1916, the Maritime United Farmers Co-operative was chartered in New Brunswick. Branches in Antigonish, Truro, Tatamagouche, Amherst, Springhill, and Windsor were established between 1917 and 1921. This organization got into trouble. In 1922, a Special Act was passed in Nova Scotia allowing each local branch to be incorporated separately. This move did not save the system, and only the branch in Antigonish survived.[12]

The reasons for the failure were poor management, the control of co-operatives by one individual, and the careless use of credit. Basic to this failure was the absence of an educational component in the co-operative movement. Farmers and fishermen are notoriously difficult to organize. Even after the co-operative movement got under way, some ventures, such as the Cape Breton Island Producers' Co-operative, collapsed. It was easier to organize co-operatives in the towns. The first co-operative store in Canada was organized at Stellarton in 1861, only seventeen years after the Rochdale pioneers opened their store in Toad Lane, in the north of England. The act of the Rochdale pioneers in 1844 is usually taken as the beginning of the modern co-operative movement. In 1906, the British Canadian Co-operative Society Ltd. was established by miners from Great Britain. This seems to have been an exceptionally well-managed undertaking.

The idea of co-operative action, therefore, was not new in Eastern Nova Scotia. What was new was the way in which adult education and co-operative organization went together, hand in hand. The provincial and federal governments had limited resources, but they did what they could to help the work of the Extension Department of St Francis Xavier University. Not until the

apparatus of university and church were involved in co-operative development would the work of the agricultural representative gain institutional
grounding. They were a bit loathe to support the idea of consumer co-
operatives, because of the possible complaints from the merchant class. But
in the area of marketing, the Department of Agriculture gave plenty of backing.
The federal government provided grants for work among the fishermen, but
the Movement seems always to have been in a condition of financial crisis.
Even as late as 1938, for example, a report stated that "it will be difficult
for the University to continue carrying the burden of the Extension Department."[13] In that year, the Extension Department received a federal grant
to organize the fishermen of the Maritimes.

Social movements seem to be able to operate on relatively small sums of
money. They rely on commitments from like-minded people who are willing to give of their time and their talents for the common good. They tie
together scattered efforts, and so achieve economies of scale and effort. The
region around Antigonish was blessed with many able and dedicated clergymen
and laymen who provided a decentralized network of willing workers. Without
the work of clergy (Revs. Michael Gillis, John R. MacDonald, A. R. Rankin,
J. D. Nelson MacDonald), former left-wing union organizer turned extension worker A. S. MacIntyre, and women (Kay Desjardins, Sister Marie
Michael, Ida Gallant), the movement would never have flourished.

Throughout the twenties there was steady pressure on the university to get
into the field of adult education. At that time, adult education was neither
recognized nor academically respectable. The idea of teaching ordinary people
to read and write, use a set of books, organize, and set up co-operatives and
credit unions was totally foreign to any Maritime university. Two groups
— the University Alumnae Society and the Scottish Catholic Society —
apparently indicated that they would get involved in adult education if the
university did not. Rev. Michael Gillis was a leading spirit pushing St Francis
Xavier to create an Extension Department. He had gone through the First
World War as an army chaplain, studied at the London School of Economics,
and was known for his advanced social ideas.[14]

In 1921, the university put on its first "People's School." This brought
fishermen and farmers on to the campus for six weeks to discuss their problems. In 1924, the clergy held their first rural conference on campus. This
conference raised $2500 a year for five years to send young men from the
farms to take short courses at Truro Agricultural College. The slow ferment
built up, and pressures for using the university as a force for social action
became stronger. But Father Tompkins was ejected from the university in
1922, and began to substitute action for exhortation.

The ostensible reason for Father Jimmy's rustication was his support for
the idea of Maritime university amalgamation. This was a project of the
Carnegie Corporation of New York, which they were willing to fund. The
Bishop of Antigonish opposed the idea, and so Father Tompkins went as pastor

of Star of the Sea Church in Canso. This was a poor, isolated area, and Father Jimmy set about stirring up the local people, making them aware of their problems, and suggesting what they could do about them.

Father Tompkins was an extremely abrasive individual, forever prodding people to read a book, discuss a pamphlet, take some action. He probably saw his role as that of carrying out the social mandate of the Catholic Church. He did not do things for people; he suggested how they might tackle problems, and get information and some of the resources they needed. He was a typical prophet, a truly holy man who and took little account of hardships and human frailties.

What Father Tompkins did at Little Dover has been documented in detail.[15] He "animated" the people, got a road built, lent the fishermen money to build their own lobster plant, and in general helped the community to renew itself by its own efforts. He continued to read and to travel. In 1924, for instance, he was in New York to attend a meeting of the Carnegie Corporation to discuss adult education. The Carnegie Corporation provided much of the financial support for the Movement over the next fifteen years. At the meeting, there was talk of the use of co-operation and credit unions as vehicles for putting local energy and capital together for economic development. Credit unions were introduced into Canada by Alphonse Desjardins, who opened the first "people's bank" in Lévis, Quebec, in 1900. When it came time for the Nova Scotians to find out about credit unions, they invited Americans in to help them to organize. Roy Bergengren, Director of the Credit Union National Association, made nine trips to Nova Scotia at the invitation of Coady and his colleagues.

The official beginning of the Antigonish Movement at St Francis Xavier University came in 1928, when an Extension Department was opened. Before this, an event took place on 1 July 1927 that had much to do with getting social action moving in Nova Scotia, and in the Maritimes as a whole. On that day, the sixtieth anniversary of Confederation, the fishermen of Canso were all ashore, complaining that they had little to celebrate. In the latter part of 1926 and the winter of 1927 "weather conditions on the Atlantic coast were particularly favourable for fishing."[16] A large quantity of fish was landed, more than the market could absorb. Steam trawlers landed larger catches than usual, and prices slumped. Father Jimmy organized a meeting, to which forty fishermen came. A week later on 1 July he organized another meeting in Antigonish, this time of priests from fishing communities. The press was called in, and the general uproar resulted in the establishment of a Royal Commission on the Fisheries of the Maritime Provinces and the Magdalen Islands. The MacLean Commission was appointed on 7 October 1927, and reported on 4 May 1928. Among other things, it recommended the establishment of co-operatives among the fishermen of the Maritime Provinces.

From this time onwards, Father Moses Michael Coady dominated the Movement. He was a charismatic figure, a big rough hewn man with a transcendental vision of the good life.[17] He was an impressive speaker, and no one who met him ever forgot him. In 1928, he was asked by the federal government to organize the fishermen of the Maritimes. On 26 June 1930 he brought together 208 representatives of fishermen's groups and helped them to create the United Maritime Fishermen. Technological changes in the fishing industry and improvements in transportation had resulted in the decline of small communities. Large fish plants were built in key locations, and larger fishing vessels employed to get economics of scale. While a number of communities established co-operative canneries, the improvements in transportation after 1930 meant that inshore fishermen could send their lobster to market live, and get a better price.

When the Extension Department was created in July 1928, Father Coady was named its first director. He spent six months looking at adult education in central and western Canada and in the U.S.A. Then his assignment for the fishermen took him away from Antigonish, as he travelled around and visited communities in the Maritimes. But from 1930 onwards, when the actual work began, the Extension Department took all his time. Small communities swung into social and economic action, backstopped by the workers from the university. Social movements do not persist unless they show that their methods work, and what happened at Little Dover was proof that adult education could change communities. Father Tompkins and Father Coady could stimulate, inspire, talk, teach. They could present a new vision of a better life, talk of social justice, and educate people. But neither was a very good organizer. To help him to set up the network of study clubs, Coady called in A. B. MacDonald. "A.B." was from Heatherton and had studied at Ontario Agricultural College in Guelph. He worked first as an agricultural representative, and then became Inspector of Schools in Antigonish–Guysborough. "A.B." had doubts about exchanging the security of government for the uncertainty of a new venture in adult education. He agreed to take the job only if the clergy of Cape Breton would back him. R. J. McSween, an agricultural representative, met with the "hard headed old Scotsman" in Sydney, and convinced him that the Movement was a genuine attempt at social change. "A.B." did most of the detailed work of organization, following up after Father Coady had generated interest in the idea of community action. He also went to communities to tell them about the Movement.

There was nothing new, startling, or radical about the methods used by the Antigonish Movement. What was new was the development of a network that linked together scattered individuals and groups with common goals, and provided them with access to the information and resources they needed. The Movement operated in a decentralized manner, and complemented the efforts at social change in the region. Croteau was working in adult education, co-operative development, and credit unions on Prince Edward Island during the Thirties. At the same time, McEwen was building up the co-operative wholesaling organization that eventually became Maritime Co-operative Services, based in Moncton. And the Movement was struggling to gain a foothold in industrial Cape Breton. Indeed, Coady claimed in 1932 that "the miners were swinging to us in great numbers." In 1937 Tompkins wrote Coady claiming that about "30 miners of the ultra radical group in Reserve [Mines] are coming to us in neat shape and are going to attend the course."[18]

The Movement used a variety of methods. The Antigonish educators believed that persons, awakened through education, would develop the strategies for co-operative economic institutions. The first stage in this process was the organization of mass community meetings. Here Moses Coady excelled, challenging the people to break out of their "culture of silence." After the mass meeting, people were organized into study clubs. The study club — lighting little fires — was viewed as the essential starting point to mobilize "the people of Eastern Canada to fight their economic battles."[19] Realizing that they lacked trained community organizers, Coady and MacDonald saw the study club as an effective means of organizing large numbers in the rural areas. By the end of 1931, 173 study clubs were underway, most located in rural Scottish Catholic parishes. But that would change as the Movement diversified through the 1930s, making inroads into industrial Cape Breton, drawing in women, some Protestant communities and Acadian fishing villages, as well as spreading to other areas of the Maritimes. To train cadre and solidify the Movement, St Francis Xavier Extension Department held short courses, general meetings, and rural and industrial conferences. St Francis Xavier was the educational mobilizing centre of the Movement.

St Francis Xavier provided a pedagogical method without predetermining what problems ought to be acted on: education for self-organization. But Coady clearly believed that education had to start with "simple material things" that were "vital to human living."[20] What could be more vital to impoverished Eastern Nova Scotians — farmers, fishermen, unemployed coal and steel workers — than credit unions, producer and consumer co-operatives, insurance and buying clubs? Credit unions — the distinctive creation of the Extension Department — flourished in industrial settings with high rates of unemployment. Indeed, 50 percent of all credit unions appeared in urban areas which had only one-quarter of all study clubs. But the need for credit unions was experienced generally throughout all sectors of life in Eastern Nova Scotia. Producer and consumer co-operatives in rural areas far outnumbered urban efforts; the major effort in organizing primary producers was in the area of co-operative marketing. Here government and national co-operative organizations were active in organizing farm and fishing co-operatives. Establishing co-operatives was, in fact, a peripheral activity of the Extension Department, which concentrated on study clubs, leadership courses, and credit unions.[21] Co-operative housing and stores were particularly successful in urban areas. The Movement appears to have taken hold primarily in areas dominated by big capital where the social differentiation process was well advanced. Receptivity to the Movement had a class dimension.[22]

National Archives Canada/NA-C 98724

Fr M. M. Coady speaking to a Canadian Congress of Labour Weekend Institute in New Glasgow, N.S. 1950.

The Movement probably reached its peak in 1938-39. In 1938, the Movement received official Papal approval. In its Annual Report for the year ending 30 April 1939, the Extension Department noted that staff totalled eleven full-time members, seven part-time, and thirty additional staff in the fishing communities.[23] The annual Rural and Industrial Conference in August 1938 had attracted one thousand people. A Co-operative Institute held after the Conference brought together two hundred educationists, clergymen, social workers, and others from thirty states in the United States and from every province in Canada. Rev. J. D. Nelson MacDonald, a United Church minister who promoted the Movement in the Baddeck area of Cape Breton, had lectured at the University of British Columbia to Pacific Coast fishermen. In the three Maritime Provinces, 19 600 people were enrolled in 2265 study clubs. At the annual extension course held in February 1939, 136 people from the region had participated. In all, 342 credit unions had been established, and 162 other forms of co-operative organization. In 1939, Father Coady's book *Masters of Their Own Destiny* appeared, and in this he articulated the philosophy of the Movement. Between 1931 and 1938, a social movement was occurring in Eastern Nova Scotia.

The Antigonish Movement was oriented towards reform and not revolution. The Movement did not topple monopoly capitalism; it achieved limited but significant reforms within capitalist political and economic structures.[24] Yet the Movement articulated a "system-transcending" vision. Since the Movement attempted to insert co-operative principles into the industrializing social and economic order, it was reformist. But these principles, metaphysically rooted in the biblical prophetic tradition,[25] were based on an alternative communitarian vision of society. The Movement leadership was aware that the dominant competitive individualist culture rendered people passive and ignorant, crippling their self-confidence. The leadership saw the need for people to start defining and working towards the solutions to their own problems, rather than waiting for someone else to start. People were encouraged to take direct action in their local communities, beginning a process of personal and collective empowerment. One William Feltmate, a fisherman, spoke at the 1938 Rural and Industrial Conference, claiming that he was no longer an "individual fighter" but now fought collectively. For him, as many others, there was more than material benefits involved in co-operation: "it teaches us to trust one another" and "transact business . . . in peace and harmony with one another."[26] This new spirit of community was recognized by agricultural workers. One representative exclaimed that Mabou "presented him with *their* plan of what they thought Mabou needed most. At last we found a community where we play our proper role as technical advisers and no longer need to be self-salesmen."[27]

The Antigonish Movement presented itself to the world as the "middle way" between the extremities of collectivism and individualism. The Movement was basically a left populist one, and it worked from the ground up, rather than from the top down. Coady was "for" the rural people, co-operation, and grassroots action, and "against" centralized power, absentee owners, cities, and the outside forces that kept Maritimers in a state of bondage. Coady was not a socialist, however. This is understandable — socialism was ideologically unacceptable to Rome and isolated as a movement to urban Cape Breton. Coady's antipathy to socialism also was strongly influenced by its perversion in practice. In its stead, Coady proffered a vision of a participatory democracy which confronted the anti-democratic currents in the communist movement and a strategy of education for economic co-operation. It is perhaps more precise to identify the Antigonish Movement as an expression of a "third way" on the Canadian left, a radical tradition it its own right intersecting with, yet autonomous from, social democracy and communism. The genius of the Antigonish Movement lay in its ability to provide its largely Catholic constituency with a new, transcendentally-based explanatory framework for life in an industrial society and a non-violent strategy for attaining the "good and abundant life."

The Antigonish Movement was moderately successful as a social movement. Utilizing community-based networks throughout Eastern Nova Scotia and other parts of the Maritimes, the Movement brought about significant individual and community change but limited structural change in the region, helped people to handle social and economic tensions, and showed communities how to identify economic opportunities. Thousands were assisted in articulating their needs, and the Movement effectively mobilized educational and economic resources to meet those needs. Through participation in various co-operative ventures economic competencies were acquired. The Movement focussed less directly on enabling individuals and communities to develop political competences; however, it was inevitable that men and women would acquire some political knowledge and skills in the process of organizing community projects. Nonetheless the Movement did deflect attention away from the achievement of state power. And even though Coady thought that through credit unions, lobster factories, and sawmills, the Movement was "laying the foundation for an appreciation of Shakespeare and grand opera,"[28] there is little evidence that this occurred.

But Father Tompkins did promote actively the establishment of libraries to increase the effectiveness of the study clubs and co-operatives. On 5 July 1935, the People's Library of Reserve Mines was opened, the collection consisting of Tompkins's own books and those he had purchased with help from his American friends. James Marsh of Reserve Mines recalls the impact of Tompkins's books.

> He got books and he had them in the vestibule of the glebe house. Then he started buttonholing people to come in and read. He would announce from the pulpit that anyone interested in reading on economics, sociology and things like that — the books were in the glebe house. We didn't

understand those words at first, you know. But we started to read books on the co-operative movement and about reformers like Ernest Bevin and Booker T. Washington — about self-made men. That's what Father Jimmy wanted us all to be — masters of our own destinies — to do things for themselves that other people were doing for them. That was his adult education program.[29]

In subsequent years, Tompkins would be instrumental in promoting a regional library system for Nova Scotia.[30]

Dr Alexander Laidlaw, who was deeply involved in the Movement, summarized the Movement's achievements as economic uplift of the poor; the implementation of a philosophy of adult education that focussed on ordinary people in group action; helping labor to get organized; making the university relevant to everyday life; and supporting the social teachings of the Catholic Church.[31] To this might be added the fact that the Movement created a new opportunity structure for local people with ability. Despite the failure of Coady's dream of transforming society from the margins, that was no small achievement.

Footnotes

1. See, for recent examples, Tom Lovett, Chris Clarke, and Avila Kilmurray, *Adult Education and Community Action* (London: Croom Helm, 1983), pp. 6, 39. Lovett discusses Antigonish in the historical context of nineteenth-century radical educational work, and the contemporary context of Highlander and the Work People's College. Stephen Brookfield, *Adult Learners, Adult Education and the Community* (Milton Keynes: Open University Press, 1983), pp. 9, 71, 107-111, views Antigonish as a liberating form of community education.

2. See Alexander Laidlaw, *The Campus and the Community: The Global Impact of the Antigonish Movement* (Montreal: Harvest House Ltd., 1961), pp. 161-70, for a useful bibliography of early works, most of which were concerned with Movement philosophy and leadership intentionality. Frank Mifflen, "The Antigonish Movement: A Summary Analysis of Its Development, Principles and Goals," *Canadian Journal of Public and Co-operative Economy*, vol. 10, 1977, provides a serviceable recent account of Movement philosophy.

3. An article in *MacLean's*, 1 June 1953, claimed that "St.F.X. has put new life into a dying fishing industry, restored idle farms and stamped out Communism in industrial Cape Breton, once a hot-bed of radical activity."

4. Establishment politicians such as St Francis Xavier graduates Alan MacEachen and Brian Mulroney pay glowing tribute to the Antigonish Movement. It would be fun to try and reconcile DEVCO's development strategy with the principles of the Movement.

5. For an excellent review of resource mobilization theory, see William Gamson and Emilie Schmeidler, "Organizing the Poor," *Theory and Society* 13, 4 (July

1984), and John McCarthy and Mayer N. Zald, "Resource Mobilization and Social Movements: A Partial Theory," *American Journal of Sociology* 82, 6 (May 1977). For an analysis of the role of education in social movements, see Rolland Paulston and D. Lejeune, "A Methodology for Studying Education in Social Movements," in *Other Dreams, Other Schools: Folk Colleges in Social and Ethnic Movements,* edited by Rolland Paulston (Pittsburgh: University Center for International Studies, 1980).

6. For detailed accounts of competing and intersecting social movements of the 1920s, see Ernest R. Forbes, *The Maritime Rights Movement, 1919-1927: A Study in Canadian Regionalism* (Kingston and Montreal: McGill-Queen's University Press, 1979); G. A. Rawlyk, "The Farmer-Labour Movement and the Failure of Socialism in Nova Scotia," in *Essays on the Left,* edited by Laurier LaPierre et al. (Toronto: McClelland and Stewart, 1971); David Frank, "The Cape Breton Coal Industry and the Rise and Fall of the British Empire Steel Corporation," *Acadiensis* 7, 1 (Autumn 1977); Paul MacEwan, *Miners and Steelworkers: Labour in Cape Breton* (Toronto: Hakkert, 1976); Donald MacGillivary, "Military Aid to the Civil Power: The Cape Breton Experience in the 1920s," *Acadiensis* 3, 2 (Spring 1974); Ian MacPherson, "Patterns in the Maritime Co-operative Movement 1900-1945," *Acadiensis* 5, 1 (Autumn 1975).

7. Père Anselme Chaisson, *Chéticamp: Histoire et Traditions Acadiennes* (Moncton: Edition des Aboiteaux, 1972), p. 31.

8. "The Social Significance of the Co-operative Movement," *Brief* to the Royal Commission on Taxation, Halifax, 5-7 March 1945, pp. 12-13.

9. See Daniel MacInnes, "Clerics, Fishermen, Farmers, and Workers: The Antigonish Movement and Identity in Eastern Nova Scotia, 1928-1939," unpublished Ph.D. dissertation, McMaster University, 1978, Ch. 4, "Responses of the Church to Industrial Development and Change in Eastern Nova Scotia, 1899-1928."

10. See references on Cape Breton in footnote 6.

11. MacInnes, "Clerics, Fishermen," p. 223. See also F. Waldo Walsh, *We Fought for the Little Man* (Moncton: Co-op Atlantic Press, 1978).

12. See MacPherson, "Patterns in the Maritime Co-operative Movement 1900-1945," for background data.

13. Cited in Laidlaw, *The Campus and the Community,* p. 90.

14. See MacInnes, Ch. 4, for a detailed discussion of the role of the Scottish Catholic Society, and R. J. MacSween, "The Role Played by the Scottish Society of Canada in the Establishment of the St.F.X. Extension Department," unpublished manuscript, Public Archives of Nova Scotia.

15. See, for example, Bertram B. Fowler, *The Lord Helps Those* (New York: Vanguard Press, 1938), pp. 37ff, and George Boyle, *Father Tompkins of Nova Scotia* (New York: P. J. Kenedy & Sons, 1953).

16. *Report* of the Royal Commission investigating the Fisheries of the Maritime Provinces and Magdalen Islands (Ottawa: King's Printer, 1928), p. 9.

17. For an explication of these principles, see Moses M. Coady, *Masters of Their Own Destiny* (New York: Harper and Row, 1939), and MacInnes, Ch. 6, "Objectifications of the Movement," pp. 273ff.

18. MacInnes, p. 404. Research is needed on the link between the Antigonish Movement and the Labor Movement.

19. Coady, *Masters of Their Own Destiny*, p. 38.

20. Ibid., p. 68.

21. Ian MacPherson, *Each for All: A History of the Co-operative Movement in English Canada, 1900-1945* (Toronto: The Macmillan Co., 1979, p. 134), points out that "despite its widespread involvement in rural development, the Antigonish Movement did not dominate the agricultural societies in the early thirties, and certainly not later."

22. James Sacouman, "Underdevelopment and the Structural Origins of the Antigonish Movement Co-operatives in Eastern Nova Scotia," *Acadiensis* 7, 1 (Autumn 1977), p. 84, argues that the "magic of the Antigonish leadership and programme was potent or impotent depending on the structural base upon which it acted." Although Sacouman's work is marred by a rigid adherence to a deterministic Marxism which dissolves subjectivity, he raises important research questions.

23. Reprinted as part of *We Learn By Doing*, a series of fifteen short articles published by the Extension Department *circa* 1940.

24. This "fact" has not escaped the eye of orthodox Marxian critics who accuse the Movement of not transforming the capitalist mode of production. See Gary Webster, "Tignish and Antigonish: A Critique of the Antigonish Movement as a Cadre for Co-operation," *The Abegweit Review* 2, September 1975; D. L. Murphy, "The Failure of the Antigonish Movement in Larry's River," Unpublished M.A. thesis, Dalhousie University, 1975; and Sacouman, "Antigonish Movement Co-operatives."

25. Theologian Gregory Baum has argued that the significance of the Movement lies in its annunciation of a "critical spirituality." See *Catholics and Canadian Socialism: Political Thought in the Thirties and Forties* (Toronto: James Lorimer, 1980), Ch. 7, "Catholics in Eastern Nova Scotia."

26. Cited in MacInnes, p. 350.

27. Ibid., p. 348. Emphasis in the original.

28. Coady, *Masters of Their Own Destiny*, p. 68.

29. "Father Jimmy Tompkins of Reserve Mines," *Cape Breton's Magazine*, No. 16, n.d.

30. See Violet L. Coughlin, Ch. VI, "Library Development in Nova Scotia," in *Larger Units of Public Library Service in Canada* (Methuen, N.J.: The Scarecrow Press, 1968).

Dramatizing the Great Issues: Workers' Theatre in the Thirties

Sandra Souchotte

They were justifiably disgusted with the barren fields of Canadian bourgeois culture, with the smirking complacency of Canadian artists and writers, with their puerile ignorance of and contempt for social questions, with their snobbish nose-thumbing at the workers and their movements. These intellectuals who have "revolted" against the ideas of the swell mob have quite comfortably landed on the pink cushion of bohemia.

[E. Cecil-Smith, "Our Credentials," Vol. 1, no. 1, April 1932, n.p.]

The "they" of the opening quotation had formed by the Fall of 1931 a specific medium of communication — the Progressive Arts Club of Toronto with an initial membership of about thirty-five. Their objective was to provide the basis for the development of a militant, working-class art and literature and to register popular complaint about the economic crisis of the thirties in Canada. Two initial ventures provided an outlet for that commitment: one was the publication of a national magazine with a socialist viewpoint called *Masses,* and the other was the formation in the winter of 1931-32 of a small troupe known as the Workers' Experimental Theatre. Progressive Arts Clubs (PAC) eventually became active in six Canadian centres — Halifax, Montreal, Toronto, London, Winnipeg, and Vancouver — until their gradual demise by 1936.

Although *Masses* ran only twelve issues, covering the period from April 1932 to April 1934, it was able to publish poetry, short stories, and articles of a defiantly anti-bourgeois nature, plus details of workers' theatre groups across the country and a number of original Canadian playscripts, all short mass recitations or agit-props. E. Cecil-Smith, one of the editors and playwrights with the theatre group, described *Masses* as:

... the first publication of its kind to appear on Canadian soil, produced from the life of Canada's factories, farms — and breadlines. It has a whole battlefield of barbed wire to traverse. It will rip down the wire.[1]

The Workers' Experimental Theatre of Toronto (later abbreviated to the Workers' Theatre) recognized the possibility of using drama to expose and ridicule what was considered to be an exploitative bourgeois society. The Canadian group was ideologically linked to similar movements active at the time in Britain, the United States, Russia, Germany, and other countries. It is doubtful that many of the members belonged to the Communist party, although they were familiar with party doctrine. They were, for the most part, young, unemployed workers, students and artists, zealously critical of the existing social order and supportive of revolutionary activity in Canada.

The first script published in *Masses* (December 1932) is one borrowed from the British Workers' Theatre movement but it helps to define the stylistic method and thematic concerns of the Canadian socialist theatre. **The Theatre — Our Weapon** is a series of short speeches arranged for five individual voices and a chorus. After a declamatory opener from the chorus, "Workers of the world, unite!," it goes on to attack non-socialist theatre, "Down with the theatre where the bourgeois comes to digest his heavy meal! Down with the theatre where the idle parasites come to amuse themselves!," and includes what appears to be a reference to specifically Canadian social problems:

In Canada, where thousands are dying from hunger, while stoves are being heated with the surplus of wheat, the workers' theatre is calling for the overthrow of the accursed system by which this is possible. The miners, dockers, metal-workers, textile-workers hear our voices as they defend themselves from the attacks of despairing and desperate capitalism. The blows of police-batons cannot break our determination.

In spite of occasional borrowing, the Workers' Theatre was determined to create its own repertoire of Canadian plays based on "a drama rooted in the lives and struggles of the toilers of Canada's shops, mines, farms and slave camps." To this end, an early issues of *Masses* (June 1932) outlined the requirements of a special "Dram (*sic*) Contest."

This is undertaken with the object of building up a repertoire of working class plays based on the struggle in Canada.
Plays should be as brief as possible, and be written for a cast of no more than seven or eight characters.
Bear in mind that we want plays that can be put on by small dram (*sic*) groups with a minimum of props.

Early attempts to meet these requirements had already proved moderately successful. The first performance of a Canadian agit-prop play **Deported** was given at the Ukrainian Labor Temple of 6 May 1932. Written, acted, and directed by members of the PAC, the play was praised for being "extremely realistic and very effective in its stark simplicity." Though criticized for an insufficiently optimistic ending it signified, according to *Masses*, an appropriate new direction for topical Canadian drama.

> In spite of these and other minor defects, the performance marked an encouraging departure from the polite whimsies of what, until now, has passed in Canada as native theatre.

By July the Workers' Experimental Theatre had made their third appearance before Toronto workers, somewhat improving their technique. At a concert for the Workers' International Relief they presented a two-scene play **Solidarity, not Charity** (taken from the U.S. publication *Workers' Life*), dealing with the appearance of a striking worker before a bureaucratic relief committee and his subsequent condemnation of charity. The *Masses* reviewer found individual lines well-rendered but the collective enunciation deplorable.

> Collective rhythm, clear tones, sharp ringing phrases — these are essential for successful mass recitation. The players, furthermore, did not move in rhythm. The gestures, the swaying of bodies in unison, the striking of symbolic poses, are as important as the lines, with which close unity is essential.

More intriguing is his suggestion for a concrete form of stage symbolism to supplement the dialogue.

> In one of the corners of the stage could have been a large ticker-tape apparatus, labelled RED TAPE. As the committee interviewed the worker, one of its members (preferably the investigator) could have pulled long strips of red ribbon from the case, winding it around the workers' hands and legs.

By November 1933 E. Cecil-Smith reported via an article in *The Canadian Forum* on the rapid success rate of the Workers' Theatre, which now existed in six centres from Halifax to Vancouver. People in more than sixty smaller cities or towns were in touch with the Toronto centre, requesting plays or information on how to form their own groups. Declaring that Workers' Theatre went far beyond the drab and dreary prospects of the Little Theatre or church stages, Cecil-Smith was convinced that this new drama, "its themes, its plots, its stage difficulties and techniques, its authors and its players — these and many other things clearly stamp it as truly Canadian."

Three tours had been made by the Toronto Workers' Theatre the previous summer: one to the Niagara Peninsula, the second to London and Windsor, and the third to Ottawa where an unemployment congress was being held. The tours contained a number of political highlights. A strike broke out at the Canadian Canning factory in St. Catharines during the tour and besides playing at the strike meetings the Workers' Theatre group also helped out on the picket lines, until the police ordered them out of town. In Niagara Falls they appeared at an open-air protest meeting against the supposed frame-up of Tim Buck (a leader of the Communist party and prisoner in Kingston Penitentiary, later the subject of a play **Eight Men Speak**) as well as in a concert hall which lacked curtains, lights, wings, or anything else but a small, raised speakers' platform. The group carried with it an expanded selection of plays, which seem to have proven popular with the largely working-class audience.

Along with **Solidarity,** not **Charity** were plays with such titles as **Eviction,** a mass recitation written by two Montreal members of the PAC; **Farmers' Fight,** also from Montreal; **Labor's Love Lost,** a one-act satire on the CCF (adapted from a play in the U.S. *Workers' Theatre Magazine*); **Meerut**, a mass recitation on the trial and sentence of the Indian trades union leaders (by the Workers' Theatre in England); a Joe Derry play (pantomime and recitation performed for children), written by a Toronto member; and **War In the East,** a play in four scenes on the robber war against the people of Manchuria and China (by a University of Toronto undergraduate named Stanley Ryerson).

By this time three general categories defined the form of the plays: mass recitation (usually of political slogans pertaining to Communist ideology); the short agitational-propaganda sketch (broad cartoon-like characterizations with subject matter focussing on social inequalities and the need for increased social consciousness); and Socialist realism (using more traditional representational techniques drawing on topical themes).

Eviction was considered the most successful of the mass recitations performed by the Workers' Theatre groups, carrying with it an immediate and dynamic example of social oppression. It examined the murder, during an eviction, of unemployed Nick Zynchuk, who was shot in the back by a Montreal police constable, and the later police attack on the twenty thousand workers who attended his funeral. First produced as a memorial to Zynchuk, the piece was soon being performed by theatre groups across Canada. The mass recitations were usually performed by a cast of from five to eight people, dressed in the standard Workers' Theatre uniform of black sateen blouse and trousers, topped by a red neckershief.

Under the agit-prop grouping two plays were given special mention: Stanley Ryerson's **War In the East,** and Oscar Ryan's **Unity,** both by Toronto Club members. **Unity** was written for a mass meeting of labor and socialist organizations held on 1 May 1933 at the Hygeia Hall in Toronto and was acclaimed as having "tremendous propaganda value." **War In the East** drew praise for its effective symbolism.

In the first scene of this the stylized characters, Mikado, Capitalist, War Lord, and Priest wear masks which aid the slight costumes (top hat, Priest's cassock, and so forth) in showing that they represent forces, rather than individuals. Throughout these agit-prop sketches, the only properties or costumes used are very simple; such as a helmet and baton to indicate a soldier, top hat, white gloves, spats and cane for the boss etc. These are worn with the uniform black blouse and trousers.

Examples of company-produced Socialist realism were scarce but a Toronto electrician, H. Francis, had written a more representational two-scene play, presented at a National Congress on Unemployment in Ottawa. Rather than a great deal of direct declamation, it concentrated on the dramatic development of a family situation which the father changes from a passive relief recipient to a determined advocate of a decent unemployment insurance scheme.

Undoubtedly the most successful and adventurous production of Workers' Theatre was a six-act, collective work **Eight Men Speak** (with a cast of thirty-two which combined aspects of all three forms. Written by Oscar Ryan, E. Cecil-Smith, H. Francis, and Miriam Goldberg, it deals with the attempted murder of Communist political prisoner Tim Buck in Kingston Penitentiary. The scenario includes satiric caricatures of the controlling personnel of Kingston society, realistic trial and prison scenes, a pantomimed shooting of Buck, and a symbolic conviction of Capitalism by the Labour Defense League, ending with a ringing assertion of Socialist triumph.

Although melodramatic in tone and weakened by a casual mingling of conflicting styles, the play's explosive topicality and moments of simple, factual presentation were apparently a stirring experience. It attracted enough public attention and official approbation to be banned after its premiere performance at Toronto's Standard Theatre (later the Victory) on 4 December 1933. Provincial police also attempted to censor the play when it was shown by the Progressive Arts Club of Winnipeg at the Walker Theatre on 2 May 1934. These events were well publicized.

The Play Which
Frightened the Ont. Gov't!
"Eight Men Speak"
In Six Acts
The Greatest Hit of the
1933-34 Season in Canada
Banned because of its
Militant Working Class Line

With people stimulated by the success of **Eight Men Speak** and incensed by the censorship of it, Workers' Theatre had a rapid increase in membership. The PAC in Toronto decided on a more militant stance and announced a decision to participate in the International Revolutionary Theatre move-

Progressive Arts Club "EIGHT MEN SPEAK" Workers' Theatre

ment by holding a special Canadian International Theatre Night and Ten-Day Campaign (projected for 15-25 March 1934). The Toronto office issued the necessary instructions on procedures:

> Remember this is an International Theatre Night and this must necessarily be reflected in the programme, which should be as varied as possible. Only one short one-act sketch is needed on the programme. The rest of the time will be taken up with dance numbers, musical selections, choirs, bands, chalk talks and so forth. The aim should be that every organization in your district must be represented on the programme of this theatre night.
>
> To link up the Workers' Theatre movement in Canada with that of other countries, a speaker should appear on every programme. In this talk he should acquaint his listeners with the aims and tasks of the workers' cultural movement in Canada and abroad.

Besides an optimistic proposal to link up with the international socialist cultural movement, the same issue of *Masses* recorded that one hundred Workers' Theatre groups were in existence across Canada and that the circulation of *Masses* had surpassed that of the *The Canadian Forum*. Unfortunately *Masses* was not heard from again and the decline of activities, naturally enough, is unrecorded. Various hypotheses abound about the fading appeal of the movement.

Popular cultural protest eventually sought other directions and became more urgent as the threat of war increased. Mass chants and short sketches had reached their dramatic limits, indicating that a probing, more developed appraisal of people in contemporary society was needed and that the full-length play (traditional or not) was required again. In Toronto, a core group from the Workers' Theatre had decided to explore a new dramatic doctrine and, drawing on a New York experiment, started Theatre of Action in the summer of 1935. That experience forms the second part of Canada's political drama of the thirties.

Somewhat ironically the Workers' Theatre was heard from again via the Dominion Drama Festival. The latter was despised by many of the workers' groups for its bourgeois tendencies and pretensions to a national drama. An early judgement read:

> Let the prize-winning T. Eaton Co.'s sponsored Masquers Club, and the Winnipeg Little Theatre group parade with their anaemic plays as the representatives of "national drama."

But the absence of any representation from the Workers' Theatre in the Dominion Drama Festival was felt by some to be an even greater insult. In 1936 a Vancouver branch of the Progressive Arts Club won a Dominion Drama Festival trophy for its production of Clifford Odets's **Waiting for**

Lefty. And that event appears to mark the final defusing of the Workers' Theatre, a movement which created a potentially exciting platform for "the affairs of the people" and the first national attempt at a truly proletarian theatre.

The formation of Theatre of Action groups in Canada has less historical definition than its socialist predecessor the Workers' Theatre. The organizational structure was more nebulous, lacking the central authority of the Toronto Progressive Arts Club and its national publication *Masses*. Many of the Workers' Theatre groups seem to have petered out without leaving much trace of their existence, while others moved towards less politically committed forms of cultural expresson. The Workers' Theatre group of the Vancouver Progressive Arts Club evolved into the Progressive Arts Players and then into Theatre of Action. In the Process, it allied itself more closely to the Little Theatre movement and to the élitist, award-giving procedures of the Dominion Drama Festival than to workers. This seems to have been true of most Theatre of Action groups across the country — perhaps because the social ills of the Depression now afflicted all strata of society and it had become fashionable to demonstrate an increased social consciousness. The new activity was also less specifically Canadian.

Theatre of Action in Toronto and its equivalent in Montreal, the New Theatre Group, both took their names, their ideology, their theatrical methodology, and, to a large extent, their plays from flourishing New York examples. During 1936 and 1940, the second period of political theatre in Canada, more Canadian plays were presented by amateur Little Theatre groups at the Dominion Drama Festival than by Theatre of Action players. But while Theatre of Action productions were attempting to deal with urgent social issues (poverty, the need for unions, the threat of fascism and world war), the Candian plays of the Little Theatre groups did little more than portray melodramatic family situations imbued with a folksy Canadian atmosphere and usually set in the backwoods or prairies of Canada. After judging the 1938 Dominion Drama Festival, London director Malcolm Morley pinpointed the problem in an article in *The Sunday Times*.

> Of the hundred and more entries a dozen were original Canadian plays. Until recently the scene of the native Canadian play was inevitably a kitchen and the chief character an old woman who sat moaning in front of a stove. From the host of such pieces one might have imagined that the kitchen stove was the centre round which Canadian drama revolved and that the whole Dominion was a chain of shacks and sheds. This year the native drama had noticably come out of the kitchen and entered the drawing room. In some cases it has ascended to the boudoir.

Whatever its limitations — especially the lack of indigenous source material — Theatre of Action was motivated beyond kitchen, drawing room, and bedroom.

Essentially Theatre of Action was theatre of the broad left rather than explicitly Marxist, experimental rather than radical, a theatre of protest rather than revolt and, at its best, inspirational or instructive — not agitational. When first organized in the summer of 1935, the Toronto company declared its policy "of presenting plays dealing with the economic, emotional and cultural problems facing the majority of people." Although allied to the ideals of the Little Theatre movement in Canada,[2] it was also initially committed to opening up another avenue of contact with the working-class, where it was felt a wide and stimulating audience was to be found. Had the original decision to be a "portable" theatre which could play in trade union halls, workers' clubs, and community centres been continued, Theatre of Action might have attracted a wider working-class audience. Instead, the necessity of finding accommodation in such attractive, but bourgeois, spaces as Hart House Theatre and Margaret Eaton Hall brought with it a standard middle-class clientele.

Theatre of Action's summer training school, first held in 1935, was dedicated to a study of the Stanislavsky system of acting and directing. The school flourished for four more years offering acting techniques, body movement, directing, history of the theatre, make-up, and voice training. Several of the teachers — Leonard Asher, Jim Watts, David Pressman, and Paul Mann — used their experience with the Group Theatre, Neighbourhood Playhouse, and New Theatre League schools of New York as a basis of instruction. After its first training session, Theatre of Action launched productions. **America, America** by Alfred Kreymurg and **The Home of the Brave** by Frank Gabrielson and David Lesan were given at the small theatre studio on Grenville Street during the last week of September 1935.

Both the New Theatre Group of Montreal and Theatre of Action in Toronto presented Clifford Odets's one-act play **Waiting for Lefty** later that season. On 27, 28, and 29 February 1936, Theatre of Action, in conjunction with the Student League, staged Odets's **Waiting for Lefty** and Albert Maltz's **Private Hicks** at Margaret Eaton Hall, followed by a repeat performance on 26 May 1936. *The Mail and Empire* critic praised the play's dramatic qualities but had difficulty with the social message, a concern that appeared repeatedly in review of the "leftist" theatre.

> The Odets play is so good, so genuine in craft and spirit, that not even its propaganda flavor can mar the enjoyment. With reason, sincerity and the most acute use of dramatic possibilities, it shows how exasperation with an existing economic system may drive men to drastic action.
>
> An engaging device of the play is the union of auditorium and stage, the stage scene being a hall platform, and the hecklers of the meeting speak from the audience.

The Canadian socialist theatre was given an ideal opportunity in June 1936 when a Toronto publication called *New Frontier*[3] announced that the New

Theatre Groups of Canada (comprising the Vancouver and Winnipeg Progressive Arts Club, the Toronto Theatre of Action, and the Montreal New Theatre Group) were sponsoring a contest for one-act plays dealing with the Canadian social scene. Even this idea had been borrowed from a similar contest held by the New Theatre League in the United States, but the premise was a valid and exciting one.

> A tremendous need exists for the dramatization of the great social issues of our time, for plays which will speak out boldly against hunger and unemployment in a land of plenty, against the waste of human life and the degradation of the human spirit, which will portray the world of today honestly and fearlessly.
>
> Such social drama does not exclude treatment of the past. The great, but neglected or maligned figures of this country who fought on the side of progress and freedom offer a rich mine of dramatic material.

The plays were assessed in a subsequent issue of *New Frontier* (March 1937), and the writer regretfully acknowledged that the Canadian nature of the plays reflected all too clearly the limitations of our national standards and culture. The democratic, middle-class background of most of the writers also created a tiresome predictability in the plays, which tended to dwell on stock family situations instead of dynamic social problems.

> Categorically, you had a young person from a well-to-do family who rebelled and went forth to live among the workers, therefore renouncing (1) a comfortable living, (2) a soft job, or (3) a reactionary betrothed. Or you had a different young person, who also rebelled. If the emphasis was on the couple, they would decide to get married anyway or take their happiness without. If it was on the young man he would go out and rob a bank, and upon discovery would (a) commit suicide, or (b) get killed under a freight train.

Of the sixty-six plays submitted, Vancouver playwright Mary Reymold's **And the Answer is . . .** was judged worthy of the winning prize. The play uses three short scenes to contrast a group of derelicts gathered around a war memorial with a group of effete wealthy snobs gathered at a club. The derelicts demonstrate a simple concern for each other in their helplessness while the wealthy are shown as selfish, petty, and oblivious to the misery around them. The play ends with a floodlight suddenly illuminating the words on the Memorial IS IT NOTHING TO YOU, ALL YE THAT PASS BY?, followed by a blackout.

The play, presented by Theatre of Action at Margaret Eaton Hall in April 1937, received laudatory comment, although the *Saturday Night* reviewer had this query:

> . . . why do members of a group professedly interested in the drama
> only as a means of social regeneration, and not as a vehicle for personal
> display, take so many curtain calls so consistently?

The Telegram reviewer, Rose McDonald, felt that the play exemplified Theatre
of Action's motivating purpose: "to draw attention to, if not solve, social
problems." She added that when the play was presented by the Co-operative
Commonwealth Theatre Group of Vancouver as part of the British Columbia Regional Drama Festival, the adjudicator, George de Warfaz, said that
he did not think the Drama Festival should be used for political purposes.

David Pressman, from New York's Neighborhood Playhouse, was invited
to manage Toronto Theatre of Action's second summer school but stayed
on for two more years to direct a succession of highly acclaimed productions: Irwin Shaw's **Bury the Dead** at Hart House from 26 to 31 October
1936; Sergei Tretiakov's **Roar China** at Hart House from 11 to 16 January
1937; Milo Hastings and Orrie Lashin's **Class of '29** at Margaret Eaton Hall
from 22 to 27 November 1937; and John Wexley's **Steel**, presented at
Margaret Eaton Hall from 14 to 19 March 1938, and then at the Legion Hall,
on 8 April 1938.

Bury the Dead is a militant peace play in which six dead soldiers rise up
and refuse to be buried. A sergeant, a captain, the generals, and finally the
womenfolk of the men implore them to enter their graves and observe pro-
priety, but in the end the dead men lead a revolution overwhelming the army
staff. Montreal's new Theatre Group presented the play just before the Toronto
company, eliciting a controversial response from S. Morgan Powell, the drama
editor of *The Montreal Star*.

> "Bury the Dead" is a jejune anti-war thesis distinctly Communistic in
> flavor, rather than a moving anti-war piece of the theatre . . .
>   If the New Theatre Group will drop Communistic propaganda and get
> hold of a good play, then things may be mightly interesting.

Provoked by the loose prejudice of these remarks, the director of the New
Theatre Group, Lilian Mendelssohn, wrote a letter to the paper demanding
a clarification of "propaganda" and outlining the objectives of the New
Theatre.

> In conclusion, we must protest publicly against this statement of yours
> that we aim to do communist propaganda. But it is quite true that we
> shun using our stage to root for war and the status quo. Our group is
> allied on the side of progress and on the side of truth. It believes that
> art that is worth while in any period has always been allied to the forces
> of progress. Our roots are in the masses, and we would like to develop
> a "people's theatre" in which every point of view relating to the pro-
> gress of the masses would be represented.

The letter was printed, but Powell felt obliged to add a rather petulant qualification. After asserting that both **Waiting for Lefty** and **Bury the Dead** were indeed communistic propaganda, he concluded emphatically that:

> There will be no further correspondence upon the production of "Bury the Dead". It can bury its own dead, so far as I am concerned. As for the opinions of those who hail "Bury the Dead" as a significant contribution to modern drama, well, all I can say is that their ideas of what constitute modern drama and mine are as far apart as the poles — and I hope they will always remain so.

Toronto accepted the play enthusiastically, although there is a self-congratulatory flavor to the reviews peculiar to a liberal middle-class morality suddenly feeling radical. *The Toronto Daily Star* reported that "amateur theatricals in Toronto reached a new level of effective presentation and strong language," and *The Mail and Empire* carried a headline "Allegory Whips Crowd to Cheers," followed by a statement that "The Play is one of the greatest indictments of war that has ever been produced on the stage."

Later that season **Bury the Dead** won second prize in the Regional Drama Festival and was selected for the Dominion Drama Festival finals in Ottawa. Curiously George de Warfaz, the same adjudicator who later found political theatre inappropriate at the Festival, called the play "marvellous anti-war propaganda" and even suggested that "It ought to be performed all over the world for the edification and illumination of dictators." Apparently coming out against war as an abstract concept was one thing but discrediting the controlling forces of your own society was quite another.

When adjudicated at the Ottawa finals the production was praised for its "experimentation," but criticized for allowing the message to supersede theatricality. Typifying a situation that was to prove increasingly familiar in Canadian theatre, David Pressman, the New York director, wrote an assessment of that year's Dominion Drama Festival citing the need for a national Canadian theatre.

> If the Festival as a Canadian institution is to grow and mature into something in which the entire population of the country may be creatively interested, it will have to change some of its policies. At present, there is keen competition between the east and west, and among the various participating groups; but the audience is almost exclusively upper class and regards the festival as a grand social affair of the year rather than as a review of the country's work in the theatre. It is remarkable to realize that outside of the Festival committee and the competing groups themselves, very few people are really interested in the progress being made in the theatre as a cultural and educational force. The Festival runs the danger of remaining a conventional outlet for a drab and highly traditional one-act nightmare.

Theatre of Action's next effort, the anti-imperialist play **Roar China,** was hailed as being the first Soviet play presented in Toronto. This mammoth production, with a cast of forty-seven, detailed the political development of oppressed Chinese to the moment of solidarity when they overthrow the British rulers. But as usual the relationship of this play to progressive social action in Canada had to be extrapolated through a lengthy process of inductive reasoning. The opening performance did include a cautious, and gratuitous, entr'acte speech about the exploited classes of Canada, but it is not known if this token attempt to relate the play to a contemporary parallel situation was a continuing aspect of the production. Judging from the reviews, the mob rushes, tableau, effective lighting, and Chinese costumes were the highlights of the play while the instructive speeches were considered propaganda, not realism — and annoyed rather than enlightened. (A young actor called Frank Shuster received good reviews.) Even Toronto's Communish newspaper *The Daily Clarion* suggested that, "Theatre of Action should thoroughly discuss, after this week has passed, whether they were ripe enough for Tretiakov and whether it best serves to popularize the Canadian people's theatre in the present stage of its development."

The American import **Class of '29** suffered from the same basic deficiency but was chosen because "It might just as well have been the product of Canadian playwrighting and its characters might be Canadian students — so universally does it reflect the plight of student youth on this continent." The play, with its stress on characterization, suggested a shift from the group work, mob psychology, and mass movement used by Theatre of Action to individual emphasis. It also introduced the temptations of choice lead roles, negating the possibilities of collective identification with a representative (but not differentiated) mass group on stage. Ideally, of course, the realistic addition of individual characteristics would enliven the portrayal of a particular social class rather than blur it into a limited, homogeneous stereotype. But once individual roles dominate, audience awareness of that individual as part of a unified group (and group consciousness) tends to be lessened or lost. The play, though, was well-received by everyone except, ironically, the student newspaper *The Varsity.*

> If you like plays about noble but caustic revolutionaries in Lower Depths surroundings where well-meaning but fatuous bishops bungle around, and tense young gentlemen too proud to serve as elevator boys seek death beneath the subway wheels, you may like **Class of '29.**

The production of **Steel** seems to have come closest to unifying conventional stagecraft (a three-act play with a plot and some love interest, elaborate painted sets, a cast of thirty-five and several starring roles) with a political intention. The action of the play was a steel town in the United States where the Pan American company exerted capitalistic control. But even the most undiscerning audience could recognize the Canadian parallel situation (although not the fact that the Canadian steel industry was largely American-owned — the question of national ownership not being a concern for about another thirty years). Theatre of Action players had made a special trip to Hamilton to get first-hand experience of steel factory conditions (qualified by the limitations of a single day's immersion) and one performance of the play was reserved for an audience of steel workers, guests of the Steel Workers' Organizing Committee. *The Clarion* applauded the production, especially its artistic stage effects:

> Special tribute should be paid to Sydney Newman and Nathan Petroff for their remarkable sets, the stylized interiors which fit so naturally in with the huge background of mills, chimneys, furnaces and pipes. Particularly effective was the interior of the mill, with its noise, smoke and glowing furnaces. Lighting was unusually good. Your could almost feel the heat.

And its poetic realism:

> Director David Pressman has adequately realized the rhythm of John Wexley's play and has given in most scenes, an almost poetic swing to the action and the grooming.
>   Throughout the play the actors worked in rhythm, harmoniously, as part of a pattern of living human relationships. The play itself is well constructed, convincing and particularly timely.

But it neglected to mention whether this dramatized version of worker oppression and unification was sufficient to induce a corresponding recognition and political motivation beyond the stage. The concentration on aesthetic form and the dilution of didactic content indicates the weakness of these performances as political theatre. Although based on loosely factual information or topical events, the productions had yet to achieve a creative integrity of documentation with dramatization. The original Workers' Theatre got its message across in a severely restricted dramatic form but it would seem that Theatre of Action sacrificed its message to the artifices of dramatic form.

Steel won the Central Ontario regional competition of the Dominion Drama Festival that year and, along with the second place production of **The Guardsman,** by the Toronto Masquers, went off to the finals in Winnipeg. The reasons for Theatre of Action participation in the Festivals are ambiguous. No doubt the company sought to demonstrate the validity of its type of theatre as opposed to less socially relevant productions and perhaps change the character of Festival productions by meaningful example and subtle dissent. But it is also possible that it was beguiled by the entertainment values, the prosperity of the cultural milieu, and the opportunity for national publicity and personal promotion.

Daniel Mann, also from New York's Neighbourhood Playhouse, arrived in Toronto in October 1938 to assume directorship of Theatre of Action. He expressed an aspiration to work with the classics as well as modern social-psycho dramas but ended up staging contemporary American social plays, with messages that could be applicable to Canadians. Under his leadership Theatre of Action presented **It Can't Happen Here,** an anti-fascist play by John C. Moffitt and Sinclair Lewis, **Life and Death of An American,** by George Sklar, and several political cabarets billed as the first of their kind in Toronto. One of the latter cabarets (planned for July 1939) proposed a light view of outstanding Canadian historical events:

> Laura Secord will be there with her cow, and Madeleine de Vercheres, surrounded by Indians giving a college yell as well as war whoops. . . . Sir Francis Bond Head will rub shoulders with John Cabot, while the finale of this section is entitled Moscow Gold Rush.

Life and Death of An American, with its theme about an economic system that wrecked the lives of two generations of an American family, epitomized Theatre of Action's move towards elaborate illusion and stage artifice. It was presented with the emphasis on impressionistic montage sequences. Using a multi-levelled ramp stage, the play incorporated the kind of experimental techniques initiated by the Workers' Theatre and expanded upon by Theatre of Action: quick blackouts, choric recitations, tableaux, symbolic pantomime, freeze poses, backstage noises, and a cyclorama of shifting lights to mark scene or group changes. Both the stage techniques and the social implications confounded adjudicator George Skillan when the play was entered in the Central Ontario Regional Drama Festival in the spring of 1939. His was the final word on the incongruity of earnest socialist theatre at the establishment Festival. With oblique and hedgingly contradictory statements he said "that such a scenario of mechanistic technique dwarfed the characters and the acting and confounded the message of the play," and then attempted to relate a discrepancy between democracy and geography to the presentation of the play. He said:

> A festival that presents such plays has a broad angle democracy in its program too eclectic for even so fine a little theatre as Hart House, tucked away underground amid a maze of colleges, half a mile from street cars.

Following these productions, Leo Tepp directed Theatre of Action players in Nikolai Gogol's **The Inspector General,** and Sydney Banks (a veteran actor with Theatre of Action) directed the last major production, John Steinbeck's **Of Mice and Men.** The only female role in the latter play was performed by Toby Gordon (now Toby Ryan), who appears to be the only person involved with Theatre of Action to keep a comprehensive scrapbook of its activities and who, consequently, inspired this article.

The year was 1940. In a cruelly ironic twist of fate and idealistic philosophy many of the people who had worked with, or supported, Theatre of Action's anti-war play **Bury the Dead** went off to a more fatal form of drama with no curtain call. Theatre of Action ended with the war, and the majority of those who returned from the holocaust were either too involved with re-building their lives to bother with theatre or too alienated to believe in the viability of political theatrics. Some of them did become well-known in American and Canadian theatre (and later television or film work): Lorne Greene, Frank Shuster, Sydney Banks, Ben Lennick, Sydney Newman, and others.

It is easy to condemn Theatre of Action for losing touch with the people, for becoming overly involved with stage ingenuity and for obscuring its social message. The temptations of recognition and the potential opportunity for general consciousness-raising through the Dominion Drama Festival were apparently irresistible. In spite of its shortcomings Theatre of Action did make a genuine attempt to overcome the distinction between propaganda and art by presenting carefully crafted productions with a contemporary social relevance. This movement, like the Workers' Theatre which preceded it, recognized that theatre need not be just escapist entertainment but could be an instrument of artistically viable political instruction. If it catered to entertainment fanfare more than the Workers' Theatre that is not surprising, and at least it avoided obscurity. Nowhere in all the references to Theatre of Action does the press make mention of the Workers' Theatre which preceded it. Few people even know that the Workers' Theatre ever existed. More to the point is the fact that attempts to create both a Canadian national theatre and a people's theatre today experience many of the identical problems of Theatre of Action.

Footnotes

1. In fact this assertion was more rhetorical than factual. An outspoken, anti-establishment paper *Le Fantasque* was published in Quebec City from 1837 to 1844 by Napoleon Aubin. He occupied the positions of editor of the paper, a leader of the Typographical Association of Quebec City (thought to be the first labor organization in Canada), and enthusiastic drama reviewer of plays produced by the Typographical Association. Aubin's sympathies with Quebec Patriotes and support of labor union theatrical activity (in particular the production of Voltaire's **Death of Caesar** on 23 October 1839) resulted in his arrest on charges of exciting "the passions of the audience against the constituted authority." Acquitted of seditious charges, he continued to publish his paper and the company of typographers continued their dramatic performances, with popular support.

   Almost a hundred years later, the same incident came close to being duplicated after **Eight Men Speak,** a controversial production by the Workers' Theatre of Toronto, was banned. In a protest meeting against this action, one of the actors, A. E. Smith, was arrested on charges of sedition. His later acquittal was regarded as a vindication of free speech in Canada.

2. Amateur theatre groups formed in Canada as an alternative to the professional foreign touring companies which dominated the country from the nineteenth century. Little Theatre flourished in the twenties, especially in Toronto after the completing of Hart House Theatre in 1919. A united attempt to create a national Canadian drama came in October 1932 when Lord Bessborough, the Governor General, officially formed the Dominion Drama Festival.

3. **New Frontier,** described as a monthly magazine of literature and social criticism, was published in Toronto from April 1936 to October 1937. Many of the writers who had originally contributed to *Masses* reappeared with *New Frontier,* among them Jocelyn Moore, E. Cecil-Smith, Stanley Ryerson, Dorothy Livesay, Avrom and H. Francis. After the war a similar publication *New Frontiers* existed from the winter of 1952 to the summer of 1956, and many of the same people again made contributions. *New Frontiers* was edited by Margaret Fairley.

Propaganda for Democracy: John Grierson and Adult Education During the Second World War

Juliet Pollard

On 9 November 1917, two days after the Bolsheviks assumed power in Russia, Lenin declared, "Of all the arts, cinema is the most important."[1] This was a perceptive statement given the times. Lenin understood that the silent picture could overcome the great diversity in languages and cultures within the Soviet Union. His vision was instrumental in developing Russian cinema during the 1920s — cinema acclaimed by the world as art, but also cinema which harnessed the new media in the forefront of adult education.[2]

Although the provincial and federal governments in Canada failed to see the artistic merits of film, they were as quick as their Soviet counterparts to seize upon the media as an "instrument of propaganda." From the 1890s onward, movies were used to lure European immigrants to Canada. During the First World War, Canada experimented with film propaganda to maintain morale and imprint patriotic duty in the public mind. Successful wartime use of film led to promotion of trade and tourism via the screen in peacetime. All the provinces engaged in film-making activities at one time or another, and from its inauguration by the Conservatives in 1917 until its demise in 1941 at the hands of the Liberals, the Canadian Motion Picture Bureau serviced federal needs.[3]

During the Second World War the National Film Board (NFB) created a grand scheme to educate the people via the screen. For a brief time, a veritable pot-pourri of academics (mainly social scientists and educationalists), labor leaders, business spokesmen, and the Liberal government masked their differences in a co-operative venture to unite the Canadian workforce in the fight against fascism.[4] The man responsible for the films was John Grierson, a Scot, who considered himself first and foremost an adult educator. During the war years he held two complementary positions, one as Commissioner of the NFB, in 1939, and the other as General Manager of the Wartime Information Board (WIB), a position he assumed in 1943. The latter conducted secret public opinion surveys during the war, and the former translated the survey information into film productions. The two positions provided Grierson with the power to unite education policy and direct it to a single end.[5]

It was largely Grierson's vision of what wartime propaganda should be that filled the screens in union and farm halls, factories and schools on film circuits designed to create a nation-wide communications network. Grierson's family ties linked him to the working class, education, and reform movements; his wartime experiences as a telegrapher in the Royal Navy made him a member of the "angry generation"–discourteous, arrogant, and disillusioned with the establishment. While working on his M.A. at the University of Glasgow he was active in the "Clydeside Cult," the most humanistic of the socialists in the new Independent Labour Party of Scotland.[6] In America, on a Rockefeller Fellowship from 1924 to 1927, he changed his study of "yellow journalism" as a force shaping public opinion to film as a more powerful media to activate the masses.[7] All of these components cast a large shadow on the way Grierson saw the world and influenced his ideas on the direction Canada should take during the war and in the peace to follow.

In 1938, at the request of the Liberal government, Grierson came to Canada to survey the country's film needs. A year later, he drafted the National Film Board Act and in due course was appointed Commissioner of the new board.[8] As Commissioner he addressed many organizations, including the 1940 annual convention of the Canadian Association for Adult Education (CAAE) held at the Fort Garry Hotel in Winnipeg. According to E. A. Corbett, Director of the CAAE, Grierson articulated the faith of all adult educators:

> Education will come out of the school-room and the library, the literary circle, and the undergraduate conference. . . . It will go into the factory and the field, into the co-operatives of production and distribution. It will express itself not as thought or debate but as the positive action within the community of organized youth groups, women's groups and men's groups. One half of education, the stronger half, will lie in the organization of active citizenship; for there can be no concept of Planning without the concept of Participation.[9]

What linked Grierson to these Canadian educators was the growing recognition that adult education was a "vitalizing force in any movement toward the realization of social justice through democratic methods."[10] The Carnegie Foundation, established to fund "the cause of higher education," and the Rockefeller Foundation, whose objective was "to achieve concrete improvement in the condition of life," financed numerous studies in adult education in the United States, Canada, and Great Britain during the 1920s and '30s.

Both foundations argued that new means of communications had to be found to make humanistic values, knowledge of economics, and social problems an integral part of the daily lives of the public. To this end, the foundations moved into the fields of radio and film, which were perceived to be active media in moulding and shaping the social ideas and aesthetic standards of the masses.[11]

In Canada, B.C. teachers had been studying how to use film in their classrooms since 1920.[12] The University of Alberta's extension department could boast a film library of one hundred reels constantly in use on rural educational circuits throughout the province.[13] Yet, in 1916 when Harvard Professor Hugo Munsterberg wrote *The Film: A Psychological Study,* and experimented with audience manipulation, his pioneer work was largely ignored.[14] For most educators during the 1920s film was seen as a useful tool, an appendix to lectures. For a small group, however, whose interest lay in an improved democracy, the time was ripe to explore the potential of film to mould public opinion and promote dialogue.

John Grierson's contribution to this group was a report on cinema for the Rockefeller Foundation in which he suggested that film be used to formulate social change. He elaborated on this theme, carefully noting the "democratic" nature of the media in a series of articles published in 1926 in *Motion Picture News.* "The cinema," he wrote, "belongs to the people as no other social institution in the world before. It is the only genuinely democratic institution that has ever appeared on world wide scale."

The idea that film could be harnessed for the common good was not limited to the United States.[15] The Empire Marketing Board (EMP) in Britain, which publicly ascribed to fostering imperial unity through trade, hired Grierson in 1926 and allowed him to put his theories into practice under the guise of cultural and public relations. Grierson attracted young filmmakers, described as "left wing bourgeois," who joined him at the EMP, and moved with him to the General Post Office when the EMP ceased operations. In 1938, while Grierson was in Canada, they continued the task of "glorifying the working man" on film.[16] With the formation of the NFB, Grierson summoned his British film unit to Canada. Here, they replaced Canadian filmmakers when the Canadian Motion Picture Bureau folded and were largely responsible for the scripting and filming of movies Canadian workers saw.[17]

Mackenzie King and his cabinet knew that Grierson was working for the Imperial Relations Trust to set up a North American propaganda base to urge the United States and Canada into partnership with Britain if war should come. But they were apparently unaware or didn't care that Grierson and his filmmakers were regarded as communists by some English members of parliament. In Britain, the Conservative MPs failed to see why the British taxpayer should fund an image of the working man on the screen which differed greatly from their capitalist version.[18] In Canada, King and the Liberals endorsed such a vision. As Grierson once expressed it, "the Prime Minister [gave me] his personal backing and almost a blank cheque in support.''[19]

Grierson's film genre was the documentary. In a report to Mackenzie King entitled, "Propaganda and Education," he noted that the documentary, a word he coined, had not come from film people, but rather from his student days when he and others had come to believe that discussion alone was not enough, that it "hid from men's eyes that essential picture of the time in which the great economic and political forces were climbing into place on the horizon." What was needed, he said, was a medium which would both educate people in the complexity of their society and motivate them to action. Documentary, Grierson believed, could both observe the ordinary and discover the patterns which gave the ordinary significance for civil education.[20]

For the "propaganda maestro," as *MacLean's Magazine* once dubbed Grierson, propaganda and education were one.[21] Propaganda, he argued, was the necessary education in the circumstances of the times. If people were given a democratic interpretation, they would grasp the "true sense of their relationship to events." The documentary would serve the government by interpreting state information and securing the co-operation of the public. At the same time, the documentary would assist the educator in interpreting the nature of the community to students, provide issues for discussion, and promote action. The documentary linked governmental and educational needs, he told King, the first would provide the sponsorship, the second the audience.[22]

Grierson had been weaned on the Russian cinema of the twenties and shared the Tolstoyan view of art as activist. In his version, however, art was to be used "to see and say what is right and good and beautiful and hammer it out as the mold and pattern of men's actions."[23] He deliberately pushed aside artistic films in order to meet the enormous demand for NFB films during the war. But, since he was also influential in creating the demand, the need to produce thousands of movies was largely, though not exclusively, Grierson's personal perception of Canadian wartime film needs.

The filmmakers believed they were replacing the simple message of "patriotic duty" used in First World War films with a more sophisticated and complex view of the world. This new imaging of the world was carefully constructed by a group of handpicked employees Grierson gathered from all regions of the country to fill the ranks of the NFB and WIB. Grierson preferred a certain type of candidate: idealistic young men and women mostly under thirty who shared values and educational backgrounds similar to his own in the arts and social sciences. Thus, on the banks of the Ottawa River, day and night, filmmakers, who shocked conservative Ottawa and were dubbed by some locals as "bohemians" and by others as "the bunch of long-haired Reds on Sussex Street," mass-produced Canada's war films.[24] Essentially, they argued that winning the war had to be linked to the promise of a better peace than the Depression of the 1930s. The new message was education for active citizenship.

In one form or another, most of the films argued that farmers and industrial workers had power if they co-operated with government in the democratic process. Grierson confessed he could not get excited about the war effort *per se*, but rallied to the cause of using film to bring about an education which would activate workers to a revitalized democracy.[25] The film educators set out to turn the negative image of government which lingered from the Depression into a positive one by perpetrating the notion that "Democracy was on trial." They attempted to keep the "human stature in proper perspective," which meant that the war was shown as a "people's war" and "a midwife to a new social order."[26]

It was indeed a "war for minds and spirits," as the 1942 Vining Report on Canadian propaganda stated, but the new disguises in making propaganda contained many of the old messages of fear, hate, and duty used in the First World War dressed up in new costumes.[27] The "Huns" were as evil and barbaric as before, outmatched only by the "Japs" in some propaganda. Both images were used to generate fears about the future if democracy faltered. To spur greater productivity, Canadian workers were warned that the "Japs" and "Huns" had kept "the lights burning in their munition factories" during the Depression and that they would have to catch up and outmatch them in order to win the war.[28] Canadians were told, as they had been twenty-five years before, it was their "patriotic duty" to buy war bonds and support such good and necessary measures as rationing and wage and price controls.

The most potent propaganda films produced by the NFB were for commercial distribution. These films comprised two major series, *The World in Action* and *Canada Carries On,* which were produced at the rate of one a month and distributed by Columbia Pictures in Canada and by United Artists and Fox Films internationally. New markets in countries like France opened up for these NFB films as the allies advanced and the Germans retreated. Grierson himself produced *The World in Action* and the deep and sonorous voice of Lorne Greene narrated both series. Both to meet the demands on the home front circuits and, more importantly, because they were the best propaganda the Board produced, some of these commercial films were converted to 16 mm stock.

Many of the NFB's films, however, were non-theatrical, low budget, kodachrome, 16 mm shorts. The relevance of these films was not that they were great and even good, but that they were produced as "political necessities" to influence farmers and factory workers on subjects like citizenship, social change, and the war effort. Educationalists loved such governmental films and equated them with a "free handout." Some of these non-theatrical shorts also found international distribution through the British Commonwealth and Canadian embassies, but the primary function of such pictures was to link rural and urban workers in a united production team for the war effort.[29]

The non-theatrical circuits used for such films were orchestrated as much by the Wartime Information Board as they were by the NFB. The WIB aimed at improving morale, production, and consumer education. To this end, the "Publicity Jamboree," as the WIB was known, used an arsenal of weapons which included confidential surveys of public opinions on a wide range of topical issues, information briefs and bulletins, reference papers, statistical analysis, weekly press releases, newspaper clippings from Canada and abroad, the monitoring of enemy broadcasts, and a monthly publication, *Canada at War*.[30] NFB films were only one part of this massive blitz of wartime propaganda, but they often launched various campaigns Grierson inaugurated at the WIB.

One of the major problems faced by the WIB and the NFB was how to reach farm labor with wartime propaganda. The importance of reaching this labor force was clear — in 1940, the nation's economy was still largely an agricultural one, employing a considerable proportion of the work force.[31] In 1946, the average number of farmers, exclusive of their paid and unpaid employees, was 679 000.[32] Moreover, manpower shortage on the farm during haying and harvesting season caused by an exodus of farm labor to the armed forces and war industries resulted in direct appeals for industrial workers assistance. Messages such as "Be a Farm Commando: We Can't Fight if We Don't Eat!", which suggested that industrial workers "lay down their tools" and make "raids" into the country for a half day of farming, appeared in *The Labour Review* and tried to link industrial and farm workers in a unified production effort.[33]

Central to the problem of communications with farm labor was that over half the Canadian population, including most farmers, still lived in rural areas, many in sparsely settled regions, some without electricity or radio service.[34] Then there was the other problem of ensuring loyalty and productivity among those of "varied racial origins," especially those in the large farming communities of German and Ukrainian origin on the Prairies, who "above all had to be reached."[35] The rural film circuits were established to meet these concerns. A variety of film circuits established mainly by university extension departments during the 1920s and '30s were already in place.[36] The task at hand was to weld these local and provincial circuits into a coordinated national network.

It was Donald Buchanan — assisted by grassroots adult educators — who laid the groundwork for non-theatrical distribution throughout rural Canada. Buchanan, the son of Senator W. A. Buchanan, had founded and was the Secretary-Treasurer of the National Film Society. In 1937, with funding from the Carnegie Institute, he had written a "Report on Educational and Cultural Films in Canada" and had organized the distribution system for the National Film Society. His work on both these projects, plus his family connections, placed him in a strategic position to organize the whole film circuit from Ottawa.

The project began in January 1942 with a phone call to Dr Gordon Shrum, at that time Director of the University of B.C. Extension Department, and went from there. Donald Cameron, Director of the Extension Department at the University of Alberta and on the Directorate of the NFB, became regional agent for Alberta. In Saskatchewan, Morley Toombs, head of the newly formed Film Branch of the Provincial Department of Education accepted a similar position as did Watson Thomson, Director of the Adult Education Division of the University of Manitoba, and so on until the entire country had been canvassed.[37] As Buchanan put it:

> Willing helpers were found among those many Canadians who for years had wanted to use motion picture as an instrument of civic instruction; some were on the staffs of our universities, others were connected with the provincial departments of education. By telephone, some half-dozen of these enthusiasts were immediately appointed as regional agents for the project, and by telephone, too, they were given instructions as to what type of projectionist to hire, and in general how to conduct organization in the field.[38]

Adult educators like E. A. Corbett, Thomson, and Stan Rands, who assisted Thomson, believed that Grierson had chosen adult education organizations to sponsor film circuits because he recognized that war-time efforts, though important, were short run. By establishing a national network of rural (and later industrial and trade union) circuits, Canada was laying the basis for their perpetual use in communities, both to promote national unity and to stimulate action on community problems. For Grierson, and the educational radicals, it was

> integral to the democratic idea that constructive action shall bubble up all over the place. Initiative must be not only central but local. By the mere acceptance of democracy we have taken upon ourselves the privilege and duty of individual creative citizenship and we must organize all communications which will serve to maintain it. . . . And, in the process of creating our democratic system of communcations, in bridging the gaps between citizen and community, citizen and specialist, specialist and specialist, we shall find we have in the ordinary course of honest endeavour made the picture of democracy we are seeking.[39]

By April, Buchanan had forty travelling theatres using 16mm portable projectors from Vancouver Island to Nova Scotia. He had enlisted the support of the Canadian Council of Education for Citizenship, eight provincial departments of education, and seven university extension departments. In Ontario, he pursuaded the Ontario Agricultural College, the Department of Extension at Queen's University, the Community Life Training Institute at Barrie, and the Educational Division of the United Farmers of Ontario to take the movies to that province's farmers and rural workers. Grierson insisted that NFB films be made in both French and English. In keeping with this bilingual policy, French-speaking projectionists were hired not only in Quebec, but for some circuits in Alberta and New Brunswick as well.

The plan was simple. The Regional agents hired projectionists to tour their provinces on a designated circuit. The Wartime Information Board agreed to pay them a salary of $130 a month, seven cents a mile for their cars and travelling expenses. In most cases, the NFB supplied a projector, screen, and a one- to three-hour program of films which they routed to about twenty places in their province per month. In each community a committee was formed to arrange a hall and conduct publicity. Local radio stations promoted the films and reminded the audiences of time and place of viewing. Thus the "Lash Circuit," named after Herbert Lash, Director of the WIB before Grierson, came into being.[40]

By the end of 1942, the Maritimes had organized seven circuits, Central Canada had twelve, and in the West, there were twenty-four travelling projectionists. In addition, the Canadian Council for Citizenship had forty-three travelling theatres which included speakers who gave a few remarks at each showing. Even the RCMP organized a few circuits and Alberta's University Extension provided several supplementary circuits operated by the United Grain Growers. In Saskatchewan and Manitoba, the Wheat Pool maintained circuits under the program.[41]

How successful were adult educators in using film to stimulate action on community problems and promote national unity and the war effort? Certainly Manitoba succeeded in integrating film into its program of rural animation. Thomson and Rands, who was appointed as Western Regional Director of Film Circuits in the spring of 1943, hired sympathetic, progressive-minded projectionists like George LeBeau, Will Dougall, and Jack Wilson. Rands collaborated with the Manitoba Federation of Agriculture, the provincial organizer of the Farm Radio Forum, linking film with their radio listening-group program. Rands also succeeded in establishing film forums and study groups as regular features of monthly meetings in numerous Manitoban communities. By the end of 1944 Watson Thomson believed that the local film committees were developing into effective community councils. Film circuit work in Manitoba had borne fruit, he thought, as communities established credit unions, hospital units, and smaller projects as a result of film showings and discussions.[42]

Manitoba was, perhaps, an exception to the general Canadian pattern. The circuits were decentralized and bore the stamp of indigenous leadership. For there is some evidence that the lofty ideal of using film as a stimulus for social action was often thwarted by the realities of the rural situation. Although Manitoba showed films for children in the daytime, and films for adults in the evening, in other regions film showings became family affairs. In Quebec, for example, the total monthly film circuit attendance was 24 000 adults and 22 000 children.[43] Where large numbers of children attended film showings, film as precursor to serious discussion was unrealistic. Further, initially there were not enough NFB films to meet the demand and foreign films were im-

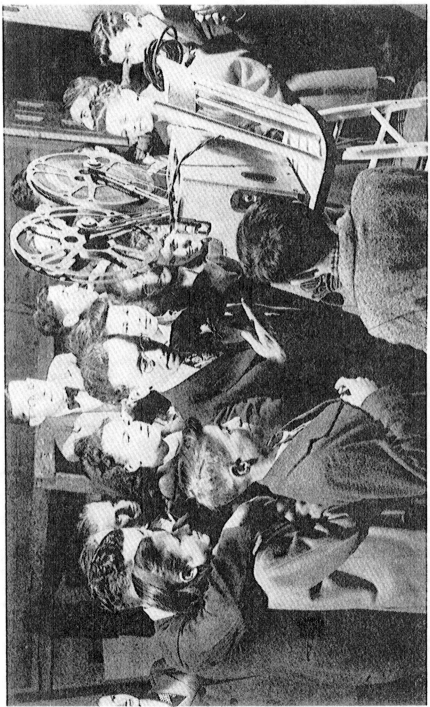

Rural circuit showing, National Film Board of Canada, Mont Rolland, Quebec, May 1946.   National Archives Canada/NA-144855

ported and shown. As the nature of the audience became clear, a kind of "family package" was prepared. One or two war propaganda films were included on every program, but so too were entertainment films, such as a short with Bing Crosby or other notables of the time or a Disney film, and often one of the NFB sing along series, *Chant Populaires* on French circuits, *Let's All Sing Together* on the English ones.[44]

Some projectionists did initiate film forums (approximately 25 percent of all circuits had film forums by the Spring of 1943), but others were more like travelling showmen rather than community animators. They organized talent contests, ran square dances, or other entertainment along with the films. At their best, projectionists integrated ethnic cultural activities into their programs. The shows were free, but often merged with other wartime activities such as collecting funds for the Red Cross or promoting such things as war savings stamps. To the women fell the task of baking and cooking for suppers after the screenings. In particular, the Women's Institute, the Imperial Order Daughters of the Empire, and the Home Makers' Clubs took an active part in organizing social hours.[45]

The experiences of the projectionists in the 1940s reveal a persistence of lifestyles in the rural communities dating from the 1920s, when university extension people made their way on similar circuits, encountered similar difficulties, and shared similar forms of community hospitality.[46] In some areas there was no electricity or no 110 volt AC current, so that gasoline-operated generators had to be carried. In other regions the projectionist's cars couldn't get through in the mud of spring or the snow of winter. Trains, sleds, toboggans, and canoes were sometimes employed. In certain Mennonite and Ukrainian districts, the old folks and youngers claimed they had never seen a film before. In Lac St. Jean, Quebec, over 90 percent of the audience had never heard a sound film. Similar stories were told throughout each region of Canada.[47]

Labor shortages created by the war meant that many of the projectionists were poorly educated men, unable to initiate or articulate educational activism in the communities. Furthermore, even dedicated projectionists had to work with community committees made up of the local establishment whose "status quo" thinking opposed their notions of social change. As a job, being a projectionist had limited appeal. Whatever rewards it offered had to be measured against living out of a suitcase during severe wartime restrictions on travel, gas, and food rationing. Then there was the difficulty in obtaining car parts, to say nothing of "camping out" in the rigors of hostile climates.[48]

The WIB's need to reach farm labor was mirrored in its concerns about industrial labor, in particular with workers' morale and productivity. The Canadian work force engaged over one million men and women in wartime industry, production tripled, and organized labor made significant gains, but not without struggles. The year 1943 proved to be a critical one in labor unrest and, not surprisingly, marked the introduction of the industrial film circuits.[49]

In that year there were more strikes than at any time since 1919, several in key wartime industries such as coal and steel.[50] An order-in-council in December 1940 established wages at 1926-29 levels, considered to be a normal period of economic activity. Prices were also controlled. This meant that in 1941, nearly 40 percent of the work force was earning less than $450 a year, while at the same time these meagre earnings were eroded by a 20 percent inflation rate. Big business interests, overrepresented in the "dollar a year" men who held key governmental wartime positions, combined in a concentrated effort to keep wages down and resist labor's lobby for the right to collective bargaining and a more equitable wage structure.[51] Delegates to the second annual convention of the Canadian Congress of Labour in 1941 were told:

> It is more important . . . to defeat Hitler and his gangsters than to bring the most tyrannical and reactionary employer in Canada to his knees. Action against him can wait, but Hitler won't wait, and there can be no peace or hope for anyone in the world until Hitler is beaten and Germany disarmed . . . both employers and workers . . . should cooperate to promote the national welfare . . .[52]

While officially subscribing to co-operation with government, however, short strikes by unions for better pay and recognition persisted. In 1943, after 13 500 striking workers halted steel production, the Liberals, fearful of losing labor's support to the CCF, made concessions. For the workers there were changes in wage controls, a new minimum wage, and legislation the following year giving workers the right to collective bargaining. For the Liberal party, there was a move to the left and a new "Industry and Humanity" labor policy. There was also a stepped up propaganda campaign by the WIB to appease workers.[53]

The Industrial Film Circuits, established in 1943 when Grierson assumed the position of General Manager of the WIB, were instrumental in carrying out government propaganda. For example, a request for a morale-building program from the Coal Labour Supply Committee, which had just experienced strikes in Alberta and B.C., led to one film, three radio broadcasts, poster and photo displays, and articles on coal mining circulated to magazines and newspapers. The film, *Coal Face Canada* (1943), which cost the Department of Labour $18 000, was made as part of the *Canada Carries On* series and seen in commercial theatres as well as on the industrial circuit in thirty-seven coal mining regions. The film was pro-union, but pushed the morale building theme, "We the Miners Fight With Coal!"[54]

Grierson's views of labor relations distinguished him from his peers who knew about Keynesian economics but were unable to recognize any interest other than materialistic ones on the part of labor.[55] He argued that industrial unrest had to do with workers' status. To create good industrial morale, the WIB would have to produce propaganda which dealt with health, transportation, safety, nutrition, taxation, in short, all those things which made up the workers' lives. Grierson also supported the expansion of labor-management committees. These enjoyed support from both labor as an outlet for their grievances and business because, as C. D. Howe, Minister of Munitions and Supply, phrased it, they "increased the output of war goods to lower costs and improve efficiency."[56]

Gordon Adamson of the NFB, who had established the Trade Union Film Circuit in 1942, was also made responsible for the Industrial Film Circuit. The essential difference between the two circuits was that the former focussed on specific needs of trade unionists, while the latter was concerned with various agencies engaged in wartime production who wanted to get messages to the workers. By 1944, these "message senders" included the Wartime Price and Trade Board, Munitions and Supply, the Department of Labour, the National War Service; in total, some sixty-six representatives of government business and labor were involved.

The Industrial Film Circuit operated in a similar fashion to the rural film circuits — itinerant projectionists were hired and given the responsibility for a number of factory showings each month. One film was made every thirty days to provide eleven programs a year. Although initially regarded as the urban counterpart to the rural circuits, the Industrial Circuits came to include rural showings in logging camps, saw mills, and the like. Here the projectionists encountered many of the same difficulties in making their way to these "wilderness factories" as their rural counterparts. The industrial films also played to packed audiences of civil servants such as post office and national selective service workers. The audiences were so diversified that "the only common factor in industrial wartime film shows across Canada," according to projectionists, "was that the acoustics were unbelievably bad in each and every situation."[57]

Projectionists' hours were irregular. Commonly, they held three or four shows nightly, including screenings at 2:00 a.m. when the night shift came off work. Unlike the leisurely and social two- or three-hour program on rural circuits, industrial film showings in urban centres were only twenty or thirty minutes in length, designed to catch the workers on their free time before or after shifts, or during lunch or supper breaks. Within the plant, labor-management committees, where they existed, arranged the showings. Often the employer allowed part of the program on company time, which in effect meant the workers were held captive to film propaganda whether they liked it or not. The films dealt with subjects like fire prevention, safety in the plant, Victory Loans, recruiting, and, of course, workers in the war effort. The come-on was often a cartoon or comedy short. Given the briefness of such viewings in the midst of factory production, the lack of time for follow-up discussion, to say nothing of the lack of a "free" forum without employers present, and the poor acoustics, it is questionable if much learning took place in most wartime factories. Under such circumstances, film as agent of social change was nullified and perhaps thwarted by workers who resented the intrusion of war propaganda at their place of work and on their freetime.[58]

In terms of audiences, the Industrial Film Circuit with its average monthly attendance of 400 000 was far more significant than the Trade Union Film Circuit with its audiences of 40 000 a month, but the smaller circuit was the more important as an adult education program for workers.[59] If the audiences could have been switched, then significant changes in the labor movement might have occurred. But, since the steady growth in unionism during the war still only captured 15.9 percent of the population in 1944, the trade union programs only reached a small proportion of industrial workers.[60]

The executive of the Trade Union Circuit who organized the educational film programs was composed of Gordon Adamson and Stanley Hawes of the NFB, Art Hemming, Assistant Secretary for the Trade and Labour Congress, Norman Dowd, Executive Secretary of the Canadian Congress of Labour, and Drummond Wren, General Secretary for the Workers' Educational Association (WEA).[61]

Of these, Drummond Wren and the Workers' Educational Association, the "politically neutral" affiliation of academic tutors and worker students operating from the University of Toronto, played a key role. In 1937, the Association inaugurated the WEA *Radio Forum*, which was recast in 1941 as a prime time Saturday night CBC series, the *National Labour Forum*. The *Forum* was something of a coup for Drummond Wren since he was instrumental in bringing the two rival labor congresses together on programs mainly scripted by the Association.[62] Wren played much the same role with the Trade Union Film Circuit a year later, when the Trades and Labour Congress (TLC) and Canadian Congress of Labour (CCL) jointly designed film programs for workers. Unlike the *National Labour Forum,* however, which the WEA was forced to withdraw from when anti-labor sentiments became apparent in the programs, the Trade Union Film Circuit lasted until 1945 and, according to Art Hemming of the TLC, was not pressured by government or private industry in choosing the films for the circuits.[63]

Ideally, both the TLC and CCL preferred to educate their own members themselves, but given the wartime circumstances, the WEA provided a viable alternative. In 1941, the CCL unanimously adopted a report from their Committee on Education and Publicity which called for worker's study groups, CCL publications, and radio advertisements in order to educate members and attract new ones "to the proper appreciation of . . . trade unionism." The Congress urged all its affiliate unions to join the WEA or other "bona fide" adult education organizations and form study groups. It decided to use radio to keep the public fully informed on organized labor's point of view on the war and "to counteract the propaganda of organized big business."[64]

During the depression, the WEA had done research on workers' rights and now, in wartime, it was translated into film subjects — labor laws, the duties of shop stewards, the responsibilities of union members, and so on.[65] At the same time, the Department of Labour had films made for the circuit which emphasized its particular interests. For example, after 1943, the Department was keen on encouraging the formation of labor–management production committees, and had several films made to convince remaining skeptics in the union movement of their value. The Trade Union Circuit was therefore in the precarious position of promoting government labor policies while at the same time encouraging the trade union movement.[66]

Instead of films being imposed on workers as on the Industrial Circuits, in the Trade Union Circuits it was customary to enlist the aid of the local trade and labour council and top union management in establishing the network, which in turn worked through regional supervisors. Some of the projectionists served both the trade union and the industrial circuits, but in addition to these NFB projectionists, others were recruited through the International Alliance of Technical Stage Employees and paid $4 a showing. In Toronto, a projectionist might hold twenty-five to thirty screenings a month, usually at the end of the union business meeting. "When the meeting was over," recalled one projectionist, the little peephole in the door "would move to one side, an eye would appear and the door would be opened to admit me, with my projector, screen and films into the union hall."[67]

The Trade Union Film Circuit like the rural circuits made use of a new adult education device — the discussion trailer. These were five-minute films shown at the end of the feature film where notables, such as the trade union circuit executive, were shown sitting around a table debating the issues raised in the film. After the trailer, the audience was invited to participate in a similar debate of their own. In some cases these took the form of panel or round table forums, but the intention in each case was always the same: to facilitate discussion and "constructive action." The success of these trailers as a "teaching method" varied. To further counter the persistent problem in getting workers to debate, the WEA published a study guide series entitled *Films for Freedom* which laid out what was to be learned from each film program, and public libraries often co-operated by setting aside books relevant to the films for workers to study.[68]

While each circuit had films produced for their specific audience, in reality, film shortages meant many of the films seen by farm laborers were also viewed by industrial workers. Discounting the major war propaganda series, the non-theatrical films made for the circuits roughly divided into seven categories — agriculture, health, education, social planning, ethnographic subject, art films, and newsreels which dealt with the progress of Canada's armed forces overseas. They included titles like *Wartime Housing, Farm Front, Hands for the Harvest, Dollar Dance, The Plot Thickens, Supper's Ready, Coal for Canada, National Income, How Prices Rise, Price Controls and Rationing, Land of Quebec: Trans-Canada Express, People of the Potlatch, Iceland on the Prairies, Now the Peace, Return of the Veterans to Industry,* and *Diamond Jubilee Convention,* which viewed the TLC Labour Convention in Toronto in 1945 and was shown to union members and their families across Canada. The films included themes like unemployment insurance in *A Man and His Job,* women at work in *Night Shift,* credit unions in *The People's Bank,* daycare for children of factory workers in *Before They Are Six,* and the future of young people in one of the most controversial films the NFB made, *Battle Is Their Birthright.* [69]

One of the chief complaints of those involved with the Trade Union Circuit was the lack of films available on subjects conducive to union members. To fill this gap, American movies such as *The Valley of the Tennessee* were used. In this instance, the co-operative efforts of the U.S. government and the poverty stricken people of Tennessee to rehabilitate the Valley promoted the idea that Canadian labor should embrace government efforts to undertake similar rural electrification via power development on the St Lawrence, to make farmers' lives easier and create new jobs for industrial workers. [70]

Towards the end of the war, films were aimed at giving workers a crash course on the causes of inflation. For example, *A Story with Two Endings,* designed for the Trade Union Circuit, portrayed two routes workers might take after the war and left the decision as to which was the better one up to them. In fact, however, the decision was not left up to them. Ending one showed that workers' greed for consumer goods and business desires for fantastic profits had led to the depression. By contrast, ending two encouraged workers to buy only what they needed, support continued rationing, settle for "fair wages" rather than striking, and support government postwar economic policies. It argued that such means would preserve economic security in Canada. [71]

Running at cross purposes to the aims of the Trade Union Film Circuit in promoting unionism and social change was the largest and most successful circuit, the Volunteer Projection Services. Ann Macdonnell was hired by Grierson to organize screenings among the thousands of Canadians who were neither farmers nor factory workers. She gathered the support of voluntary organizations and established business groups like the Junior Board of Trade and the Chamber of Commerce, set up training programs for projectionists and depositories, usually in public libraries, for NFB films. The local organizations determined their own programs and audiences. Trained projectionists, many of them women, in turn trained others so that towards the end of the war there were 660 voluntary film circuits in Canada. [72]

This service continued throughout the fifties long after the Trade Union and Industrial circuits ceased operations and rural circuits had been drastically reduced to a few projectionists operating in extremely remote areas of Canada. [73] The Voluntary Projection Service completed the national wartime communication system which would both gauge the pulse of the country and spread government propaganda. It responded to Grierson's and other adult educationalists' mandate that social change begin at the grassroots, but what often passed for "activism" in the community were such things as a couple of families remodelling their kitchens after seeing an NFB film which touched on the subject.[74] Hardly the stuff Grierson had in mind for recasting a democratic society in Canada!

There is no precise way to measure the impact of the film circuits on the Canadian populace. They were only a part, and a small part at that, of a larger and more complex system of wartime propaganda which subjected workers to a bombardment of messages. Trade-offs were involved. NFB films motivated some individuals and turned others off. Undoubtedly, community gatherings, be they rural, factory, or union, were important to home front morale during the war years. Judging from the subjects presented, the films could heighten workers' awareness of their country, their job, their union, and the war effort. For new Canadians, unreachable through the English or French press, the films helped them understand Canada's war aims.

By 1940, film, a novel approach to propaganda in First World War, had proven itself as a major weapon in the war for men's minds. All the major powers had propaganda agencies of one sort or another; that Canada would follow suit is not surprising. What was amazing was that the Liberal government would put so much faith and entrust so much responsibility for wartime propaganda to John Grierson, a foreigner and socialist adult educator. The Canadian Motion Picture Bureau might have filled Canada's propaganda film needs, but the Canadian mentality reflected itself in a colonial preference for a Britisher who was perceived to be more capable than Canadians already engaged in such work. As Grierson phrased it, "The curious thing is that the (information) services on the whole has [sic] been very good. It's just that the Canadians have not thought so."[75]

With Grierson at the helm, the NFB grew from a small organization of forty, to a large bureaucracy employing over eight hundred people by the end of the war.[76] Despite the expense involved in this creation, Grierson's master plan for film education to motivate Canadians towards a more egalitarian and co-operative society was never realized. Making films for workers on farm and in factory brought together the full complement of those in the forefront of adult education throughout the country in a way no force short of war could have done. Film offered the tantalizing possibility of communication with whole segments of the population never before reached. Community educators believed that the film circuits could "be a medium in an adult education, social reconstruction movement that (would) both express 'the people' and give leadership to them."[77] In short, the NFB film circuits were a great experiment to mould and shape the minds of men and women in Canada. Grierson and other educationalists were quick to seize the opportunity, but it didn't work.

The educational radicals had sought to utilize film circuits as an "authentic instrument of the democratic process."[78] But they confronted many barriers, not the least of which was their own idealism and hope for "co-operative movement, community planning, and collective action from below.''[79] In rural settings, community educators made some headway with limited pedagogical resources and conservative audiences. On the industrial circuits there was often little opportunity for laborers to escape the "eternal, earnest, plodding voice of the narrator" and the propaganda in the films.[80] On the Trade Union Film Circuits, the impression is left that much that passed for education was a case of preaching to the already converted. By 1945, the Trade Union Film executive thought that the amount of money being spent on films for workers was not producing the desired results. A promotion campaign was started to attract more industrial laborers.[81]

Ironically, as the cold war loomed, Drummond Wren and John Grierson, the "loyal" supporters of democracy, were accused of being communists, as were Watson Thomson and Stan Rands. These charges destroyed the WEA and crippled the NFB's operations for a time.[82] Wren and Grierson resigned, but their experiments with film in workers' education continued throughout the 1950s and flowered again in the 1960s when many of the "new" ideas in progressive education echoed those of John Grierson twenty years earlier. Grierson best summed up what he and films for rural and industrial workers were all about:

> I have been a propagandist all my working life because I have believed that we needed to do our democratic mind over if we were going to save democracy. I have believed that in education was the heart of the matter, but that education needed to be revolutionized altogether if it was to become the instrument of revolutionized democracy I was thinking of. . . . I have had to pretend to a whole lot of powers I didn't have in running my education revolution. I have had to be a creative worker and a civil servant and a promoter and an organizer and a critic and a teacher of the youth. . . . I have had to find the millions, often from people I dared not tell fully what I was after lest it would seem pretentious. . . . This was always a difficult situation, for . . . it is only if the State is fighting for democracy that it has a dog's chance of coming through.[82]

Footnotes

1. Peter Cowie, ed., *A Concise History of Cinema*, Vol. I (New York: A. S. Barnes Company, 1971), p. 137.

2. Two days after the establishment of Soviet power the first film organization was founded as a unit under the Minister of Education, the playwright Lunacharsky. Late in 1917, the film unit opened a film training school in Leningrad and in 1918-19, a second school in Moscow. On 27 August 1919, the motion picture industry was nationalized. See "Cinema," *Thirty Years of the*

Soviet State, 1917-1947 (Moscow: Foreign Language Publishing, 1947), p. 1; Jay Leyda, *Kino: A History of Russian and Soviet Film* (London: George Allan and Unwin Ltd., 1960), p. 124. During the Second World War, Soviet factories organized collective visits of their workers to propaganda films. The slogan above the screen read: "The World's Theatre is the Most Valuable Form of Political Propaganda," See Alexander Wirth, "Political Films First in Russia," *Saturday Night*, 5 October 1946, p. 17.

3. Juliet Pollard, "Government Bureaucracy in Action: A History of Cinema in Canada, 1896-1941," unpublished M.A. thesis, UBC, 1979, pp. 1-137.

4. The composition of the wartime staffs of the NFB and WIB are discussed in Marjorie McKay, "History of the National Film Board of Canada," unpublished manuscript, NFB, 5 August 1964, p. 49, and William R. Young, "Academics and Social Scientists Versus the Press: The Policies of the Bureau of Public Information and the Wartime Information Board, 1939 to 1945," *CHA Historical Papers*, 1978, pp. 217-39.

5. Gary Evans, *John Grierson and the National Film Board: The Politics of Wartime Propaganda* (Toronto: University of Toronto Press, 1984), p. 89.

6. For a discussion on Grierson's growing up, wartime, and university experience, see Forsyth Hardy, *John Grierson: A Documentary Biography* (London: Faber and Faber, 1979), pp. 11-31.

7. Walter Lippman, author of the widely read *Public Opinion* (1922), personally instigated Grierson's departure from studying yellow journalism to documenting the changing character of society by examining the box-office records of successful and unsuccessful films. This study took Grierson to Hollywood where he increasingly became involved with film production. See John Grierson, *Grierson on Documentary* (New York: Praeger Publishers, 1971), pp. 260-61; Jack C. Ellis, "The Young Grierson in America," *Cinema Journal*, Vol. VIII, No. 1, Fall 1968, pp. 12-21; Hardy, *John Grierson*, p. 36.

8. Grierson had previously visited Canada while a student in the United States and again in 1931 as spokesman for the Empire Marketing Board and had established connections in the Dominion. His 1938 visits, one in May and another in November, were arranged by Vincent Massey, Canadian High Commissioner in London, his first secretary, Lester Pearson, and his staff secretary, Ross McLean, and the National Film Society of Canada. For more information on his visit and subsequent creation of the NFB, see Hardy, *John Grierson*, pp. 90-108; Evans, *John Grierson and the National Film Board*, pp. 51-56; Clifford James, "The National Film Board of Canada: Its Task of Communications," unpublished Ph.D. thesis, Ohio State University, 1968, pp. 49-53; Canada, Parliament, *Debates of the House of Commons*, "National Film Board" (Ottawa: King's Printer, 1939); Canada, Parliament, *Debates of the Senate*, "National Film Bill" (Ottawa: King's Printer, 1939), pp. 101-105.

9. E. A. Corbett, "But, Is It Education?", *Queen's Quarterly*, Vol. 48 (1941), p. 400.

10. E. A. Corbett, "The Canadians March," *Adult Learning*, September–October, 1939, p. 12.

11. Between 1937 and 1941, for example, twenty-seven studies on Adult Education were published in the U.S. under the title *The Social Significance of Adult Education*, a project funded by the Carnegie Institute and the American Association of Adult Education. Both the Carnegie and Rockefeller Foundations also funded early works in public surveying and radio forums which eventually led to *The Voice of America* during the war. They were less successful in their attempts to penetrate the Hollywood theatrical film chains with educational movies. For information on the Foundations' goals and interest in adult education, see Raymond Fosdick, *The Story of the Rockefeller Foundation* (New York: Harper and Brothers, 1952), pp. 245-49; James Adams, *Frontiers of Democracy: A Study of Adult Education in a Democracy* (New York: Charles Scribner's Sons, 1944), pp. ix, 23; Corbett, "But, Is It Education?", p. 396; Henry James, "The T.I.A.A. and Canadian Universities," *National Conference of Canadian Universities*, Toronto, June 1942, pp. 42-43.

12. "Teachers to Learn Teaching by Movies," *Victoria Daily Times*, 9 July 1920, p. 8.

13. Corbett, "But, Is It Education?", p. 390.

14. Mason, "Teaching by the Movies," *The Outlook*, December 1914, p. 964; Hugo Munsterberg, *The Film: A Psychological Study* (New York: Dover Publications, Inc., 1970), pp. v-xv.

15. In 1929, the British Institute of Adult Education commissioned a report on education and film which was published as *The Film in National Life* (1932). This led to the establishment of the British Film Institute in 1933 to encourage the use of cinema for entertainment and instruction. Two years later, the National Film Society of Canada was founded with similar goals. Thomas Kelly, *A History of Adult Education in Great Britain* (Liverpool: Liverpool University Press, 1962), p. 317.

16. Evans, pp. 34, 46, 47, 113; James, "The National Film Board of Canada," pp. 67-68.

17. Evans, pp. 76-82; Pollard, "Governmental Bureaucracy in Action," pp. 102-22; Charles Backhouse, *The Canadian Government Motion Picture Bureau, 1917-1941* (Ottawa: Canadian Film Institute, 1974).

18. Hardy, p. 88; Evans, pp. 47, 53.

19. Jack Ellis, "Grierson's First Years at the NFB," *Canadian Film Reader*, edited by S. Felman and J. Nelson (Toronto: Peter Martin Associates Ltd., 1977), p. 38.

20. John Grierson, "Propaganda and Education," W. L. Mackenzie King Papers, PAC, MG 26, J1, Volume 341, pp. 12-13.

21. James, p. 122.

22. Grierson, "Propaganda and Education," pp. 13-14.

23. James, pp. 82-83.

24. Hugh L. Keenleyside, "Bureaucrats with Cameras," *Canada Digest*, Vol. 2, No. 7, 1946, p. 11; McKay, "History of the National Film Board of Canada," p. 49.

25. Hardy, p. 131; Grierson, "Propaganda and Education," p. 18.

26. Donald Buchanan, "The Projection of Canada," *University of Toronto Quarterly*, Vol. 13, 1943-1944, p. 302; "Motion Pictures as a Spearhead," *Food for Thought*, Vol. IV, No. 5, January 1944, pp. 4-7; Evans, p. 108.

27. For a discussion on the Vining Report, see Evans, p. 87.

28. For example, see "Let No Trace of the Huns Remain!" *The Labour Review*, May 1944, p. 207, or NFB films *The Mast of Nippon* (1942) — part of the series *The World in Action*, which depicted the "japs" as the most vile "race" on earth.

29. Peter Morris, ed. *The National Film Board of Canada: The War Years* (Canadian Film Institute, 1971), pp. 6, 20, 27; Donald Buchanan, "The National Film Board," *Maritime Art*, October 1941–August 1943, pp. 77-78, 108; Graham McInnes, "Canada Carries On," *MacLean's Magazine*, 15 March 1941, pp. 18-19, 26. A list of foreign non-theatrical distribution is given in Evans, p. 301.

30. Evans, pp. 98-109, 111-12, 292-94.

31. Daniel Coates, "Organized Labour and Politics in Canada: The Development of a National Labour Code," unpublished Ph.D. thesis, Cornell University, August 1973, pp. 28-29.

32. "Farmers and Labour," *Labour Research*, July–September, 1962, p. 1.

33. To meet farm labor shortages women and children twelve years of age and older were employed, see "Program for Relieving Farm Labour Shortage in Ontario," *Labour Gazette*, Vol. 43, 1943, pp. 40-43. The advertisement "Be A Farm Commando" was sponsored by the Dominion–Provincial Committee on Farm Labour, see *The Labour Review*, July 1943.

34. McKay, p. 33.

35. Donald Buchanan, "Experiment in Community Education," *Saturday Night*, 30 May 1942, p. 27; "Canadian Movies Promote Citizenship," *Canadian Geographical Journal*, Vol. XXVIII, March 1944, pp. 120-29.

36. C. W. Gray, *Movies for the People: The Story of the National Film Board's Unique Distribution System* (NFB Publication, 1973), p. 39; Corbett "But, Is It Education?", pp. 391-96; E. A. Corbett, "Adult Education," *Thirteenth National Conference of Canadian Universities*, Ottawa, 22-24 May 1929, pp. 57-59; Evans, p. 147.

37. Gray, *Movies for the People*, p. 40.

38. Buchanan, "Canadian Movies Promote Citizenship," p. 121.

39. John Grierson, "Searchlight on Democracy," *Food for Thought*, April 1944, p. 4. See also Michael R. Welton, " 'To Be and Build the Glorious World': The Educational Thought and Practice of Watson Thomson, 1899-1946," unpublished Ph.D. thesis, UBC, 1983, pp. 182-220, 291-98.

40. For further discussion on the formation of rural farm circuits, see Buchanan, "Experiment in Community Education," p. 21; McKay, pp. 34-40; Evans, pp. 148-151; Gray, pp. 38-49; R. Alex Sim, "Films for Farmers," *C.S.T.A. Review*, No. 36, March 1943.

41. Buchanan, "Experiment in Community Education," p. 21; Gray, pp. 40, 42.

42. Welton, "To Be and Build the Glorious World," pp. 182-220; 291-98; Welton interview with Stan Rands, 22 March 1985.

43. Evans, p. 150; McKay, p. 35.
44. Gray, pp. 42-43.
45. Buchanan, "Canadian Movies Promote Citizenship," pp. 122-26; McKay, p. 35; Evans, p. 150.
46. This comment is drawn from a comparison between the experience of extension educators outlined in Corbett, "But, Is It Education?", pp. 391-96; "Adult Education," pp. 57-59; and NFB projectionists given in Gray, pp. 42-49.
47. Buchanan, "Canadian Movies Promote Citizenship," pp. 121-25; "Experiment in Community Education," p. 21; Gray, p. 45; McKay, p. 35.
48. Gray, pp. 43-44.
49. Charles Lipton, *The Trade Union Movement of Canada* (Toronto: New Canada Press, 1978), p. 266.
50. H. C. Pentland, "A Study of the Changing Social, Economic and Political Background of the Canadian System of Industrial Relations," A Draft Study Prepared for the Task Force on Labour Relations, February 1968, p. 202.
51. Lipton, *The Trade Union Movement of Canada,* pp. 266-69; Coates, "Organized Labour and Politics in Canada," pp. 76, 92.
52. *The Canadian Congress of Labour: Proceedings of the Second Annual Convention,* Hamilton, Ontario, 8-12 September 1941, p. 13.
53. Coates, pp. 136-41; Laurel MacDowell, "The 1943 Steel Strike Against Wartime Wage Controls," *Labour/Le Travailleur,* Vol. 10, Autumn 1982, pp. 65-85.
54. Evans, pp. 126-27.
55. Pentland, pp. 194, 206.
56. Evans, pp. 97, 153. The first labor–management committees (LMC) were introduced in the aircraft industry in 1941. By 1943, there were more than six hundred of them. In that year government support was given to them and expansion encouraged. See W. Donald Wood, *The Current State of Labour–Management Co-operation in Canada,* Industrial Relations Centre, Queen's University, Kingston, Ontario, pp. 13-14. A good discussion on LMC is found in David Millar, " 'You Cannot Prevent Unrest . . .': Labour Policy in Practice, 1941-1943," unpublished paper, 1980, pp. 270-302. For C. D. Howe's views, see "Labour–Management Production Committees," *Labour Gazette,* October 1944, pp. 1464-65, or, "Have Production Committees a Future?", *The Labour Review,* December 1944, p. 369. The CCL urged the establishment of such committees in 1942. See *The Labour Gazette,* May 1942, pp. 507-508.
57. Gray, pp. 50-51; Evans, pp. 97-127, 196-97, 287.
58. Gray, pp. 50-52; James, pp. 91-99, McKay, p. 40, Evans, p. 151.
59. James, p. 97; A. E. Hemming, "Canada's National Film Board," *Trade and Labour Congress Journal,* September 1945, p. 35; Graham McInnes, "Canada: Producer of Films," *Queen's Quarterly,* Vol. LII, Summer 1945, p. 192.
60. Coates, p. 29. In 1941 there wre 462 000 union members in Canada; in 1944 there were 724 000.

61. Hemming, "Canada's National Film Board," p. 35.

62. See Ian Radforth and Joan Sangster, "The Struggle for Autonomous Workers' Education: The WEA in Ontario, 1917-1951," pp. 73-96 in this volume.

63. Ibid., p. 86; Hemming, p. 35.

64. *The Canadian Congress of Labour, Second Annual Convention,* Hamilton, Ontario, 8-12 September 1941, pp. 73-75.

65. Gray, p. 52.

66. Evans, p. 153.

67. Gray, pp. 52-53.

68. Buchanan, "The Projection of Canada," p. 305; Stan Rands, "Film, Forums, and Community Action," *Film Forum Review,* Vol. 1, No. 3, Fall 1946, pp. 6-8.

69. McKay, pp. 50-51; James, pp. 86-92; "Convention Film," *Trade and Labour Congress Journal,* February 1945, p. 7.

70. "Movies for Workers," *Trades and Labour Congress Journal,* October 1945, p. 17. John MacNab of the Winnipeg Labour Union Film Council chaired the discussion trailer on the film along with industrial and farm workers.

71. "A Story with Two Endings," *Trades and Labour Congress Journal,* Vol. XXIV, No. 9, 1945, p. 24.

72. McKay, p. 36; Gray, pp. 54-57.

73. The Trade Union and the Industrial Film circuits ceased operations at the end of the war in 1945. McKay, pp. 55-56.

74. "Northern Film Distribution," *Food for Thought,* Vol. 20, No. 6, March 1960.

75. Evans, pp. 92-93.

76. McKay, pp. 50-56; James, p. 107.

77. Cited in Welton, "To Be and Build the Glorious World," p. 224.

78. Gregory Vlastos, "Education for Morale," *Food for Thought,* November 1943, p. 6.

79. Report of the Proceedings of a Special Programme Committee of the CAAE, 27 December-2 January 1942. Harry Avison Papers, Vol. 5, File 25, pp. 4-6.

80. Glover, "Film," p. 108.

81. "Trade Union Film Circuit," *Trades and Labour Congress Journal,* June 1945, p. 11. In 1950, the efforts to educate workers using film during the war resulted in the National Trade Union Film Committee made up of the TLC, CCL, Catholic Confederation of Labour, The Canadian Film Institute, the Canadian Association for Adult Education, the NFB, and the Federal Department of Labour, which continued the work of the war years. See Charles Topshee, "The Canadian Trade Union Film Committee," *Food for Thought,* Vol. 17, No. 6, 1957, p. 298.

82. Evans, pp. 224-68; Hardy, pp. 160-163; James, pp. 129-40.

83. Hardy, p. 126.

Mobilizing the People for Socialism: The Politics of Adult Education in Saskatchewan, 1944-45

Michael R. Welton

"June 15, 1944," David Lewis observed in his autobiography, "was an intoxicating day for the CCF across Canada."[1] It was only slightly less so for Watson Thomson who was invited shortly after the Co-operative Commonwealth Federation (CCF) victory to come to Saskatchewan to "launch the biggest adult education program in the country."[2] Tommy Douglas had made an excellent choice: Thomson was a veteran, if enigmatic, communitarian socialist, seasoned adult educator, and respected defender of the civil rights of the oppressed.

Thomson was committed to awakening individuals and communities to a participatory civic consciousness in order to create participatory forms of organization in every prairie village and town. He believed that the process of working together, first in study groups and then in community projects, would set in motion a movement, deeper and broader, towards a fundamental restructuring of the social order. While Thomson placed too much faith in the potential of this process, he thought this was the only way one could proceed. Revolutionary change in the external structures of oppression would be impossible without change in individuals. They had to undergo a conversion to community, breaking with egoistic individualism. Through dialogue, conflicting interest groups had to break through internal divisions of class, race, and sect to find the "truly human" ground of commonality.

There was no easy way to transform the quality of human relationships in any society; individuals had to discover their own power to re-fashion the institutions in which they were enmeshed and, as self-motivated individuals, build co-operative institutions in local communities, the region, the nation, and the globe. Thomson envisaged that economic and social life could be rebuilt around units small enough so that face-to-face relationships were never crushed. Adult education was the means to achieve his goal of a decentralized and participatory democracy. Although Thomson utilized an amazing array of pedagogical methods, the small study group remained the indispensable context for learning to transform self and society through dialogue and action.

Thomson attempted to put this transformative-communitarian vision into practice in the Canadian context — Alberta from 1937 to 1940, and Manitoba from 1941 to 1944. Before arriving in Saskatchewan, Thomson had participated in a remarkable range of adult education ventures and experiments. He founded chapters of the Workers' Educational Association in Calgary and Edmonton in 1937 and 1938 and played pivotal roles in the Danish folk school-inspired Alberta School of Community Life and the University of Alberta Extension Department's innovative outreach programs. As director of the University of Manitoba's Adult Education Office, he worked to revitalize rural Manitoba communities in often dreadful conditions. And along with the residents of Roslyn Road in Winnipeg, he created the Prairie School for Social Advance (PSSA) to mobilize and co-ordinate the progressive forces of Western Canada.

Thomson's strategy involved using the study group to establish a beachhead in the community. Study groups, Thomson would repeatedly insist, should see themselves in the community context and strive towards greater social responsibility on the local, national, and international level, initiating wherever possible social and political action. To reach beyond the intellectual few who joined study groups, Thomson promoted the National Film Board's (NFB) film circuits and devised, with Stan Rands, the film-forum as a democratic pedagogic device.

Thomson also played an important role in several national organizations. He campaigned tirelessly for the Canadian National Refugee Committee. He participated actively in the deliberations of the Canadian Association for Adult Education throughout the war years and provided philosophical perspective for the CAAE at a turning point in its history — drafting the controversial Manifesto of 1943. He was one of the primary instigators of the Citizens' Forum (extending his vision outward to the national community), and his Northern Plains project (engaging farmers and agriculturists in critical dialogue about the need to create a decentralized bio-region) was a bold attempt to challenge the centralization of Canadian politics and culture. Moreover, his own experiments in co-personal living, begun in Edmonton in 1939, and continued in the co-operative house on Roslyn Road in Winnipeg, provided a crucible to test his communitarian theories.

His work in Manitoba, successful within the constraints imposed by the university bureaucracy and conservative political climate, had suffered through disconnection from government policy formation. Now, for the first time in his life, Thomson had the opportunity to link his transformative-communitarian educational theory to the social policy of the government. This was indeed a new and unprecedented experience for the anti-establishment Scotsman.

The Saskatchewan CCF had swept W. J. Patterson's Liberal machine out of office, winning forty-seven of fifty-two seats. Despite the bitterness of a business-supported anti-socialist campaign, the CCF had won a decisive victory. The national CCF leadership thought they saw signs of wonderful things to come. Even the fanatically anti-socialist *Financial Post* predicted that the CCF could win between seventy and one hundred federal seats. Of course the victory in Saskatchewan had not happened overnight. The first three decades of the twentieth century in Saskatchewan had witnessed the creation of a powerful, self-conscious agrarian movement. As the dusty and dirty thirties ended, the CCF at last acquired more supporters among the depressed rural population than the oldline parties.[3]

With the war came rising expectations of increased prosperity. But satisfaction of those expectations came too slowly for activists in the farmers' movement, with their traditions of co-operative endeavor and populist rebellion, and they soon abandoned the Liberal party.[4] Tommy Douglas, who had only assumed the Saskatchewan CCF leadership in 1941, had succeeded quickly in drawing diverse elements of the populace into a crusade for "definite reforms." although without explicit reference to some essentials of socialism — such as state ownership.[5] His reluctance to emphasize "state ownership" was partly tactical. He was unwilling to offend suspicious, anti-statist farmers. Douglas preferred to emphasize "social ownership," including co-operatives.

The 1944 election program appealed to a broad spectrum. Saskatchewan was promised security of land tenure, expanded social services, including socialized health services, educational reform, and a planned economy. Although the CCF won a convincing victory, Douglas faced formidable problems in establishing a "beachhead of socialism on a continent of capitalism."[6] He had inherited one of the worst bureaucratic machines in the country. Most, if not all, civil servants were wary of CCF goals. The CCF had come to power without the support of any of the major Saskatchewan, or national, newspapers. To be sure, 53 percent of the electorate had voted CCF. But large numbers of big Saskatchewan farmers had not. Nor had significant numbers of the urban middle classes. Despite the work of an influential Roman Catholic supporter, the Rev. Eugene Cullihane, most Roman Catholics remained suspicious of the CCF as did many ethnic sub-groups — French Candians, Ukrainians, Mennonites. One group of Old Colony Mennonites even prepared to leave Saskatchewan, believing that a totalitarian dictatorship was about to decend upon the province. Could all of these groups be drawn into the reform projects of the new government? What form would the opposition of old line parties take? How would this opposition be confronted?

If Douglas faced a politically nervous public, he was by no means presiding over a unified party with a consistent base of support. The CCF's most vigorous support came from the province's left-wing — what Richards and Pratt call the "culture of left populism."[7] The left, while agreeing with the party's limited electoral goals of a secure land tenure and of public welfare, wanted soon to create a socialist society with a fundamentally new value orientation. They sought qualitative changes in all social relationships. They proposed co-operative farming and housing, inclusion of co-operative values in public school curricula, and believed social services should be built and governed from the community upwards. They promoted direct, "grass-roots" democracy.

"The CCF government," Richards and Pratt contend, "was a marriage between the leaders of a left populist movement and representatives of professional civil servants...."[8] Was it a marriage of convenience? How much support would Douglas and the cabinet provide to the left populist forces?[9] Would they foster this culture's central preoccupations? One could not answer these questions unequivocally in the summer of 1944. But it would be evident soon enough that the Fabian bureaucrats, committed as they were to rule by cabinet, would win out and, after a period of initial radical enthusiasm, settle in to running a moderate, increasingly bureaucratic, social democratic party. Nonetheless, the need for a sufficiently reliable and practical, yet sufficiently radical, educated civil service was obvious and acknowledged early in the life of the Douglas government. The way was increasingly clear for the Thomson appointment soon to come.

Tommy Douglas was, after all, sympathetic to, even identified with, the left wing of the party in the early days of the Saskatchewan regime. Douglas wanted not only to introduce legislation on health, collective bargaining, and education as he had promised. He wanted also to use a campaign of grass-roots radical adult education — a massive campaign of study-action throughout the province — to begin the building of a new society. Thomson thought he saw "exciting vistas ahead."[10]

Although the University of Saskatchewan Extension Department had done good work with Homemakers, Co-operative organizations, Boys and Girls' Clubs, and the Farm and Citizens' Forums, Woodrow S. Lloyd, the Minister of Education, did not think it could be an educational mobilizing centre. Lloyd thought that a new Division of Adult Education should, firstly, clarify the thinking of Saskatchewan citizens so that desirable social and economic conceptions might prevail and, secondly, should provide adult education with immediate and tangible aims (co-operative farming, credit unions, health improvement facilities, development of community centres and leisure-time activities).[11]

The context into which Watson Thomson stepped seemed perfectly suited to his aims, his methods, his hopes. Saskatchewan was "gripped" by vague hopes of social and community change; the old chains of money-based dominance — one group over another — seemed to have loosened. Into this vaguely hopeful scene stepped Watson Thomson, whose scattered schemes for mass change appeared suited (as none other could be) to the needs of the CCF administration. Yet that context was, in fact, deeply flawed and unready for Thomson-style adult education.

In the first few months as Director of the Division of Adult Education Thomson was convinced that he had "all the room for growth and action that one could possibly desire or use."[12] He was happy with the staff he was recruiting — experienced educators like Art Wirick, his first District Supervisor, and Florence Gaynor, Thomson's assistant and supervisor of the Basic Citizenship Program. But he also encountered some opposition from the editors of the *Saskatchewan Commonwealth* who shocked Thomson with their "narrow right-wing line." [13] Moreover, unbeknownst to Thomson, Douglas had received his first of many letters from outside the province casting doubts on Thomson's political acceptability. H. M. Caiserman, Secretary of the Canadian Jewish Congress, wondered if Thomson, though a "splendid educationist," was "communistically inclined." Douglas dismissed the accusation out-of-hand.[14]

Thomson moved quickly to establish government policy for adult education in Saskatchewan. His brief "Adult Education Theory and Policy" outlined what to Thomson was the only possible attitude to adult education for a socialist government to adopt. It was of the "utmost import" that members of the Saskatchewan government understand the educational theory and principles of the new Adult Education Division, both in itself and in relation to their own social philosophy. Accusations of "propaganda" and "totalitarianism" would be levelled on the slightest provocation. Even the progressively minded were liable to be placed on the defensive — a weakness the progressive cause could not afford. This weakness, he thought, was rooted in an insufficient understanding of the fallacies of liberal education theory (education viewed as impartial and socially neutral).[15]

In Saskatchewan, a socially committed adult education had two primary concrete tasks: (1) to support the people with relevant knowledge in their movement towards the new objectives for which the way had been opened up, whether it be co-operative farms, larger school units, or new public health projects; (2) to awaken the people to a sense of the "central issues of the world crisis," still unresolved, so that there would be a clear way ahead for modern society. Thomson informed the cabinet that a socially minded education had to find where the growing points were, where a sense of social purpose was breaking through towards liberating social change. Then, that activization had to be fostered in every possible way, feeding it the material for its creative job of re-shaping the environment. In the fall of 1944 Thomson wagered that a significant number of Saskatchewanians had opted to move towards a new participatory and self-reliant society. He saw his task as catalytic: helping people to clarify their goals and achieve their ends through dialogue.

The cabinet never reponded officially to this brief. Perhaps it was simply forgotten in the hectic first months of establishing the new government. Yet one cannot escape the suspicion that the cabinet may not have wished to face the implications of openly declaring their real goals. At any rate, since the cabinet did not provide any feedback, Thomson considered that they found it acceptable. The whole affair did not bode well for the future.

During November and December of 1944 Thomson shared his hopes for adult education with the Saskatchewan people. This was the old publicist at his best. In early November he published several articles in the *Regina Leader-post, Moose Jaw Herald, Prince Albert Daily Herald,* and the *Saskatoon Star-Phoenix.* He gave a series of four radio broadcasts on the theme of "Power to the People" in December. The knowledge the Adult Education Division wanted to convey was not knowledge for its own sake, but for the sake of change nearer to the heart's desire of ordinary, decent people everywhere. The average man, Thomson believed, did not want to study the history of medicine in the abstract. But when he began to ask why he could not have a decent hospital in his own district and to get together with his neighbors to figure out some way of getting one, he was ready to learn some history of medicine, as well as some social and economic history of Western Canada. "Education for the People — all the People. Education for action — co-operative, responsible action. Education for change — inevitable and desirable change. Power to the People." Thus Thomson ended his first broadcast.

In subsequent broadcasts people heard Thomson challenge them to be "scientific and to be co-operative." Aware that the trend in agriculture was towards increasingly mechanized, capital-intensive, large-scale units, Thomson challenged farmers to bring their isolated farms together into single co-operative communities. He was convinced that the people could take the "raw material" of a prairie village and create a rich community full of life and interest. But one could not do that without study and co-operative action. "No study without consequent action. No action without previous study" — this was the banner of the Department's Study-Action program.

Thomson urged Saskatchewanians to see action in their local communities as just one expression of the "whole new social pattern." Voluntary co-operation and voluntary socialization of life in all its aspects in order to create a new pattern not forced down from above but worked out by ordinary people from below. "A new world, built from below by the Common Man with the guidance of science and his own trusted leaders — that was the only answer to war and fascism . . . " Thomson's goal, then, was the creation of the "activated citizen": generally cognizant of the scientific and technological developments of the day, aware of the main issues of the world crisis, committed to playing an intelligent role in the constructive life of the community.[16]

By mid-December Thomson and his staff had prepared a detailed "Provincial Study-Action Program" and submitted it to an overburdened cabinet for discussion. In principle and structure, the study-action program was to be decentralized. Resident field workers, called district supervisors, were to be placed in district centres such as Yorkton. They would correlate their work with that of other government departments and agencies such as the Wheat Pool, University Extension Departments, and the NFB. The Division of Adult Education eventually hoped to have a full-time study-action leader for every large unit of administration in the province. The district supervisor was to establish a nuclear community centre program, to start discussion and study groups on basic economic and political issues, encourage all forms of citizen activization (credit unions, community centres, co-operative farms, study clubs, community forums), promote study and discussion of projects in public health, reconstruction, rehabilitation, social welfare and co-operatives, organize periodic three-day adult schools, act as district librarian and take charge of film-distribution, replacing the existing NFB circuit organization. In the urban areas, labor education classes for unionists would begin in Regina, Saskatoon, and Moose Jaw.

Study-action was underway in Saskatchewan! Nevertheless, immediately after returning from Winnipeg on 12 or 13 December, where he had been addressing a PSSA weekend forum, Thomson had the nagging fear that there was resistance of several kinds to the program. He was beginning to think that characteristic vices and weaknesses of social democracy were represented in this government. One week later some of this gloom lifted. The cabinet had approved the "Provincial Study-Action Program" plan and granted $100 000 for it budget.

Obviously elated at receiving this stamp of approval, Thomson wrote to Douglas on 1 January 1945, one week after prominent CCF labor leader Eugene Forsey advised Douglas to watch Thomson closely. Thomson told Douglas that "for the first time" he could "feel identified with the basic goals of the people in authority." Thomson raised several strategic considerations with Douglas. What should the study-action program emphasize? What should be the content of the central drive? How safe and disarming should the Division play? And how challenging? "You see," Thomson pointed out,

I'm interested in the whole gamut from the microscopic "Kingdom of God on Earth" in the establishment of genuine fellowship and "being members one of another" as between a handful of people; to the total radical change into a society at all points socialized and "of the People". Co-operatives are relevant, community-centres are relevant, even just getting a group of neighbours to sit down regularly together as a study-group is relevant. But so also is the challenge to monopolies and vested interests and racialism and irrationalism (either in politics or in religion). Only there's more dynamite in some of these things than in others. The question is: How is the battle going to develop? And what is the wisest and most effective thing to do in the light of our understanding as to the stage of development of the battle we're at right now?[17]

Thomson insisted that the Division's activities had to be "clearly and explicitly" co-ordinated with the general political policies and strategies of the government. All government publicity, public information, and much of adult education should, Thomson thought, be an integrated system directed by someone who had continuous access to the government. Why did Thomson raise this question with Douglas? Perhaps he knew that the bolder his Division became, the louder the political opposition would scream that Adult Education was nothing but a conduit for CCF propaganda. Could the Division count on full government support?

With a substantial budget approved, Thomson could hire the staff needed to launch study-action throughout the province. William M. Harding was appointed in mid-January of 1945 as Director of Study-Action and Administrative Supervisor. A man of keen intellect and exceptional organizing skills, Harding's task was pivotal: he would organize efficient record-keeping and community centres and the projected citizens' conferences. Harding moved quickly, fleshing out the details of the proposed study-action plan. In mid-February he was joined by Eddie Parker, seconded from the Department of Physical Fitness and Recreation to work as promotional director. A young man of scintillating imagination highly regarded by David Lewis, Parker joined Thomson, Harding, and Hugh Harvey of the Department of Co-operatives, to form the visionary centre of the the Division. These men, who really believed that Saskatchewan could be turned "upside down," would be joined in the following months by two new district supervisors, a production editor and a supervisor (and assistant) of the Lighted School Program.

In early November Thomson had sent out the first questionnaire to a number of community organizations. Through these "amateur" sociological surveys, Thomson hoped to gain ammunition for future social action projects and keep the CCF on the side of the people. By 18 December the Division had received two hundred replies. With the able Harding overseeing the study-action program and district supervisors ready to go into action, the department began to proceed systematically to establish more starting and growing points, study-action groups, and community councils. A "starting point," as Harding conceived it, consisted of one individual; a "growing point" of four individuals interested in a common "problem" or "issue." When ten "units" cohered around a common theme, a study group was created.

The visionaries in the Division of Adult Education imagined nothing less than a "comprehensive adult education campaign for social progress through which five hundred thousand men and women of the province are being encouraged to become active citizens and fully-rounded personalities."[18] By 1 May the central study action office hoped to send circulars to all existing contacts. By 1 October, when the study-action outlines would be ready, the Division of Adult Education wanted to have a thousand starting-points and three hundred growing points. Looking into the future, Harding and Thomson envisioned that by "1960, fifteen years after the start of this campaign and ten years after its full-speed capacity is realized, Saskatchewan should be able to boast it is truly possessed by its people . . ."[19] "Half-a-million active builders of a new and better Saskatchewan. Half-a-million intelligent citizens of the world. Nothing less is the goal of the Saskatchewan Study-Action program . . .", Thomson exuded in a press release at the end of January.[20]

Three central issues were clear to Thomson and Harding. Firstly, they understood that the Saskatchewan government had to demonstrate to the farmers, workers, and plain people that a "provincial socialist government" could effect tangible material improvements. Secondly, they knew that the mass of people must be mobilized and activized as rapidly as possible. Only by participating in the processes of social change would people realize that "socialism is democracy extended" and the bogey of "socialism as mere bureaucracy and regimentation" ludicrous. Thirdly, Thomson and Harding believed that the "political consciousness" of the mass of people must be so deepened that the foundations of prairie radicalism would become unshakable.

The first issue was one of legislation and administration; the second and third issues ones in which adult education could play an important role. Study-action had been designed to meet the second need: mobilizing and activizing the people at the grass roots. It was essential, the study-action strategists contended, to begin with a broad approach to "communities as communities," serving them in some appreciable way regarding their "felt needs." Study-action, citizens' conferences, and the Lighted School all aimed at serving communities in an "above-party spirit." Yet, these latter activities were not quite "above-party": Harding and Thomson wanted to create an organizational vehicle for a more directly "political" or "socialist" type of education. This goal was not announced publicly for obvious reasons.

It was educationally sound, they thought, to attempt to lead study-action groups from local and immediate concerns to the affairs of the province, nation, and eventually the world. As one did so, the issues discussed would inevitably take on a more "political character and groups would look to the Division of Adult Education for guidance. And that guidance could be then given on the basis of confidence earned through non-partisan services in the community-centred interests. Developing this political consciousness — the most crucial task as far as the progressive movement was concerned — was the most difficult. If too abrupt and outspoken an approach were taken to current political and economic issues, one would be "reduced to the futile role of preaching to the converted."[21]

During the month of February Thomson's main preoccupation had been with the training course for the field workers and staff. Morning sessions were taken up with educational theory and the practical problems facing field workers (problems of new Canadians and returned veterans, for example). In the afternoons, representatives from various government ministries addressed the students. In the evenings, field workers and staff saw demonstrations of film-forums, watched films critically, participated in panel discussions, and heard more talks from government officials and representatives of community organizations. It was an exhaustingly thorough and exciting three weeks. And the excitement of the training school was no doubt intensified several days after the sessions ended. The staff opened the *Financial Post* of 24 February and saw this headline — "Saskatchewan CCF Adult Education Program May Emerge as Straight Socialist Propaganda".

Under this provocative headline, Gordon L. Smith malevolently linked Saskatchewan study-action with undemocratic education. "Nothing like it has ever been broached in Canada," he exclaimed. "One can only point to Germany or Russia or pre-war Italy for such a deliberately planned scheme of a mass education, perhaps more correctly described as mass propaganda." The anonymous author of the regular news column, "The Nation's Business," informed Canadians that if they wanted to know what would happen on the national level if the CCF came to power, they should look at Saskatchewan. "The evidence strongly indicates that they are in for a mass propaganda drive of the Goebells' [sic] variety, in which they are to be given that special set of facts and that special interpretation of those facts which suits the government in power." The author was quick to add that Watson Thomson was an exponent of "socialist and communist blueprints for utopia" who readily admitted that he felt "no obligation in educational work to present more than one side of the question."[22]

This sort of "socialist-bashing" was, of course, nothing new to CCF and farm movement activists. Accusations that CCF was synonymous with totalitarianism and regimentation had been hurled at Douglas throughout the bitter 1944 campaign. When farmers were establishing co-operatives in the 1920s, they were often labelled "communist." What was new was the intensity of the anti-socialist propaganda engineered by people like B. A. Trestrail and supported by many business organizations.

Through the spring of 1945 until the June federal election the CCF would experience its most vicious onslaught in its twelve-year history. Despite the chicanery of the anti-socialist propaganda, the Trestrails and Smiths succeeded in undermining CCF support. This impairing was particularly effective in Ontario, less so in Saskatchewan where populist and co-operative traditions inoculated a good segment of the population against the diatribes of the bourgeois press. For his part, Watson Thomson thought the *Financial Post* comments were "pretty damning." But he still trusted that "all publicity was good publicity."[23] All he could do was to encourage his staff to "go ahead with your work quietly. Shrug off verbal opposition with a smile."[24]

April of 1945 saw the beginnings of positive responses in the field. District supervisors confirmed the Division's opinion that although apathy was still to be found, people were stirring at the grass roots. Ed Parker had visited the Landis-Biggar area and discovered that their central passion was co-operative farming. In this case, Thomson observed, the Department's job began with the "happiest of all stages," namely with helping a "grand bunch of people" to get what they wanted by giving them something "we've got which they know they want." A weekend conference was in the offing. This citizens' conference on co-operative farming would be part of the preparation for a whole winter's study and research and discussion of the entire community. Thomson told his staff that other citizens' conferences were also being considered. Through the co-operation of Major McKay, head of the Rehabilitation Division of the Department of Reconstruction, Adult Education was already committed to a short weekend or two-day conference at Melfort and Prince Albert on "How a Community should prepare to receive its veterans," with others to follow.[25]

The idea of the citizens' conferences was that ordinary citizens could come together with "experts," who could provide some analytical guidance, and government officers, who could provide some information regarding "official" policy. This may sound naive to political realists. But Thomson explicitly rejected the notion that specialists were there to deliver their words, leaving the people to criticize or go home and pick the words to pieces. This was not the way to build a "true democracy." Those who were not specialists had a right to have their say. Each conference utilized the familiar methods — speakers, films bearing on the conference theme, group discussion, panels, and strategy and action sessions. The heart of the citizens' conferences, from Thomson's viewpoint, lay not with the large assembly but in the small discussion groups. As issues emerged in the plenary sessions, clear and significant questions were then placed before these "policy-making" groups. Following the panel discussion, Thomson's role, a crucial one, was to intuit the audience's mood and address himself to the question — "Where do we go from here?" Action, as Thomson repeatedly pointed out, was of two orders: study and practical projects.

If Thomson thought he lived in a "dangerous, fascinating, grandly terrible"world that was "suddenly darker and more uncertain" [26] than the pre-Roosevelt era, events on the national and provincial scene were equally ominous for him personally. In early March of 1945 the original budget of $100 000 had been reduced to $60 000, possibly in part due to the squabble over the seed grain issue. Without any warning that there had been any change in understanding between Thomson and the Premier, Lloyd, the Minister of Education, told Thomson in early April that no provincial grant would be made to the Prairie School for Social Advance. "Lloyd," Thomson wrote to Roslyn Road, "said that the Premier himself had made the decision on the grounds that it was too politically dangerous." Thomson was incensed: this seemed to be a unilateral repudiation of the original agreement which brought him to the province. "But this," Thomson continued, "is not the only instance I know of in which Douglas has acted on impulse and then backed away from the consequences of his action. He is capable of being impulsive and inconsistent to the point of irresponsibility." Thomson told

Lloyd how serious the consequences of such a decision were. Evidently impressed, Lloyd told Thomson he would re-open the question with the Premier.[27] It is at this point that the ground begins to slide out from under Thomson.

Lloyd informed Thomson that the decision not to support financially the PSSA had been made around the end of March. That could mean, Thomson thought at the time, that the decision was related to the Richards–Johnson rebellion in the Manitoba CCF (Berry Richards, CCF MLA from The Pas stayed at Roslyn Road during house sittings) and Watson Thomson's alleged association with it. Thomson had, however, been "officially exonerated."[28] What had been happening behind Thomson's back? In early March S. J. Farmer, the leader of the Manitoba CCF, informed Douglas that he had talked with Stanley Knowles about Thomson. Farmer believed that Thomson was a fellow-traveller of the communists — pointing to Thomson's article "Not Bread Alone" written for *The Record* (March 1945). On 8 March Douglas sent the booklet to Woodrow Lloyd.[29] On 19 March the national executive of the CCF and caucus (including F. R. Scott, M. J. Coldwell, Angus MacInnis, and Knowles) had met in Ottawa. At that meeting Stanley Knowles gave a "full report of the background of the trouble with Richards and Johnson, analyzing the situation as it developed from day to day."[30] Knowles probably raised the question of Thomson's role in the Manitoba imbroglio.

In fact, only a week after the national executive and caucus meeting, national CCF leader M. J. Coldwell informed Douglas, his protégé, that on 12 March, while in Montreal addressing a public meeting, he saw a bulletin board announcing that Thomson was to speak under the auspices of an organization for interracial co-operation. Coldwell believed the Communists were "boring from within" and wondered if Watson Thomson was "playing ball with these people."[31] The day after receiving Coldwell's letter, P. N. R. Morrison, president of the Calgary CCF constituency, told Douglas that the Berry Richards incident had "either been engineered by or the result of contact with Watson Thompson [sic]."[32] Morrison added that "we had Thompson [sic] here for a meeting and his line of talk was certainly very comforting to the Labour Progressive Party (LPP) line." Five days later, on 2 April, Knowles wrote to Douglas to ensure that if Stanley Rands applied for a job in Saskatchewan (Rands lived at Roslyn Road) he should not be hired. "I cannot make my warning too strong. It is very clear that we have a real struggle on our hands with these so-and-so's."[33]

Knowles's letter was followed just three days later by one from Dr J. Stanley Allen, president of the Quebec CCF party, to Woodrow Lloyd. Allen pointed out that R. E. Gordon, editor of *Today* magazine, had been associated with Thomson on the same speaking platform. "I must admit," he said, "that at a meeting like this one can be very easily fooled unless he [sic] knows the individuals concerned, but for what it is worth I could call this to your attention."[34]

How did Tommy Douglas respond to all of this? The only piece of direct evidence is found in a letter he wrote to M. J. Coldwell on 31 March. Douglas told Coldwell that he had had "considerable warnings from various parts of the country, outlining the fears of some of our people. Both Woodrow Lloyd and myself are keeping that branch under careful supervision."[35] The suspicion that Thomson was not politically trustworthy, rejected out-of-hand by Douglas in the fall of 1944, seemed to be growing. The CCF was under assault from anti-socialist propagandists, the LPP was indeed seeking to disrupt the CCF in the labor movement and in political constituencies.[36] The tide, once flowing in the CCF's direction, was receding. Saskatchewan had to be protected. The CCF national leadership, threatened from outside and from within, was closing its ranks, drawing boundaries between who was in and who was out.

Watson Thomson no longer seemed to "fit" in the CCF camp. His call for unity among progressive people was misinterpreted, his severe criticism of the Communists and commitment to building a grass roots movement went unheeded. The letters to Douglas and Lloyd, sadly but understandably, utilized the "character assassination" techniques we have come to associate with McCarthyism. No sound empirical evidence was provided to support any of the accusations. His writings were not read closely, he was "guilty by association" (with Gordon and Richards). Nor did the CCF national leadership, particularly Knowles and Coldwell, understand the Roslyn Road experiment. Thomson and Roslyn Road were communitarian socialists committed to self-renewal and participatory democracy, local control of resources, and the elimination of exploitation and alienation. Thomson's CCF critics, all of whom were on the right wing of the party, were correct on one issue: Watson Thomson was not a loyal Fabian social democrat.

Everything that the Division of Adult Education and Watson Thomson would do in the ensuing months would be clouded with political suspicion. During May and June Thomson, who was unaware of the letters, had his first "serious feelings that something was amiss."[37] Only later, though, would he be able to see that the accusation that he was a communist because he talked of left-wing unity indicated the handwriting on the wall. The failure to gain full discussion of his policy paper on adult education was now looming large and becoming increasingly politically significant. Had the cabinet some doubts about the study-action program? The budget had been drastically reduced and PSSA support withdrawn. Were they a little uneasy that Thomson, through the study-action program, might actually succeed in mobilizing the people and gain support amongst the left-wing of the party? If he did, could the party control this grass roots momentum?

On 1 June Thomson assessed the global and provincial situation. The world had celebrated V–E Day on 8 May 1945. Once again, as in the tortured days of the outbreak of the Second World War, Thomson agonized over world events. Thomson was more convinced than ever that Saskatchewan "desperately needed a vehicle through which they could act to give some guidance to the thinking of people in regard to some of these desperately urgent matters of global import." Thomson told his staff that Saskatchewan needed a thousand groups, confident in the Division, who were active in their own communities and open to the broader global issues. Then they could begin to show effectively that Soviet totalitarianism was not the same as fascist totalitarianism. They could also demonstrate that freedom was an immoral luxury when men and women lacked the basic necessities. In the summer Parker and Thomson would gain government consent to conduct an experiment, called the "Living Newspaper," to demonstrate something of the emancipatory power of the media.

On the home front, Thomson was pleased that two citizens' conferences on "Community meets Veteran," one at Wynyard (June 5-6), the other at Melfort (June 26-27), were scheduled. "We are getting pretty marvelous co-operation from the other departments concerned in these plans and from the communities themselves. Both in Wynyard and in Melfort, there are some keen veterans all ready to take an active part in these conferences . . ." Lloyd Williams's first study outline, "Community meets Veteran," was in galley-proof, and Irene Leman and Ed Parker were working on preparing a new kind of visual aid, two film-strips, one on rehabilitation of veterans, the other on co-operative farming. Moreover, the Division had received four hundred replies from individuals in Saskatchewan, large numbers of letters from people all over the continent, including letters from the High Commissioner of New Zealand and E. A. Corbett, Director of the CAAE, who heartily approved of study-action in Saskatchewan. In the Landis area events were progressing towards the first citizens' conference on co-operative farming. "Let's remind ourselves," Thomson said, "[that] Study-Action is the very spine and marrow of the only kind of democracy which can lead humanity into the abundant future . . ."[38] Would most of Saskatchewan recognize the present "tide in the affairs of men" and take this new postwar opportunity to reconstruct themselves by the common co-operative effort of all classes and nationalities?

The federal election of June 1945 left Saskatchewan as the only "progressive" spot in the country. Thomson thought the general election had provided a "rough and ready" measure of how far study-action had yet to go in activizing the Common Man. Any objective student of society would agree, Thomson argued, that a victory for the Canadian Liberal party was a "victory for laissez-faire modified by paternalistic social legislation." It was not a victory for "active, participating citizenship, for government of the people, by the people."[39]

The results of the general election also demonstrated for Thomson that Saskatchewan was "away ahead of the rest of Canada." In contrast to other regions of the country, Saskatchewan was open to the idea of radical social change. "The eyes of the whole continent," he wrote, "and more are upon us — 'progressive' people watching us with envy and guardians of the **status**

quo with a sharpened hostility. Clearly, we are a vanguard . . .''[40] Saskatchewan may well have been a vanguard, relatively speaking, but the shattering defeat of the national CCF was pressuring the Saskatchewan CCF in the direction of becoming a moderate, safe, social democratic party committed to cautious rule by cabinet. Woodrow Lloyd's response to Watson Thomson's fourth newsletter provides some indication of this rightward shift. ''It would seem to me,'' Lloyd told Thomson, ''that there are some statements . . . which would be better not made. I refer, of course, to those statements which particularly refer to the recent general election, direct references to the CCF as a political movement, and also the second last paragraph on page two.'' Advising ''considerable discretion,'' Lloyd felt that Thomson's commentary on the Landis conference, where Thomson had spoken critically but favorably of the Soviet experiment in collective farming and had observed that the co-operative farm was Saskatchewan's chance to create their ''social revolution voluntarily and without violence,'' was politically unacceptable rhetoric.[41]

Lloyd was becoming increasingly edgy about identifying the CCF as a militant movement for social change. He seemed to be retreating from his earlier commitment to counteract citizen ''torpidity.'' In fact, Woodrow had discarded one of the central concerns of CCF educational policy makers — to restructure the curriculum along socialist lines — in favor of a safe policy of establishing larger units of administration and providing better working conditions for teachers.

Thomson certainly did not think that now was the time for the Saskatchewan CCF to play it safe or retreat from the opposition; the latter tendency, Seymour Lipset has observed, was quite characteristic of social democracy.[42] Shortly after the federal election of 11 June, a worried Thomson presented his concerns confidentially to the government in the form of a three-page document, ''Adult Education in Saskatchewan: The Next Three Years.'' Reminding the government of the Division's commitment to activize the people in an ''above-party spirit,'' Thomson then turned to the future. Given the present tempo of provincial, national, and global events, the government ran the risk of saying in three years' time: ''too little and too late.'' The extension and consolidation of the widespread goodwill and citizen confidence in the Division's usefulness and integrity, now being built through study-action, citizens' conferences, and, soon, the Lighted School, were ''immediate and urgent'' necessities. The plan was there, techniques known, a small but devoted staff at work as individuals and as a team. But opportunities far surpassed achievement because the Department needed more staff, research, writing, and field work.

The time was ripe. The people, as the Division was finding them, were ''disposed toward change and ready to take a more dynamic role in affairs''. Returned veterans, with their ''restless demands,'' could be directed towards social change. To transform the interest generated around the citizens' conference on co-operative farming into an "active determination" required time and money. And, Thomson observed, this example also illustrated the way in which adult education could "stimulate not merely more social and progressive attitudes of mind but also the processes of actually creating a socialist environment." The Landis study-action groups on co-operative farming and the Regina–Saskatoon study-action groups on co-operative housing were cases in point. Summing up, Thomson said that a $60 000 budget would not give adequate attention to the thousand starting-points. The difference between a $60 000 budget and a $200 000 budget was a difference between laying the

> foundations of a sound but inconspicuous program of adult education, more or less innocuous as an instrument of radical social change and, in the other case, starting a dynamic popular movement, with challenging social and political implications and consequences, making a palpable impact on the mind and life of this province.[43]

In subsequent months, in spite of the success of the citizens' conferences (particularly the Landis-Biggar conference on co-operative farming) and the Living Newspaper (an innovative but controversial experiment in putting the socialist world view into the "imaginative currency of average people"[44]), the CCF government would ask Thomson to resign. The reasons are multiplex — an interweaving of many strands. Thomson found his deepest support in the culture of left populism. However, by the end of 1945 the CCF leadership, national and provincial, was clearly committed to "cabinet government, not to the culture of left populism."[45] They were interested in managing the people and deflecting radical experimentation. They were not committed to their activization.

By the late summer of 1945 Thomson and his Division had been left exposed and rendered ineffectual. Moreover, the CCF leadership, obsessively wary of the communists, really did believe that Thomson was "playing ball with the communists." He was too unpredictable to be trusted as the Saskatchewan CCF shifted from movement to party. But the communist label pasted on Thomson no doubt masked the deeper fear of populist rebellion either challenging CCF rule or being co-opted by the Labour Progressive party. Finally, Thomson's utopian fervor — Saskatchewan was the last hope for progressives — propelled him out beyond the average citizen. Believing that the world was at a turning point, Thomson was temperamentally unable to proceed cautiously and to settle for something less than a mobilized society.

With the dismissal of Watson Thomson in January of 1946, the momentum of study-action in Saskatchewan gradually dissipated. Approximately one hundred community-based projects had been started throughout Saskatchewan and numerous study-action groups were ready to begin their winter's work. But without Divisional leadership and government support, these groups gradually disbanded. The Landis dream of the co-operative farming community was never fulfilled. Within a year, Harding, Wirick, Parker, and Harvey were no longer associated with the Division of Adult Education. One of the most creative and controversial ventures in Canadian adult educational history was over.

Footnotes

1. David Lewis, *The Good Fight: Political Memoirs, 1909-1958* (Toronto: The Macmillan Co., 1981), p. 468.

2. Watson Thomson Papers, Special Collections, University of British Columbia (hereafter WTP), box 2, file 5, pp. 184-85.

3. Seymour Lipset, *Agrarian Socialism: The CCF in Saskatchewan* (Berkeley: University of California Press, 1968), p. 203.

4. Jim Wright, *Saskatchewan: The History of a Province* (Toronto: McClelland and Stewart, 1956), p. 253; John Archer, *Saskatchewan: A History* (Saskatoon: Western Producer Prairie Books, 1980), p. 206; Lewis, *The Good Fight,* p. 288.

5. Wright, *Saskatchewan,* p. 254.

6. Lewis Thomas, ed., *The Making of a Socialist: The Recollections of T. C. Douglas* (Edmonton: University of Alberta Press, 1982), p. 169.

7. John Richards and Larry Pratt, *Prairie Capitalism: Power and Influence in the New West* (Toronto: McClelland and Stewart, 1979), pp. 139-41.

8. Richards and Pratt, *Prairie Capitalism,* p. 139.

9. For an excellent critical introduction to populism, see Margaret Canovan, *Populism* (New York: Harcourt, Brace, Jovanovich, 1981).

10. Watson Thomson to T. C. Douglas, 24 August 1944, T. C. Douglas Papers, Adult Education Division, Saskatchewan Archives, Regina (hereafter TCDP).

11. W. S. Lloyd to T. C. Douglas, 28 August 1944, Woodrow S. Lloyd Papers (hereafter WSLP), Adult Education, 1944 box.

12. Watson Thomson to Roslyn Road, 22 October 1944, Roslyn Road Papers (hereafter RRP).

13. Watson Thomson to Roslyn Road, 29 October, RRP.

14. H. Caiserman to T. C. Douglas, 12 October 1944; T. C. Douglas to H. Caiserman, 17 October 1944, TCDP.

15. "Adult Education Theory and Policy" (hereafter AETP), p. 1, William M. Harding, papers in my possession (hereafter WMHP), basic literature, book 1.

16. Texts of "Power to the People" — I to IV, WMHP, basic literature, book 1.

17. Watson Thomson to T. C. Douglas, 1 January 1945, TCDP.

18. "Outline of the Proposed Study-Action Plan": confidential, not for general release, WMHP, basic literature, book 1.

19. "Outline of the Proposed Study-Action Plan."

20. Government of Saskatchewan Study-Action Program (press release, 24 January 1945), WMHP, basic literature, book 1.

21. Watson Thomson, "Adult Education in Saskatchewan: The Next Three Years," c. 11 and 29 June 1945, WMHP, folder on adult education.

22. "Saskatchewan Socialists Start Mass Propaganda Plan," and Gordon L. Smith, "Saskatchewan CCF Adult Education Program may Emerge as Straight Socialist Propaganda", *The Financial Post,* 24 February 1945.

23. Watson Thomson to Roslyn Road, 27 February 1945, RRP. For a discussion of the anti-socialist propaganda campaign, see Gerald Caplan, *The Dilemma of Canadian Socialism* (Toronto: McClelland and Stewart, 1973), chs. 8-12, and David Lewis, *The Good Fight,* ch. 14, "CCF Bashing".

24. Adult Education Division Monthly Newsletter (hereafter Monthly Newsletter) 1 (2 April 1945), WMHP, basic literature, book 1.

25. Monthly Newsletter 2, WMHP, basic literature, book 1.

26. Ibid.

27. Watson Thomson to Roslyn Road, 16 April 1945, RRP.

28. Ibid.

29. S. J. Farmer to T. C. Douglas, 4 March 1945; Douglas to Farmer, 7 March 1945; Douglas to Lloyd, 8 March 1945, TCDP.

30. CCF Papers, Public Archives of Canada (hereafter PAC), Executive and Caucus minutes, vol. 2.

31. M. J. Coldwell to T. C. Douglas, 26 March 1945, M. J. Coldwell Papers, PAC, Vol. 15, T. C. Douglas correspondence file.

32. P. Morrison to T. C. Douglas, 27 March 1945, WSLP, Adult Education, 1945(January-June) box.

33. Knowles to T. C. Douglas, 2 April 1945, WSLP, Adult Education, 1945 (January-June) box.

34. J. S. Allen to W. S. Lloyd, 5 April 1945, WSLP, Adult Education, 1945 (January-June) box.

35. T. C. Douglas to M. J. Coldwell, M. J. Coldwell Papers PAC, Vol. 15, T. C. Douglas correspondence file.

36. See Gad Horowitz, "The Struggle with the Communists, 1943-48", in *Canadian Labour in Politics* (Toronto: University of Toronto Press, 1968).

37. Watson Thomson Resignation Letter, 31 December 1945, RRP.

38. Monthly Newsletter 3 (1 June 1945), WMHP, basic literature, book 1. E. A. Corbett wrote Thomson on 16 January 1945: "I have looked over your material quite carefully and I am certain you have the right approach. Your emphasis upon the need for community responsibility and action is most important" (Adult Education Division (AED), file 16, CAAE correspondence).

39. Monthly Newsletter 4 (1 July 1945), WMHP, basic literature, book 1.

40. Monthly Newsletter 4.

41. W. S. Lloyd memo to Watson Thomson, 14 July 1945, WSLP, Adult Education, 1945 (July-December) box.

42. See Lipset, *Agrarian Socialism,* ch. 11, "Politics and Social Change," for a discussion of the CCF's retreat from "socialism".

43. Watson Thomson, "Adult Education in Saskatchewan: The Next Three Years," WMHP, folder on adult education.

44. Gregory Vlastos to Watson Thomson, 20 October 1945, AED, interdepartmental file.

45. Richards and Pratt, *Prairie Capitalism,* pp. 139-40.

"An Act of Faith and Optimism": Creating a Co-Operative College in English Canada, 1951-73

Ian MacPherson

Following the Second World War the English Canadian co-operative movement faced three main challenges. The first was the need to gain acceptance and support in urban areas. It was already well established in rural communities as a marketer of many commodities — particularly grains, fruit, and livestock — and as a retailer of consumer goods and farm supplies. It was almost totally unsuccessful, however, in urban centres where only a few stores and virtually no worker co-ops, credit unions, or housing co-ops had been formed. The second challenge was a growing need among established co-operatives for elected and employed leaders trained in both business practice and co-operative theory. The third was a growing uneasiness that co-operatives were losing their sense of clear social purpose.[1] All of these problems could have been resolved if the movement could have agreed on its main purpose and then have developed an effective education program for its members, its elected officials, its employees, and its public. For numerous reasons the movement failed to do so, and the result was that it made fewer gains than it might have during the period of relatively easy growth in the 1950s and 1960s.

In understanding the difficulties involved in creating a unified vision and a united ideological position, the efforts to develop Western Co-operative College are instructive. The college emerged because of the determination of some "grass roots co-operators" to ensure the continuation of popular control over the co-operative movement. It encountered difficulties because of the fierce independence of Canadian co-operative organizations; the developing, competing educational programs of existing co-operatives; an insufficient interest in developing a sophisticated analysis of co-operative thought; the regional parochialisms of Canadian life; and the rapid change in educational practice.

Looked at in the long view, the creation of a co-operative college in western

Canada was a likely development as soon as the co-operative movement was reasonably well established. From the earliest years of the century, Prairie co-operators had adhered closely to the rule, traditional within co-operatives, of emphasizing education. One of the first projects of the Grain Growers Grain Company, the first major grain marketing co-op in the region, had been the publication of *The Grain Growers Guide,* a journal dedicated to a significant degree to education about co-operatives.[2] Similarly, during the twenties and early thirties the Saskatchewan Wheat Pool had purchased *The Western Producer*, the Manitoba pool had begun publishing *The Scoop Shovel* (subsequently *The Manitoba Co-operator*), and the Alberta pool had helped sponsor *The U.F.A.,* and then published *The Budget*, primarily to undertake similar activities among their memberships.[3]

During the 1930s and 1940s numerous co-operative organizations deepened their commitment to education. The wheat pool fieldmen, particularly in Saskatchewan, became, in effect, community organizers educating farmers about various kinds of co-operatives.[4] They were especially effective in organizing credit unions, usually creating in the process some form of study club. Most co-operative stores in that period also developed educational programs primarily through the publication of newsletters. The co-operative wholesales, too, organized loosely structured educational programs involving some training for directors and managers and ultimately including publication of *The Co-operative Consumer.*[5]

In the years before the 1940s, the various educational programs in Prairie co-operatives demonstrated broad concerns. "Education" did not mean simply teaching loyalty to an organization or technical advice on how to run a local co-operative; essentially, it meant teaching a concern about broad social/economic issues and inculcating a movement culture among those who owned co-operative organizations. This broader concern was particularly evident and relatively easy to promote during the organizational phases of co-operatives. The most successful co-operative organizers and publicists — people such as E. A. Partridge, A. J. McPhail, Fawcett Ransom, John T. Hull, Violet McNaughton, Harry Fowler, and J. B. "Jock" Brown[6] — were successful primarily because they reflected a deep commitment to varied but compatible varieties of co-operative philosophy. For them, co-operatives were not only an alternative way to organize economic enterprises; they were also a way to transform society — for some gradually, for others relatively rapidly. The charismatic figures who built the Prairie co-ops in the early years believed that there were serious flaws in part or in whole with the capitalist system. They opposed prizing money above people, which they believed private enterprise stood for, and they were appalled by the social and economic dislocation evident in the western Canadian settlement period and the economic disasters of the early twenties and the 1930s.[7] They advocated, in varying degrees, therefore, a co-operative ideology as a way to resolve the pressing problems confronting the West and perhaps Canada if not the world.

For those western co-operators interested in maintaining the broad perspective and concerned about meeting the challenges of urban Canada, inadequately prepared leaders, and declining social purposes, the most obvious solution was education. In essence, three kinds of educational programs were needed. The first and most obvious was educating members to an awareness that they were part of a movement and not just owners of enterprises organized somewhat differently. The second educational requirement was to create co-operatives which in their business methods reflected co-operative ideology. This was not an easy task. What, after all, were the responsibilities of elected leaders and managers to the broader movement? How could democracy be maintained in large economic organizations? What was the appropriate role for employees in modern co-operatives?

The third educational need, and perhaps the most important, was a need to develop, through research and educational programs, a new theoretical basis for co-operatives in the postwar period. The relevance of the co-operative critique of capitalism had been relatively obvious amid the tumultuous class cleavages of single resource towns, the social turmoil of the agriculture settlement frontier, and the dislocation of deep depressions. But how did co-operators cope with the prosperity of the 1950s or 1960s? How did they show the relevance of a movement to an age somewhat suspicious of ideologies and increasingly convinced that centralized government planning and responsible corporate initiatives could resolve most social questions?

There were many co-operators on the Prairies who looked to educational solutions for the challenges of the later 1940s and early 1950s, but there were two concentrations of them which were particularly important: one was in southern Manitoba; the other was in Saskatchewan. Of the two, the Manitoba group was the more tightly organized and the more dedicated to developing a coherent, extensive educational program capable of meeting the movement's immediate practical needs and its long-term philosophical requirements.

The pivotal figure within the southern Manitoba grouping was Jacob John Siemens, a teacher, farmer, and co-operative organizer.[8] During the early 1930s he helped form discussion groups among some Mennonite farmers in the Altona area who were concerned about the tragic impact of the Depression, both locally and regionally. In 1931 he was largely responsible for the formation of the Rhineland Agricultural Society, concerned with "helping farmers help themselves," and the Rhineland Consumers' Co-operative in Altona, organized to reduce costs on farm supplies and consumer goods. In 1933 he joined the board of the Manitoba Co-operative Wholesale Society, then, and throughout the decade, a strong supporter of broad co-operative causes. In 1940 he assisted in the formation of the Winkler Co-operative Creamery, and in 1943 he sparked the creation of Co-operative Vegetable Oils to process oil from sunflowers.[9]

Behind this remarkable burst of co-operative activism lay a gradually evolving education program within southern Manitoba co-operatives. During the

Depression most co-ops in the region sponsored educational programs, and in 1939 they held the first of what became annual conferences devoted largely to co-operative education. They also published a newsletter, *Southern Manitoba's Co-operative Bulletin*, and in 1943 they organized the Federation of Southern Manitoba Co-operatives. The Federation hired an educational director, Diedrich Reimer, and developed a series of courses, particularly for managers and employees, in the co-ops of southern Manitoba. While the instructors used by the Federation employed a variety of teaching techniques, they preferred using the study club method as developed by the Extension Department of St Francis Xavier University. The St F.X. program — or Antigonish Movement, as it was known — had been publicized in western Canada by George Keen of the Co-operative Union of Canada in the thirties[10] and by Catholic priests in the 1930s and early 1940s.[11] By 1945, too, there were several books and articles about the Antigonish movement available for western readers, and the co-operative press across Canada publicized its successes. Several of the St F.X. or Antigonish educators, including Moses Coady, A. B. MacDonald, and A. S. MacIntyre, visited the Prairie provinces and told co-operative groups about their remarkably successful program in social action based on adult education.

Beyond the group of activists in southern Manitoba, there was a network of interested co-operators and farm leaders at the end of the Second World War concerned about educational programs. While not as successful as in eastern Canada, Farm Radio Forum did have a significant following in Manitoba; J. J. Siemens, D. G. Reimer, and other co-operative leaders were in fact prominent leaders in the forum project which began in 1941. The Manitoba Federation of Agriculture also sponsored Folk Schools for young adults starting in 1940.[12] Once again, co-operative leaders from southern Manitoba easily fitted into this program, and they organized a number of schools as a part of their work in southern Manitoba.

Despite these initiatives, however, the educational programs within or connected to southern Manitoba co-operatives did not meet all the expectations of J. J. Siemens and his little band of associates. One reason why they did not was the reluctance of many members of co-operatives to spend much money on education. Even small expenditures attracted opposition, and the Federation was never adequately funded.[13] Rivalries among co-operatives in different southern Manitoba communities weakened the regional program, and interest among members in the co-ops was not as high as organizers desired. J. J. Siemens, too, was a controversial figure. In 1939 he had left the Mennonite church over the failure of a Mennonite-backed lending institution, the Waisenamt. Politically, too, Siemens was a social democrat, an unusual affiliation in the largely conservative Mennonite areas of southern Manitoba. Inevitably, therefore, politics became a factor in limiting the work of Siemens and his associates in their home districts. And, when they tried to work outside of southern Manitoba, they encountered another barrier because their German, even though pacifist, background was not welcomed amid the anti-German sentiments of the war and postwar period.

Nevertheless, Siemens and his associates had glimpsed a theory of education which they sought to implement despite the restrictions of institutional barriers, personal rivalries, and limited resources. Essentially, the vision was that considerable economic, social, and political power could be unleashed if ordinary people, youth and adult, could be educated in political economy and co-operative philosophy. In 1947, after having studied the Danish folk school tradition for a decade, Siemens visited several European co-operative training institutes, including the Elsinore School in Denmark. At the Elsinore School he met with Peter Manniche, the co-author of a well-known textbook on co-operatives and rural development.[14] The interview and the visit to other co-operative educational institutions confirmed Siemens's vision of the immense potential of an effective adult education program. He came back to southern Manitoba determined to duplicate, if not improve upon, what he had seen in Europe.

For the next four years Siemens promoted the notion of creating a Canadian institute for co-operative education. He preferred to have the institute financed by individual co-operators and not by co-operative organizations so that the institute would remain aloof from institutional politics and conservative managerial views. He offered eighty acres of his own land to the institute once five hundred supporters had pledged financial contributions and collectively agreed that Altona was a suitable site for such an educational institution. He also discovered that American co-operators were interested, and, therefore, when the institute was formally organized in 1951, it was called the International Co-operative Institute.

Most of the early support for the Institute came from people associated with the Federation of Southern Manitoba Co-operatives. While significant numbers of co-operators in the region purchased life memberships in the new organization, only $2997.80 had been raised by March 1954.[15] In part, this poor response was due to the organizing committee's failure to approach the major co-operative organizations because they wished to protect the autonomy of their organization. In part, too, the organizing committee suffered because the Institute was perceived as a Mennonite organization. It was at that juncture that the activities of the Saskatchewan group became important.

Interest in co-operative education did not suddenly emerge in Saskatchewan during the mid-1950s. In fact, there had been distinct educational sessions for Saskatchewan co-operators since the 1920s. A key force behind the educational activities within the province had been the Co-operative Organization Branch (the forerunner of the Department of Co-operative Development which was established in 1944). From the early 1920s, the Branch had used a mixture of films, co-operative schools, and speaking tours to encourage new co-operatives and assist old ones. During the 1930s, representatives from the consumer co-operatives, with the assistance of the Branch, had started to meet regularly to exchange information and participate in educational activities.

In the late 1930s, and especially the years immediately after the war, however, the need for educational programs in Saskatchewan had become particularly acute. The numbers of co-operative stores had grown from one to 247.[16] This remarkable growth, which coincided with equivalent growth in sales volumes and deposits in credit unions, meant that elected leaders and managers in these two key elements in the provincial movement were hard pressed to provide effective leadership for their organizations. Similarly, other kinds of co-operatives — marketing, farms, and multi-purpose — were apparently deficient in leadership. To the problems caused by growth were added the difficulties created by rapid social and economic change. Saskatchewan, like rural Manitoba, was undergoing rapid change during the 1950s as paved highways reached rural areas, as electricity transformed the countryside, and as the automobile became ubiquitous. All co-operatives were buffeted by these changes, even though some benefitted, and the Department, along with many co-operators, looked to education to help resolve the numerous problems which developed.

The consumer co-operatives were particularly affected by the changes in the postwar world. Their greatest challenge lay in finding ways to penetrate the urban centres of the Prairies, which, like most cities, were not characterized by the sense of community necessary for the easy development of dynamic co-operative societies. Further, once established, consumer co-operatives in urban centres were not easily managed because of the emergence of the modern shopping centre. Saskatchewan Federated Co-operatives (the Saskatchewan wholesale), therefore, during the postwar years intensified its educational activities, particularly for managers. By the early 1950s, the wholesale was spending $20 000 — then a significant sum — on education and training. In 1955 Federated amalgamated with Manitoba Co-operative Wholesale Society, thereby raising the question of how a large organization crossing provincial borders could serve over five hundred organizations located in a complex diversity of circumstances. This growing demand for educational programs within the consumer movement became a prominent, even dominant, force behind the development of the college.

Additional support for the college also came from the Co-operative Union of Saskatchewan. The Union had grown out of annual conferences of Saskatchewan co-operative trading associations (mostly consumer societies) in the 1930s. In 1939 this grouping had become a provincial association of the Co-operative Union of Canada under the name of the Saskatchewan Section. In 1944 it changed its name to the Co-operative Union in keeping with a restructuring of the national organization. From the 1930s, under its various names, the Co-operative Union had been a strong supporter of co-operative education — for members and the public as well as directors and managers. During the late 1940s and early 1950s, a number of powerful individuals within the Saskatchewan movement — Les Bright, L. L. "Lewie" Lloyd (brother of

Woodrow Lloyd), B. N. Arnason, Ed Whelan — were particularly concerned about developing the Union's commitment to educational activities. They became, in turn, key supporters of the College concept.

Finally, the Saskatchewan Co-operative Women's Guild, organized in 1944, had a primary concern with education. By the mid-fifties the Guild had forty local guilds and a membership of over 1200.[17] While the guilds primarily focussed on local, specific projects, they were bound together, first, by a kind of modest feminism and, second, by an interest in educational needs within co-operatives. Indeed, from the mid-1950s to the later sixties, the guilds would be a staunch supporter of the college and all its programs.[18]

The amalgamation between the two provincial groups took place in the summer of 1955. In June 1955, the organizing committee of the International Co-operative Institute proposed creating a single educational program for the movement in Manitoba and Saskatchewan to delegates attending a meeting of Federated Co-operatives.[19] On 9 August, Siemens and his associates met with representatives from Federated, the Co-operative Union of Saskatchewan, the University of Saskatchewan, the Saskatchewan Department of Co-operative Development, and the Saskatchewan Department of Education.[20] The meeting agreed in principle to developing a Co-operative Institute under the supervision of the Co-operative Union of Saskatchewan. The Institute would have a broad base of support, an involvement in training of co-operative officials and staff, and a commitment to teaching co-operative officials and staff, and a commitment to teaching co-operative philosophy.[26] Federated Co-operatives, whose training officer had resigned a few months previously, offered to make available its entire training budget for one year: an offer that would bring immediately both funds and a specific project to the organization.

The first task in developing the Institute was the selection of a director. A special committee consisting of L. L. Lloyd of the Co-operative Union, Wilfred McLeod of Co-op Insurance Services, and Orville McCreary of Federated Co-operatives quickly chose Harold Chapman from the Extension Services branch of the Department of Co-operative Development. Chapman had just returned to the Department after having served as secretary for the province's Royal Commission on Rural Life. Previously, his work with Extension Services had been concerned with co-operative farms, other new co-operatives, co-operative schools, and native co-operatives.[22]

Chapman was an experienced adult educator when he assumed control of the Institute in November 1955. In his work with the Department he had been involved with Group Development Institutes since 1949. These institutes were concerned with group dynamics and with developing a process whereby all participants would be involved in group discussions and decisions.[23] He had also been a representative of the Department of Co-operative Development on the Farm Radio Forum Committee in Saskatchewan, and he had served as a resource person for forums in the province. He was also a member of the Canadian Association for Adult Education (CAAE), attended many of its sessions, and was a close student of the issues then transforming the CAAE.[24]

But perhaps Chapman's most intensive experience in adult education came from his work with the Royal Commission on Rural Life. William Baker from the University of Saskatchewan, a rural sociologist trained at Michigan and Wisconsin, was in charge of research for the Commission. He collected information for the Commission through the conventional methods of employing researchers and inviting submissions from several organizations. He also organized, with Chapman's help, an extensive tour of the province to receive opinions from, and stimulate debate among, farm people over the fate of their way of life. The Commission visited 150 communities and followed a format where issues were raised. Those attending were divided into groups to address the issues; the groups reported back to the entire assembly; and, as far as possible, consensus was sought in refining issues and proposing solutions. This experience was particularly productive for the Commission and convinced Chapman that adult education was very much a process whereby information had to be carefully pitched to the learning level of the participant and learning took place in discussion sessions on important topics among people with specific interests.

Thus when Chapman became principal of the Institute he brought with him strong views on how its courses should be taught, and he established an approach which would remain basic to the program for many years. He later recalled:

> Very quickly I found that my job was to organize training programmes and to draw in resource people in the areas in which I didn't have expertise and there were a lot of them. Just for example, the first course I conducted was in lumber merchandizing, or building products merchandizing, so Colin Ward of Federated Co-operatives was the main resource person in the building products merchandizing but I was the resource person in setting up the class room and in deciding in every hour and a half period that about one third of that period would be spent providing information, about a third would be spent with the participants discussing the information, and a third of it spent getting feedback from the groups, the [content] resource person adding information as needed.[25]

Gradually, Chapman brought these ideas together into a theory of adult education which he organized into the following principles:

1. Problems need to be considered important to those expected to solve them.
2. Start where people are — not where we think they are or would like them to be.
3. A person cannot transfer his knowledge and skills to another — the other must go through a **learning process**.
4. Significant learning takes place when facts and information are integrated into the experience of the learner.

5. A person feels more responsible for what he helps to create.[26]

The emphasis on practical education within a specific educational process typified most of the work undertaken by the Institute during its first few years. As the following statistics indicate, most of the courses undertaken during the first four years were aimed at Federated Co-operatives.[27]

	1955-56	1956-57	1957-58	1958-59
Students	178	361	602	592
Student Days	1140	2159	3010	2790
Federated	1140	1779	2167	1859
Saskatchewan Credit Unions	—	260	270	236
Alberta Wholesale	—	—	243	245
Saskatchewan Wheat Pool	—	—	—	215
Other	—	120	—	—

Although Chapman and the small staff attempted to introduce co-operative content into the courses they offered, it was obvious that the Institute had not become a centre for co-operative idealism and community activism. Nor had it become a conscience for a movement increasingly consumed by the narrow concerns of its institutions. One critic of this preoccupation with the practical was J. J. Siemens. He saw his dream of a fully independent educational institution concerned about co-operative philosophy and fulfilling the role of critic for the movement diminishing, and he gradually withdrew his support for the organization. Doing so caused him and others considerable anguish. As he wrote L. L. Lloyd:

> Would you agree that the capacity to Love is determined by one's capacity to Give? I have from the beginning Loved the Co-operative movement with my Whole being, for it has been my material and spiritual salvation, and I gave all I knew how, including my health. . . . The success of our Co-operative financial progress is incidental to a behaviour pattern we can, through education, implant in our Co-op memberships.[28]

In retrospect, however, the practical emphasis was essential. The Institute's personnel did not have the resources, the training, or perhaps the inclination to undertake the kind of community development program typical of the Antigonish movement; nor did it have the communications skills or resource capabilities to produce curriculum materials for an extensive program in adult education. Rather, it had no choice but to focus on the immediate needs of

Prairie co-ops. Living up to the hopes of all those who expected so much from the Institute was impossible.

There were ways, however, that the Institute could escape from relying overwhelmingly upon Federated Co-operatives. The credit union movement in the late fifties was also becoming more complicated as local credit unions moved out of wheat pool offices and church basements to main street. Credit union centrals were becoming alarmed at the lack of training of managers and directors and recommended the Institute to its members. Consequently, the Institute began to train more employees and directors from credit unions. Similarly, Co-operative Life Insurance Company, Co-operative Hail, the Saskatchewan Wheat Pool, and Co-operative Fire and Casualty Insurance Company began to hire the Institute's staff regularly. By 1958 even the relatively distant B.C. Credit Union League was employing Chapman regularly.

This growing use by a diversity of organizations, some of them outside of Saskatchewan, brought into question the exclusive control — no matter how loosely it was exerted — of the Co-operative Union of Saskatchewan. It also raised the possibility of a more stable, broadly based support system for the college. Consequently, during the late fifties, the Institute — its supervising committee and staff — began to explore several alternatives. After an attempt to affiliate with the University of Saskatchewan failed because of the University's requirement that it essentially control the program,[29] the Institute recommended that the college construct its own building and be funded by major co-operatives on a dues basis. This proposal gained widespread support and in 1959 a new, independent legal entity, Western Co-operative College, supported by twenty co-operative organizations, was formed.[30]

The creation of the College was an act of faith and optimism. The building which housed the College also reflected the organization's educational philosophy since it embodied the principles of adult education which Harold Chapman had developed earlier for the Institute. Situated on fields then on the outskirts of Saskatoon, the architecture and the construction facilitated adult learning. Chapman and the architect for the building spent two days in 1960 at an International Seminar on Residential Adult Education held in Port Elgin. At the conference they learned much from adult educators from Europe, the United States, and Canada, and they designed a building ''so that every aspect of it reflected adult learning principles or reflected how a group of adults can come together who aren't used to coming together and feel comfortable and chat and exchange information and develop.''[31] Classrooms were well supplied with visual aids, the walls had specially designed acoustic tiles, and classroom furniture was selected to facilitate small group discussion. Similarly, the cafeteria and main meeting room had excellent acoustics and could be subdivided for a variety of uses. The residences were designed virtually to force interaction among those staying at the college. Bedrooms were small but grouped around a common area with comfortable

furniture and a small collection of books and pamphlets. The library, supported largely by donations from individuals and co-operatives, was spacious,
considering its relatively slim holdings, with considerable room for research.
This pattern of construction reflected Chapman's belief, well supported by
research, that much adult learning took place outside of classrooms when
the learners discussed the practical applications of what they had been told
or were studying.[32]

The new building, which was financed by donations from major co-operative
institutions, opened its doors in the autumn of 1962. It proved to be a popular
and well-used facility, particularly in its early years. By the middle of the
1960s over one hundred courses were being offered annually at the College
to over 2000 students from a variety of organizations.[33] In addition, the College
conducted a few courses as demand dictated in other centres, mostly in Saskatchewan. It also offered two correspondence courses on the co-operative movement, one an introductory course, the other a longer, senior course. Both
courses were popular, at least initially, although like correspondence courses
generally fewer people were attracted to them in later years. The written
materials used in these courses were prepared largely by Alexander Laidlaw,
then with the Co-operative Union of Canada. They were particularly strong
in their historical components, reflecting Laidlaw's extensive reading in the
movement's background. In fact, they were one of the first attempts at creating
a factual foundation for an understanding of the Canadian movement.

The expansion of the curriculum and the first efforts to come to terms with
the nature of the movement — the efforts associated with the correspondence
courses — marked a broadening of perspectives within the College. So too
did the attempt to serve co-operatives in their communities. In 1964 the College
started to develop local level staff training in areas relatively distant from
Saskatoon. Trainers were trained in communities like Portage la Prairie,
Yorkton, and Edmonton, particularly for courses that would help stores or
credit unions adjust to a changing environment. This emphasis on local training
was the major result of a trip to co-operative colleges in England, Finland,
Sweden, and Denmark by "Lewie" Lloyd, chairman of the College's board,
and Harold Chapman in 1963. In theory, the development of locally offered
courses should have offered easier access to the College by more people,
and for a while it did. In the long run, though, the practice proved to be
somewhat disappointing. There were relatively few communities with sufficient numbers of people interested in further studies on co-operatives. The
courses offered, too, had restricted appeal. Most of them dealt with technical
aspects of work within co-operative stores or credit unions. Relatively few
members of co-operatives, therefore, were interested in the courses offered
locally, and the program had limited appeal and a short life.

Another way in which the College sought to be more useful to co-operatives
during the sixties was through the development of a research program. In
1965 Olaf Turnbull, a former Minister of the Department of Co-operative

Development in the provincial government, joined the College, and part of his duties was to undertake research projects. Contacts with universities were improved, and a few projects were undertaken for consumer co-ops, but there were never sufficient funds to develop a strong program. Moreover, the co-operative movement generally was not specific enough in making demands for research upon the College. Larger co-ops generally preferred hiring research directly from consultants or academics, and few smaller co-ops recognized the value of research.

The same lack of specific requests and shortages of funds profoundly affected the development of unique curriculum resources for the courses the College offered. The College was never in a position to develop its own text-books or even extensive printed materials. Technical courses — the heart of the College's offerings — relied heavily on American sources for content and resource materials. Throughout the 1960s Chapman and other members of the staff at the College made many contacts with educators in American co-operatives through the Co-operative League of the United States and the Association of Co-operative Educators. Nearly all the outside resource people for the College in those years came from the United States, partly because of those contacts and partly because of a shortage of such people in Canada. Inevitably, this development meant borrowing from the conservative, training-oriented approaches typical of the American movement. It also contributed to the College's tendency to buy complete training programs in accountancy, merchandising, and store management from such American institutions as Kansas State University. Towards the end of the sixties, the College tried to overcome the limitations of this reliance and sought to tailor its courses more closely to the distinctive needs of Canadian co-operatives but, as in the past, a very limited budget restricted creativity and limited results.

Rather paradoxically, while the College had a limited capacity to be creative in meeting the needs of its main constituency — the established co-operatives — it had considerable success in responding to the needs of Inuits from the Canadian Arctic and co-operative organizers from the Third World. During the late 1950s the aboriginal peoples of northern Canada had developed co-operatives to market handicrafts and sell consumer goods. By the 1960s the northern co-operatives were facing a crisis because they lacked trained managers. Beginning in 1966, approximately twenty prospective managers were sent annually by the Department of Indian Affairs and Northern Development to the College for training. Bruno Neufeldt, one of the College's instructors, taught them a program on co-operative management designed particularly to meet the needs of managers in northern co-ops.[34] It proved to be a very successful venture, well financed by government, until the number of students declined during the early 1970s.

The program for overseas students flourished at about the same time. In the late 1950s, the Canadian government, through the Canadian International Development Agency, developed a program to encourage co-operative organizers in developing countries to visit Canadian co-operatives. When the visitors found the visit to be repetitive and too unstructured, the government developed an extensive training program involving St Francis Xavier University and Western Co-operative College. Visiting students would spend approximately six weeks at the Coady Institute examining the community development approach associated with that institution. They would then spend six weeks studying the adult education philosophy and management systems taught by the College. As in all the College programs, the visiting students were encouraged to share information and to divide their time about equally between learning information, discussing resultant practical issues in small groups, and working towards consensus as a collectivity. All students — and they numbered about fifty each year — were also required to prepare "mini theses" on how the approach learned at the College could be applied to a specific problem in their homeland. The approach produced some remarkable projects, some long lasting friendships, and some rich exchanges of experiences.[35]

Despite these relatively well-funded projects the College never escaped from the problems of a limited (though gradually expanding) focus and a constant shortage of funds. It also depended heavily upon the dedication of a few employees, some of whom worked for relatively low wages. The pressures of the financial situation and the constant need to meet the diverse demands of the movement eventually erupted in a debilitating staff dispute in 1968. The dispute, precipitated by the dismissal of an instructor, led to a lockout of the instructors which paralysed the College for several weeks. The dispute was eventually resolved through mediation, though it scarred the institution for some time afterward and created tensions with community groups in Saskatoon and other western centres.[36]

The dispute with the staff was only one manifestation of a need for change in the late sixties and seventies. Another was the gradual decline in the use of the college made by co-operatives. Co-operatives were increasingly moving towards in-house training, therefore sending fewer students to the College. They were also hiring members of the College staff to teach those courses, meaning that the college hired several new instructors usually from outside the movement. Inevitably, those instructors knew little about the organizations they were hired to serve and they could not immediately serve them as effectively as their predecessors.[37] To this bind was added the ambiguities of the demands of co-operatives: on the one hand, they asked for technical courses but were increasingly developing their own; on the other, they wanted broad courses on co-operative philosophy, but the movement was by no means certain of what that meant.[38] In the face of this confining, claustrophobic environment, Chapman and the Board of the College decided to open its doors even more widely.

During 1969 and 1971 the individuals and organizations associated with the College planned to expand it into a national organization under the name

"The Co-operative College of Canada." They hoped the new College, more closely aligned with national co-operatives and able to serve co-ops in Central and Eastern Canada, would become a well-financed institution able to serve efficiently as a central co-ordinating, developmental, and educational agency.[39] They also hoped the College would become, at last, a major centre for research and for the general development of the movement in Canada. With a new building, a more secure financial base, and a broader national focus, the College at last seemed to have achieved stability.

The history of the Co-operative Institute and its successor, Western Co-operative College, is largely a history of narrowing limits. The original approach, born of early co-operative associations with adult education and the crusading zeal of Canadian agrarianism, envisioned expanding the consciousness of ordinary Canadians so they could reform the nation if not the world. This vision, which had given life to the Antigonish movement and the wheat pools, proved impossible to replicate on a large scale in the 1950s and 1960s. Major co-operatives, preoccupied with their own internal needs in an increasingly competitive environment, were unwilling to fund the kind of extensive, expensive educational program that would have created a large mass movement reminiscent of the co-operative outbursts of the 1920s and 1930s. Instead, they were willing to provide only sufficient funds to permit a modest training program and two preliminary courses on co-operatives. Thus, that a handful of co-operative leaders were able to create a distinctive approach within a building that embodied a carefully thought-out theory of adult education is a tribute to their dedication. It does not reflect a strong commitment across the movement.

The narrowing limits also reflect an uncertainty among Canadian co-operators about how their movement should develop and expand. In the years after the Second World War the movement was confronting the amorphous life of urban Canada. The period of postwar expansion dulled class and regional imbalances across the country — the imbalances which had earlier provided the socio-economic problems for which co-operatives had been developed to correct. Just as important, many of the social issues, particularly the educational issues, tackled by co-operatives in the past were now being met by other organizations. University extension departments proliferated; school boards ran evening classes; community and technical colleges became more important; libraries became commonplace. Even the community activities and community halls once operated or sponsored by co-operatives became redundant, replaced by better financial programs and the more munificent structures provided by local governments. Even the special youth groups sponsored by many co-ops proved to be lacklustre in comparison with youth projects sponsored by churches, schools, and other organizations. Finally, the system of study groups used so successfully by the Antigonish movement, the wheat pool fieldman, the credit union organizers, and Farm Radio Forum paled in effectiveness: the automobile, the radio, the increased all-season tempo of urban life left little time for the careful consideration of social-economic issues by community groups.

Thus the College was forced to concentrate upon practical issues and to absorb from the adult education theory of the day a methodology — a process — for adult learning. In retrospect, though, there was a subtle but vital difference between this educational technique developed by the College and those favored by earlier co-op educators and activists. The early organizers — Moses Coady, E. A. Partridge, the wheat pool fieldmen, J. B. "Jock" Brown — began with a denunciation of the existing society and challenged ordinary people to build a new order based on economic structures operated democratically. The method developed by the College — a method that emphasized pooling experience to deal with specific issues and practical questions — worked well enough for improving institutions, but it did not offer easy scope for organizers and charismatic leaders. In essence, the approach facilitated consensus and management of problems within organizations — important enough objectives, but it was not a technique that leads easily to new campaigns, dramatic new issues, or even new solutions.

In terms of development theory, the history of the two institutions also reflects a subtle shift within the Canadian movement. Although rather unsystematic ideologically, the Canadian movement had over the years advocated a decentralized, community-based form of development. Indeed, perhaps the movement's most pervasive appeal had been the idea of creating economic and social institutions capable of safeguarding local societies from the centralizing forces represented by large metropolitan centres and modern corporations. That vision had become blurred by the 1950s — squeezed on one side by an acceptance of paternalistic corporations operated according to "enlightened principles," and on the other by the preoccupation with state power typical of social democrats and marxists. Although different in many respects, these two alternatives in the fifties and sixties favored big solutions, centralized control, and bureaucratic responses. Canadian co-operators became similarly mesmerized by scale and efficiency and grew to share many of the ideas of the conventional wisdom on how the economy and the nation could be developed. Thus, Canadian co-operators were satisfied to accept management training programs essentially developed elsewhere. They neither pressed the College nor provided it with the funds to encourage creative thought on how co-operatives should function in the modern world. In essence, the Canadian movement was satisfied with mild adaptations of the modern capitalist firm: the Institute and the College ultimately could not shake that dominant belief.

Looked at in even broader terms these narrowing limits raised most of the issues and the pattern typical of non-formal education programs. The co-operative movement in English Canada in the 1950s and 1960s can be viewed as a reformist movement which sought "to alter relationships within the social order without drastic structural change."[38] The educational program of the

Institute and College ultimately embraced this objective. This approach was in contrast to earlier forms of co-operative "educational" activity based more on ideas of liberation and self-determination which sought "a radical restructuring of the social order."[39] To a considerable extent, the differences reflects different kinds of stress within the movement, kinds of stress that had their roots in the structure of Canadian society. Co-operatives developed most rapidly earlier in the twentieth century among those groups (settlers, farmers, fishermen, workers) with limited opportunities for mobility because of severely limited resources, local investments, or widespread depression. They were galvanized to action by activists who preached the gospel of local development through co-operative action. Education at that time, therefore, was led by charismatic, even saintly, leaders who invoked a call to action even though they did so formally through individual and small group study.

By the 1950s the structural bind of low migration opportunities — viewed geographically or in terms of class — had apparently declined for many Canadians. Education about co-operatives, therefore, lost the biting edge furnished by a widely perceived and deeply felt sense of inequality. Understandably, therefore, as old urgencies lost their momentum, elements within the Canadian movement sought to build a co-operative educational institution. They inevitably found themselves faced with developing a kind of education different from what they had known and probably first intended. Perhaps the best way to understand the difference is to examine the kinds of stress this new education had to confront. The stress came largely from "internal binds" or points of tension within the movement itself. The "enemy" was no longer as much without as it was within the movement, and education was largely concerned with "leadership factions, goal displacement, participant apathy, and lack of organizational skills" — the issues that typically restrict the development of strong educational programs within social movements.[40] It is within that context that the history of the College takes on new meaning and the struggles of those who hoped to provide both a training centre and a critical capacity for the movement becomes understandable.

Footnotes

1. For a more complete description of the co-operative movement in the Prairies and in Canada generally, see the concluding chapters of I. MacPherson, *Each for All: A History of the Co-operative Movement in English-Canada, 1900-1945* (Toronto: Macmillan, 1979).

2. See R. D. Colquette, *The First Fifty Years: A History of the United Grain Growers Ltd.* (Winnipeg: The Public Press, 1957).

3. See G. L. Fairburn, *From Prairie Roots: The Remarkable Story of Saskatchewan Wheat Pool* (Saskatoon: Western Producer Prairie Books, 1984), pp. 124-33; J. Hamilton, *Service at Cost: A History of Manitoba Pool Elevators* (Saskatoon: Modern Press, undated), p. 153; and L. D. Nesbitt, *Tides in the West: A Wheat Pool History* (Saskatoon: Modern Press, undated), p. 142.

4. See G. L. Fairburn, *From Prairie Roots,* pp. 120-22.

5. *The Co-operative Consumer* was published by Saskatchewan Co-operative Wholesale Society and its successor, Federated Co-operatives, from 1939 to 1982.

6. A. J. McPhail was the first manager of the Saskatchewan Wheat Pool. He combined a good business sense with a strong commitment to co-operative philosophy. See A. H. Innis, *The Diary of A. J. McPhail* (Toronto: University of Toronto Press, 1940); Fawcett Ransom was for many years the manager of Manitoba Co-operative Wholesale and a strong proponent of co-operative action; John T. Hull was the publicist of Manitoba Pool Elevators during the 1930s and 1940s. He wrote several pamphlets on co-operative theory; Violet McNaughton wrote a column on women's issues for *The Western Producer* and played a key role in shaping several co-operative ventures in Saskatchewan during the twenties and thirties; Harry Fowler was the guiding force behind the development of the Co-operative Refineries in the 1930s and Federated Co-operatives in the 1940s and 1950s; J. B. "Jock" Brown was the first manager of Canadian Co-operative Implements and, although a marxist, he was a strong supporter of the co-operative movement during the 1940s and 1950s.

7. For a consideration of the difficulties of the 1920s, see D. C. Jones, ed., *We'll All Be Buried Down Here: The Prairie Dryland Disaster, 1917-1926,* forthcoming.

8. The best accounts of Siemens's career are to be found in H. Dyck, "Jacob Siemens and the Co-operative Movement in Southern Manitoba, 1929-1955," unpublished M.A. thesis, University of Manitoba, 1982, and R. Meyers, *Spirit of the Postt Road: A Story of Self-Help Communities* (Altona: the Federation of Southern Manitoba Co-operatives, 1955).

9. This summary of Siemens's career is based on H. Dyck, "Jacob John Siemens," passim.

10. See Ian MacPherson, *Building and Protecting the Co-operative Movement: A Brief History of the Co-operative Union of Canada, 1900-1984* (Ottawa: The Co-operative Union of Canada, 1984), p. 105.

11. H. Dyck, "Jacob John Siemens," p. 85; I. MacPherson, "Appropriate Forms of Enterprise: The Prairies and Maritime Co-operative Movements, 1900-1955," *Acadiensis,* Autumn 1978, p. 89.

12. H. Dyck, "Jacob John Siemens," p. 67.

13. Ibid., p. 84.

14. Peter Manniche et al., *The Folk Schools of Denmark and the Development of a Farming Community* (London: Oxford University Press, 1929).

15. H. Dyck, "John Jacob Siemens," p. 162.

16. Based on *Annual Reports,* 1945 and 1951, Department of Co-operative Development, Saskatchewan.

17. J. F. C. Wright, *Prairie Progress: Consumer Co-operation in Saskatchewan* (Saskatoon: Modern Press, 1956), p. 198.

18. Interview, H. E. Chapman, 15 December 1984.

19. J. K. Mollo, *Profit vs. Competition: The Struggle of the Western Co-operative College,* unpublished Master of Continuing Education thesis, University of Saskatchewan, 1971, pp. 18-19.

20. Ibid., p. 20.

21. Ibid., p. 19.

22. Interview, H. E. Chapman, 15 December 1984.

23. Ibid.

24. Ibid.

25. Ibid.

26. These guidelines — or ones similar to them — for education within the College's programs appear in many of the statements developed to guide instructors over the years. This particular version was found in H. E. Chapman, "Co-operative Education & Training to Meet the Needs of the Changing Environment," unpublished paper, Co-operative College of Canada Archives.

27. Statistics taken from the Annual Reports of the College, 1955-1960.

28. Lewie Lloyd Scrapbook #3, Archives, Co-operative College of Canada, Saskatoon.

29. J. K. Mollo, *Profit vs Competition,* pp. 39-44.

30. Ibid., pp. 64-67.

31. Interview, H. E. Chapman, 15 December 1984.

32. Ibid.

33. *Star-Phoenix,* 3 November 1962. Clippings Files, Co-operative College of Canada Archives, Saskatoon.

34. H. B. Neufeldt, "Report and Evaluation of Northern Management Courses," Archives, Co-operative College of Canada, Saskatoon.

35. Interview, H. E. Chapman, 15 December 1984. Many of the mini-theses are on file in the College Library and in the Archives of the Saskatchewan Archives Board, Saskatoon.

36. There are three files of clippings on the dispute in the Archives of the Co-operative College of Canada.

37. For a brief insight into the issues then disturbing the movement, see I. MacPherson, *Building and Protecting the Co-operative Movement: A Brief History of the Co-operative Union of Canada, 1909-1984* (Ottawa: The Co-operative Union of Canada, 1984), pp. 177-214.

38. R. G. Paulston and D. Lejeune, "A Methodology for Studying Education in Social Movements," R. G. Paulston, ed. *Other Dreams; Other Schools; Folk Colleges in Social and Ethnic Movements* (Pittsburgh: University of Pittsburgh, 1980), p. 42.

39. Ibid.

40. Ibid., p. 33.